Communicating Partners

of related interest

Relationship Development Intervention with Young Children
Social and Emotional Development Activities for Asperger Syndrome, Autism, PDD and NLD
Steven E. Gutstein and Rachelle K. Sheely
ISBN 1 84310 714 7

Relationship Development Intervention with Children, Adolescents and Adults
Social and Emotional Development Activities for Asperger Syndrome, Autism, PDD and NLD
Steven E. Gutstein and Rachelle K. Sheely
ISBN 1 84310 717 1

From Goals to Data and Back Again
Adding Backbone to Developmental Intervention for Children with Autism
Jill Fain Lehman and Rebecca Klaw
ISBN 1 84310 753 8

Giggle Time – Establishing the Social Connection
A Program to Develop the Communication Skills of Children with Autism, Asperger Syndrome and PDD
Susan Aud Sonders
ISBN 1 84310 716 3

Asperger's Syndrome
A Guide for Parents and Professionals
Tony Attwood
ISBN 1 85302 577 1

Communicating Partners

30 Years of Building Responsive Relationships
with Late-Talking Children
including Autism, Asperger's Syndrome (ASD),
Down Syndrome, and Typical Development

Development Guides for Professionals and Parents

James D. MacDonald

Jessica Kingsley Publishers
London and Philadelphia

Front cover photograph taken by Heather MacDonald.
Back cover photograph taken by Allen Zak.

First published in the United Kingdom in 2004
by Jessica Kingsley Publishers
116 Pentonville Road
London N1 9JB, England
and
400 Market Street, Suite 400
Philadelphia, PA 19106, USA

www.jkp.com

Copyright © 2004 James D. MacDonald

Library of Congress Cataloging in Publication Data

MacDonald, James D. (James David), 1940-
    Communicating partners : 30 years of building responsive relationships with late-talking children including autism, Asperger's syndrome (ASD), Down syndrome, and typical development developmental guides for professionals and parents / James D. MacDonald. — 1st American pbk. ed.
        p. cm.
    Includes bibliographical references and index.
    ISBN 1-84310-758-9 (pbk.)
    1. Language disorders in children—Treatment. 2. Communica tive disorders in children—Treatment. 3. Developmentally disabled children—Language. 4. Autistic children—Language. 5. Asperger's syndrome—Patients—Language. 6. Down's syndrome —Patients—Language. 7. Language acquisition—Parent-participation. 8. Parent and child.   I. Title.
    [DNLM: 1. Language Development Disorders—Child. 2. Child Development Disorders, Pervasive. 3. Parent-Child Relations. 4. Communication Disorders—Child. 5. Professional-Family Relations. WL 340.2 M135c 2004]
RJ496.L35M33 2004
618.92'85506—dc22

        2004009428

British Library Cataloguing in Publication Data
A CIP catalogue record for this book is available from the British Library

ISBN 1 84310 758 9

Printed and Bound in Great Britain by
Athenaeum Press, Gateshead, Tyne and Wear

To all who have trusted and joined in their child's natural path

and to Carolyn and the MacDonald boys

Lawrence   Kyle   Jackson
Malcolm and Kobe

Remembering my sister Judith D'alessandro —
my longest and strongest communicating partner

This poem is for my first grandchild, Malcolm MacDonald
and for all the children who would say this to their parents if they could.

Mom and Dad Help Me Learn

I learn when you teach me
I learn when you play with me
I learn when we catch each other on the run.

I learn what you want when you teach me
I learn what I want when I play
I learn what we both want when we play together.

I learn least when you do what I cannot do
I learn most when you act like me
I learn best when we do it together.

The more you act like an adult, the less I will learn
the more you act like me, the more I will learn
The more we act like each other, the more I will become like you.

Believe it or not, I am learning all the time
So just respond to the little things I do
And I will learn more and more.

If I fail with you, I will stay away
If I stay away, I won't learn much
Let me succeed with you and I will learn every time.

You are in such a hurry for me to learn
But I just have to take my time
So wait for me and I will do a lot.

I can learn a lot on my own,
but to communicate, I need to learn with you
Show me how to be a person not just a student.

I wish you believed you were my best school
I will learn most from you
Let's make our life together the best school.

Mom and Dad I am learning all the time
I don't want to do it on my own
Join in what I am doing and I will learn more than you expect.

The more you pay attention to me the more I will learn
If I do things you do not want, ignore me
Then I will learn what not to do.

My world is one of actions and sensations
You world is one of thoughts and words
Only when you enter my world can I get into yours.

Mom and Dad it is like we live on a staircase
You are way up there and I am way down here
Please come down and do things I can do.

I know you want me to learn new things
So just show me as we play the old things
I will learn the new when I am successful doing the old.

I can't learn the impossible
So give me something possible to do
And I will please you every time.

Mom and Dad only you can help me best
Come into my world first
Then I will come into yours.

James D. MacDonald

Contents

Part 3: Following Your Child's Development from Isolation to Civil Conversation *275*

Preface

The major thing I have learned in 30 years with late-talking children is that they and their life partners experience strikingly distinct worlds. While this may seem obvious, we have found that adults often do not respond to the child's world but stay in their own when interacting with children. I have also learned that the key to helping children develop is genuinely to enter their world at a very personal level. Ryan and Mike tell their story.

Ryan, a four-year-old nonverbal child with autism, was playing with a straw broom as if it were a sensory toy or an instrument with strings. Clearly he was experiencing it very differently to his father, Mike, who said: "Ryan, that's a broom. You sweep with a broom. You can clean the floor. Look, watch me sweep the floor." Ryan reacted by going away and Mike lost a natural chance to interact.

Mike saw the situation from his world of thought and language and so translated it into something that did not match what Ryan was experiencing. When I brought the broom back to the boy, he returned to the way he was playing. I joined him and played like him. Then I removed two straws and we began poking each other so he would attend to me. Once he attended, I began making sweeping motions with the broom and silently waited. He took the broom and imitated me. What I learned was that only when I entered his world of sensation and action would he be open to joining my world.

In fact Ryan's father was somewhat taken back when I said: "Remember when you said to Ryan 'that's a broom.' Please do not be offended, but you were wrong. In Ryan's world it was a sensory toy, not a broom. But once I accepted his experience he started joining mine."

The story speaks of the value of joining the child in his own experiences. As long as Ryan's father expected the boy to enter his adult world, little happened. However, once I accepted his world of sensations and interacted in his experiences, he attended to me and began joining my world. Social play is the first step in communicating and means two persons acting together with no goal other than to be together. Interacting more and staying longer with people may not seem very important, but it definitely is. Any increased interactions with people who enter the child's world will help children communicate. Autistic children have fundamental difficulties in "being together with people." Communicating Partners addresses the task of "getting together" head-on.

There is much said recently of the "theory of mind" that autistic children have or do not have. Clearly, our children do not read our minds in the ways we would like, but we must realize that often we are not reading their minds accurately either. We have found that a first step in helping children develop is to enter that child's "theory of mind." In the story above, Mike was expecting that Ryan saw the world as he did. When I entered into Ryan's world of action and sensation and accepted his view of the broom, he joined me and then we could begin a relationship.

Another story was related by Jack Kornfield, a psychologist concerned about adults becoming mindful of who children really are.

> Molly was at a restaurant with her mother, father, and grandmother. The waiter asked the girl what she would like. Molly said, "A hot dog and a soda." Her father said, "No, she will have the chicken and salad." Her grandmother chimed in with, "And milk, not soda."
>
> As he was leaving the table, the waiter returned to Molly and asked, "Do you want catsup on your hot dog." She said, "Yes thank you." Then she turned to her family and said, "What do you think of that? He thinks I'm a real person."

This story describes how a child might feel when she is disregarded. Late-talking children may feel similarly but are unable to express it as well as Molly. This book is an attempt to help you and others see our children more as they really are than as the diagnoses, labels, or test scores tell us to see them.

Communicating Partners is an approach that focuses on the person each child is and not on the diagnosis or perceived deficiencies. Each child is viewed from the perspective of having many signature strengths and not as making mistakes. Only when we accept the real person in each child will we be able to help him[1] develop in ways that endure. Communicating Partners sees each child as a dynamic product of his current relationships. Accordingly, we focus as much on the child's life partners as we do on the child himself.

James D. MacDonald

Note

1   The male pronoun is used throughout this book to refer to the child. The information in the book remains equally applicable to and useful for children of both genders.

Introduction

Communicating Partners is the result of over 30 years of research and clinical work exploring two major questions:

1. What do children and adults need to do to become social and communicative in daily life?

2. How can their daily life partners interact with them to help them become more social and communicative?

Communicating Partners is a practical approach that anyone can use with a wide range of persons learning to communicate: typical children and ones who are "late-talking," as well as children identified with autistic spectrum disorders, Asperger's syndrome, Down syndrome, attention disorders, motor delays, emotional disorders, and other conditions interfering with social and communicative development. The persistent goal has been to help parents and professionals develop socially effective relationships with children and adults who have been generally isolated from society.

Communicating Partners is an *optimistic* approach to communication disorders. The key to this approach is building social relationships on a daily basis with life partners. It is optimistic in the following ways.

1. It is based on over 30 years of successes in guiding a wide range of persons to become more social and communicative.

2. It focuses on supporting each child's current strengths and building them into enduring social relationships, in contrast to many approaches that focus on the child's deficits. Communicating Partners views each child as developing along his own natural path

and finds that, to foster that development, his life partners need to trust and join the child's natural path rather than try to make him into something he cannot be. Communicating Partners is a response to the approaches that focus on the child's negative features and not on current signature strengths.

3. Communicating Partners recognizes the ultimate power of daily relationships in helping children develop. Consequently, our optimism about what families can do has been rewarded with years of successes.

4. It responds to the frequent frustrations of professionals when they see their good work fail to generalize into the child's daily life. Communicating Partners is an effective way professionals and parents can collaborate so that home and school learning are supporting each other.

5. It recognizes that many persons live in their own world of sensations and actions, and that they will best develop when their life partners enter their world and then gradually introduce them to their partners' world of thought and action. Joining the person's "mind" respects that every person can learn.

6. Finally, Communicating Partners has found that children learn to communicate in every daily interaction. Consequently, a child's improvement is not dependent on access to professional therapy and education, but can occur best at home. This means that any life partner can help a child become social and communicative with the model.

Communicating Partners views a child's communication development as a social process that requires active participation not only of the child but his life partners in daily routines. As such, the book focuses on teaching the child's life partners to genuinely see and support the many little steps that are critical to building a social and communicative life. There is much that needs to happen before a child talks and there is much more than "having" language to becoming a successful communicator.

This book will guide you through five "lives" that a child or adult needs to engage in if they are to develop their social and communicative potential.

Interactive life

We begin the book by discussing how a child's early interactive play is critical to development. Often intervention and academic programs assume that the child is already interactive in terms of initiating, responding, imitating, and taking turns with people. Unfortunately, a major problem with a variety of late-talking children is simply that they do not interact socially enough to learn to communicate effectively. The book will help you insure that children are effectively social, so that when they learn to communicate, those communication skills will have a living place to grow.

In this program, you will learn how many parents and professionals have helped children become social by entering their world and using a few strategies such as responding, matching, and being playful.

Nonverbal communicative life

After you have helped a child become regularly interactive, it is time to insure that he has a strong habit of communicating with any physical means, such as movements, sounds, gestures, and natural signs. Too often late-talking children are encouraged to talk or sign before they are regularly communicating intentionally. It is not enough for a child to have a few words or signs if he rarely communicates with all the other physical ways he can. We focus on children becoming "constant social sounders" before they are rushed to learn more language.

This program will show you how to communicate effectively in the ways your child can. It will discuss and illustrate many specifics of how you can act and communicate so that your child will communicate as a habitual part of life.

Social language life

Many late-talking children learn language as performance tasks; they can recite songs, lists of facts, and monologues, but they rarely communicate to people in genuinely social ways. We have found that, for these individuals, "language is not enough." In this program we show you how to help a child use language to develop authentic social relationships. Children need to learn to use language for many social reasons other than to meet their needs and demonstrate their knowledge. Far too many children with a large vocabulary are at a loss for how to socialize with the language they have. Consequently, many people lose out in life, not because they do not have language, but because they do not know how to use it in social relationships.

In this program, we will show you how to talk with your child so that he learns more language and so he uses language to build many kinds of relationships. Language here is seen as a social way of life more than an acquisition of vocabulary and information.

Conversational life

The lives of a great many children and adults are severely limited, not due to a lack of language or knowledge, but because they have to learn to have effective conversations. Too often we are satisfied when a child learns a great deal in school and shows considerable language in tests and performance tasks. However, if they are not having conversations there are serious consequences. First, others will not know how much the child knows. Second, the child will miss out on the majority of learning that occurs in relationships. Third, they will not be able to provide the companionship and contact that others need to sustain relationships.

In this program, we show how many people have successfully built conversations with a wide variety of children and adults and we show the great variety of conversations that benefit children's development.

Civil life

A child's ultimate success in life depends on his civility, or the degree to which he treats others with respect and empathy. We have found that many late-talking children lack social skills required to be polite, considerate, and socially appropriate. Being language delayed often involves being self-absorbed and insensitive to others' concerns. This program shows how you can communicate with your child in ways that help him become socially effective at the same time as being empathetic and kind to others. The high rate of behavior concerns with later talking children shows the need for learning to help children become more civil.

We have found that the communication styles of life partners can greatly affect a child's socially appropriate behavior. In this program you will learn many effective strategies for increasing a child's positive behavior while decreasing his socially unacceptable behavior.

How to use the book

This book is designed for anyone interested in helping children and adults communicate. It has been developed and tested with over 1000 professionals and parents with persons learning to become interactive, communicative, linguistic, conversational, and civil. Many parents and professionals have used each of the five programs in the book; some have used only one or two. The book can be used in many ways.

Reading the whole book

If you are interested in an overview of how children become social and communicative, you are encouraged to read the whole book. This will show you how a few responsive strategies – *balance, match, responsiveness, sharing control,* and *playfulness* – can be used to build successful relationships with children across five developmental stages: *interaction, nonverbal communication, social language, conversation,* and *civil behavior.* As such, the book can be used as a textbook for students, professionals, and parents learning about communication development and helping persons with communication disorders of various kinds. It can be used for paraprofessional training as well as for parent education and training of professionals who have not been educated in preconversational development.

Using a chapter at a time

Each chapter is designed so that you can use it by itself to focus on one major communication stage. Many parents and professionals have used each chapter for several months as they worked to insure that a child or adult became competent in that stage of development. We have found that a major problem with treatment of late-talking children is that they are often rushed to develop skills that they are not ready for. For example, teaching a child language and vocabulary before he is regularly interacting with people may actually discourage both the child and teachers, drawing attention to what the child cannot do. Instead, the fact is that he simply does not have the skills, such as interaction and communication, to support and sustain the language learning.

Using the ARM to follow a child's development

The Adult–Child Relationship Map (the ARM) is a developmental map of the many processes that are involved in becoming more social and communicative.

Readers can begin by evaluating a child in terms of the skills on the ARM and then select the sections in the chapter to read to further understand the child. As a child is beginning to develop new skills on the ARM, the reader can focus just on the section in the book that discusses that skill. For example, when a child is beginning to recognize others and imitate how they act, the reader can read the section on imitation to understand more about the child's immediate development. We encourage readers to use the book more as a resource to do two things: first, to understand what a child is currently learning and, second, to learn what they can do to help the child develop in that particular area.

Using the book in education and intervention plans

Traditionally, education plans are based on academic curricula to prepare persons to be successful cognitive students. Communicating Partners recognizes that development is much more than becoming a student; consequently, it plans education on the basis of what the child currently needs to become social and communicative. The goal is to help the child develop skills for spontaneous learning in daily life. Using the ARM to design education plans insures that the child will be able to generalize what they learn to daily life and not just store knowledge. Communicating Partners also includes many specifics for the child's life partners in the plans, since the children will change to the degree that their life partners change interacting with them.

Using the book as a model for speech and language therapy

Communicating Partners provides speech and language professionals with a tested model for guiding their therapy and extending their work to families. It recognizes that therapy alone will not be sufficient to build social relationships and that therapy will be successful only to the degree that it generalizes to the child's daily life. Learning to communicate requires regular practice in social contexts where the child will ultimately use the skills. This model focuses on helping parents and professionals become partners in helping children. Our over 30 years of clinical and research work with parents show that parents are quite capable of helping children communicate when they learn the basic strategies and when they focus on the child's current development.

Guide for selecting individual chapters for each child

What follows is a very general guide for determining when to use one chapter for a given child or adult.

Interaction

Begin with Chapter 7 when the child is:

- isolating himself and avoiding social situations
- not regularly playing with people
- not taking turns in reciprocal or give-and-take ways
- living in his own world much of the time
- seldom learning by imitating or modeling other people
- interacting with people only briefly
- not regularly showing an awareness or interest in others
- talking at people more than really communicating with them
- facing a new environment with unfamiliar people.

Note: the interaction program is for both nonverbal and verbal persons. While interaction goals are necessary for the development of language, there are many persons with language who need to interact before their language will help them develop relationships.

Nonverbal communication

Begin with Chapter 8 when the child:

- is not frequently communicating needs or ideas intentionally
- has begun to imitate others' actions
- is generally attending to what others are doing
- is making sounds more when alone than directed to people
- is frequently not responding when others communicate
- is not initiating communication on his own
- communicates with touch and gestures but not with sounds.

Note: even though a child may have some language, he or she may not be communicating regularly. This program insures that the child becomes a habitual communicator with any physical, vocal, or other expressive means.

Social language

Begin with Chapter 9 when the child is:

- interacting frequently with some people
- communicating occasionally with sounds and gestures and signs
- beginning to say word approximations
- saying some words but not many or frequently
- talking mainly to get his needs met
- talking mainly to answer questions or perform tasks
- rarely talking just for the social connection
- talking more at people than with them
- talking with single words or brief phrases
- not responding with language
- not initiating with language
- talking only with familiar people.

Note: even many persons with a large vocabulary, or who talk for instrumental and academic reasons, still need to learn to talk for the many social reasons that build relationships.

Conversation

Use Chapter 10 when the child is:

- talking frequently when alone
- conversing with adults but not peers
- not taking turns in conversations
- staying in conversation only briefly
- dominating conversations

- playing a passive role in conversations
- avoiding conversations
- getting irritated or nervous in conversations
- talking in repetitive ways
- insisting on talking about his topic
- disregarding others' ideas
- having difficulty listening and responding to what others say
- talking in rigid or compulsive ways
- failing to take others' perspectives
- resisting a change of topic.

Note: conversations are much more than talking, and many late-talking persons need to learn that conversations will be the way to build effective relationships.

Civil behavior

Use Chapter 11 when the child is:

- frequently not cooperative
- frequently aggressive or abusive
- depressed and confused
- often afraid in social situations
- acting in socially unacceptable ways
- rude or impolite
- generally insensitive, showing little empathy
- frequently offending or disturbing others
- acting in socially inappropriate ways
- being over-stimulated
- engaging in self-stimulation
- responding sensitively or emotionally to the environment

- acting out
- resisting others' friendly contacts
- acting immaturely
- acting belligerent
- showing little understanding of boundaries
- being complained about frequently
- embarrassing others.

Note: many late-talking persons encounter frustrations of many kinds. Consequently, they may respond in socially inappropriate ways that can seriously interfere with the interactions they need to develop.

Part 1 of this book will provide a historical, research, and theoretical background to the Communicating Partners model. In this part there will be an overview of the model in terms of the five major developmental lives and the five responsive natural teaching strategies.

Part 2 will provide detailed guides to each of the five developmental lives that children need to master to become fully social and communicative: interaction, nonverbal communication, social language, conversation, and civil behavior.

Part 3 will provide the ARM (the Adult Child Relationship Map) which is a practical way to follow a child's development from initial interactions to conversational and civil behavior. The ARM also provides a guide for adults to help the child develop interaction, nonverbal communication, social language, conversation and civil behavior. The ARM is a practical response to the questions: What does my child need to become social and communicative? And what can I do to help him develop in daily interactions?

Part 1

Introduction to the Model

Communicating Partners is the result of clinical practice, research, and professional teaching since 1971. The focus has been on how children become social and communicative and how parent–child relationships can influence that goal. During this time, I have worked with over 1000 families of children across the autistic spectrum. (The model was also developed with many "late-talking" children not formally diagnosed with a disability. By late-talking I do not mean children who wake you up at night for a conversation. "Late talking" means that the child is not talking by the time typical children do. We have also seen autistic concerns in children with other diagnoses, such as Down syndrome, cerebral palsy, hearing problems, and other problems.)

The reason that families have been the focus of the approach rather than the individual child will become clear throughout the book. *In a nutshell, the focus was on families because that is where children best develop communicative relationships.*

At the same time, I directed a series of research and demonstration projects to study parent–child relationships. Luckily, the clinical and research work occurred at the Ohio State University in the context of teaching and clinically supervising over 800 students preparing for careers in developmental disabilities. The setting for much of the work was the Nisonger Center, a U.S. federally funded research and training center for developmental disabilities.

This part introduces the Communicating Partners approach in three ways. First, you will see a chronological story of its development. The story shows how the model evolved directly from our findings with the children and parents over time. Second, you will see a summary of the research and theory that support the approach. The research addressed two major issues: first, identifying the major components needed to develop communicative relationships, and second, evaluating the effects of parent-based treatment programs. Third, I will introduce and define the basic components of the model from the earliest nonverbal play to civil conversations.

The model comprises two major sets of components. The first includes the five developmental stages for communicating, and the second consists of the five responsive relationship strategies that are fundamental tools for learning to communicate. Roughly, the five stages could be viewed as the "What" of the program and the five strategies could be seen as the "How" of the approach.

Note that the model is presented as a long story because becoming communicative is a journey of several years.

> Just recently, I visited two boys, Mario and Scott. We have worked together for 7 and 12 years and each is becoming a successful social partner. Mario began to talk at four, Scott at five. But it took their parents years of becoming partners who intimately participated in the boys' development, however unusual it was. Both sets of parents entered each boy's individual world and developed with him. While they were interested in changing each boy, the parents realized that entering his world and developing with him was much more effective than directly trying to change him. In each case, as in many others (as you will see), the parents were the driving force and primary participants in the child's progress.

1

The 30-Year Journey
with 1000 Children

How Communicating Partners Came About

In 1971, I took an assistant professorship at the Ohio State University after completing a Ph.D. in Communication Disorders at the University of Minnesota. The program at Minnesota was an equal combination of speech pathology and psychology. The prevailing approaches then were behavioral psychology and cognitive child psychology as applied to a wide range of communication disorders. Some find the two schools of B.F. Skinner (the "father of behaviorism") and Jean Piaget (the "father of cognitive psychology") incompatible. I found them perplexing but eventually very compatible. While the functional analyses of behavior showed me the strength of environmental influences on behavior, the cognitive child analyses introduced me to the mind of the child and the critical issue that *children live in a distinctly distinct world from adults.*

My dissertation was a study of how very differently people perceive and evaluate the speech behaviors of persons identified as stutterers. The study confirmed the clinical finding that regular people differ widely in what they consider the problem of stuttering. This work suggested that a communication disorder is as much a function of the observer as it is of the behavior of the speaker (Macdonald 1972). At that time, I had two most intriguing problems: first, the effects of a speaker's partner on his communication, and second, the gnarly problem of getting newly learned behaviors to generalize into the child's daily life. One thing I learned from my adviser, Richard Martin, is that it is much more accurate to describe what a speaker is doing than to label him with a diagnosis such as "stutterer." In a series of studies, Dr. Martin had found that stuttering was not just one thing and that people labeled as "stutterers" did not always stutter; in fact they usually did not do so. As you will see in this book, we have also found that children called "autistic" are not always autistic.

With this background in speech pathology and both cognitive and behavioral psychology, I took two positions at Ohio State University: one on the faculty of the speech and hearing department and the other as director of the speech and language programs at the Nisonger Center. The Center was a federally funded graduate training center for the study of a wide range of developmental disabilities. The joint position was ideal in that I taught courses in language development and intervention in the department and at the Center I conducted clinical therapy and supervised in intervention programs. The courses prepared me to identify how children learn language, and the clinical responsibilities allowed me to do both clinical and research work with many children. The combination of teaching, service, and research provided an ideal position to understand children with communicative disorders. From the beginning I believed that the principles I was teaching future professionals in coursework should closely relate to the problems and needs of the 200-plus children whom we serviced yearly at the Center. Thus began 24 years of constant coordination of research, clinical programs, and teaching that led to the Communicating Partners program described in this book.

The 1970s were a very stimulating time, both in the study of language development and in the field of developmental disabilities. New research enterprises were leading to genuine revolutions in both areas. In language development, the semantic and pragmatic revolution showed that it was not enough to view young children as just little adults; children clearly had their own world of thought and communication that differed greatly from that of adults (Brown 1973; Piaget 1963). In the new field of developmental disabilities, many historical myths about what, how, and when children could learn were being upended by findings of success with many children who had previously been institutionalized or ignored in education. Changes in both fields were very exciting because the professions were actually in the throes of exploring two cultures that had not been studied or educated to a great degree. These cultures were "child language" and "developmental disabilities." In child language, no longer was it acceptable to assume that children were just "little adults." We now had to acknowledge that children had a unique culture that we needed to enter in order to understand and help them develop. In developmental disabilities, we also had to admit children with disabilities into society and discover their potential, which, heretofore, had been ignored or grossly underestimated.

So in 1971 I began struggling with making sense out of the apparent chaos of children with disabilities and their communication problems. Luckily, the faculty position required me to identify an area of research and proceed to publish. The current literature was beginning to describe the nature of children's first language and our first research focus applied the prevailing findings to assessing the children we saw. The research was showing that children begin to talk, not about adult or academic ideas, but rather their language reflects their experiences (Bloom and Lahey 1978; Brown 1973). Consequently, we noticed that educational programs were often teaching children language for school and adult life and not language they needed for their own experiences. Then we began teaching children to talk about their own experiences rather than academic concepts like numbers, time, and other impersonal meanings. This was the beginning of the ELI (Environmental Language Intervention) program that lasted throughout the 1970s. Deanna Horstmeier and several graduate students helped develop an understanding of how our children were beginning to talk and what they were beginning to say. In a series of clinical research studies we explored how to teach socially isolated children how to talk. Cheri Resler (1975), Marjorie Nichols (1977), and I conducted studies that showed that children with delays were beginning to speak with the same meaning classes as typically developing children. Judith Blott, Deanna Horstmeier, and I then applied the findings to a language-teaching program (ELI) that focused on teaching parents to help children talk by using language for their life experiences rather than the traditional approach of teaching language for school (Horstmeier and MacDonald 1978; MacDonald and Blott 1974). Early on, we saw that when we gave children language for their own actions, objects, and other experiences, they learned and generalized it to daily use more readily than language for school, such as colors, shapes, and sizes. We were beginning to understand what children want to talk about and we focused our therapy on that language before preparing the child for school.

We began teaching parents how children learn language, since they had much more opportunity to influence the child than we did in therapy or school. Teaching parents seemed to make sense since there was so much concern over the failure of children to generalize their learning to the natural environment. We reasoned that the more that language learning occurred in the child's natural environment, the more successful it would be. It was about this time that new and intriguing research was showing that even infants and parents have important communicative relationships. We reasoned that if infants could communicate, then our children, while delayed, could also do so if we learned how mothers effectively communicate with infants (Bronfenbrenner 1979; Stern 1977). In fact we began exploring how parents and children played together and found that, with our children, parents often played a directive teaching role rather than the reciprocal responsive roles that mothers of communicating children played. We then realized that while our children were chronologically from three to six years old, developmentally they were often at the infant level in interactive and nonverbal communicative development. Using the research in parent–child communication as a model, we began exploring the effects of training parents to play in balanced and matched ways like successful mothers did. What we found served as the basis for a 30-year program of clinical research and service in parent–child relationships with late-talking children.

In a three-year federal project, we began to address three major questions:

1. Which parent interactive strategies are effective in helping children communicate?

2. What does the child need to do before he develops a social habit of language?

3. To what degree can parents successfully learn and use strategies to help their child to communicate at home?

In working with over 100 parents in the early years, we realized that they generally did not understand how children develop language. Many told us they thought language just came with time, like hair and height, and generally they did not understand the many things children need to do before talking. They had little understanding that their child's language came from their own daily interactions with him and less awareness about what children needed to do before they talked habitually and socially.

Two dissertations (Lombardino 1979; Owens 1979) began exploring the details of parent–child communication with 20 children with social and developmental delays. The studies alerted us to two major problems. The first problem was that the children regularly played a very passive role when talking with their parents, such as answering questions and following commands to speak, but not talking much for the social reasons (pragmatics) that build conversational relationships. The children acted more like students than conversational partners. The second problem was that their parents often talked to the children with questions and commands and rarely with language that allowed the children freedom to have their own say. Upon interview we found that most parents believed that their child would talk only if they taught them, as academic subjects were taught in directive ways. They had little idea that their children would learn best to talk in playful interactions in which they, the parents, would easily talk in ways the child could do. A major thrust of our early work was to demonstrate to parents how capable and critical they were in helping their children communicate.

In the 1980s we changed the name of the program from ELI to ECO. ELI had focused on teaching the child language. ECO (for Ecological) expanded the ELI program to emphasize the natural relationships that fostered communication and to extend the program to noninteractive and nonverbally communicative children. We were now interested in the continuum of development from the child's earliest interaction (his ecology) to full conversational relationships. We regularly saw children of many kinds and so I was looking for some general principles that would apply to communication development per se.

While we had years of successes teaching verbal children to talk more, we were still faced with a growing number of children who were not only not talking, but were also interacting very little with others. It was in the 1980s that we saw a marked increase in the incidence of children referred to as autistic and pervasively developmentally delayed. Many of these children may have had some language but they did not communicate with it in social ways. Consequently, we expanded our intervention to "communication" itself, since we were discovering that many children had a considerable communicative life long before they became habitual talkers. By doing this we were able to investigate what children needed to do before language and how parents could enter the child's nonverbal world to insure he was a communicator before a talker. Much of the educational and therapeutic focus at the time, and still to this day, was based on the assumption that the child was already social and communicative and that his major needs were specifically in cognitive development, including learning language. We found that very little professional training was available that addressed the social and communicative needs of preverbal children. Consequently, the professionals were not understanding the many skills required for preverbal development. It was our belief that many of the predictions that children with delays "could not talk" were based on attempts to get children to talk too soon and failed to build the social and communicative skills needed before language.

These new revelations about what needed to occur before language (Bruner 1983; Stern 1977) led us to explore systematically ways to help preverbal children become more interactive and nonverbally communicative. As the identification of autistic children rose dramatically, we began to study how to help these often socially isolated children to be communicative. Note that our goal at first was not to teach language per se, but to help the children feel safe and motivated to enter the kinds of interactions needed for language and relationship development.

Another federally funded research project enabled us to study the parent–child relationships with several preverbal children with autistic features. In these clinical studies we discovered that a responsive, playful parental style was more effective at helping children interact than a directive approach. Concurrent with our studies, Gerald Mahoney and his associates were conducting a long program of research into maternal communication styles with children with social and communicative delays (Mahoney and Powell 1988). Independently, the Mahoney group and our ECO group were finding strikingly similar answers to the question, "What parent strategies are effective in helping children interact and communicate?" Much of the research support for the five responsive relationship strategies in this book evolved in the 1980s. The major conclusion was that a responsive parental style had a decided advantage over a directive style in helping children become social. Based on hundreds of hours of video analyses and years of clinical teaching programs, we found five strategies that emerged as powerful in helping children become social and communicative. The strategies were: being balanced, being matched, sharing control, being responsive, and being emotionally playful. These strategies emerged from our research and that of many others (Bruner 1990; Girolometto, Verbey and Tannock 1994; Kaiser and Hester 1994; Mahoney, Finger and Powell 1985; Stern 1977; Trevarthen *et al.* 1998; Wells 1986; and others studying the social underpinnings of language).

At this time, we realized that a central problem with autistic children was that they simply did not interact enough to develop social language. We also found that when they did interact, their life partners often behaved in ways far above what the child could try to do (mismatched) and not closely related to the child's interests (unresponsive). We were concerned by several interviews where the parents did not think it was important to interact with a child if he was nonverbal. They often expressed that they looked forward to the day when the child would talk so they could have a "real" relationship with him. A major focus of Communicating Partners has been to teach parents what preverbal children need and to show them how to have effective relationships with children long before they speak regularly. During this time I followed over 40 families a year in carrying out the parent-based programs. Getting to know the families intimately over time was essential to understanding and appreciating how parent–child relationships develop with our children. Research studies alone would not have told me the stories that reflect the reality of these relationships and the careful work involved. This book provides over 30 years of stories of parents building relationships with late-talking children.

In the early 1990s we extended the model into three new areas of study: infancy, literacy, and classroom communication. Paula Wilkening and I explored mother–child interactions with infants who were severely delayed both cognitively and socially. Paula's dissertation involved developing parent–infant interaction programs that prepared parents to build durable turn-taking relationships by entering the child's world of sensation and action (MacDonald and Mitchell 2002). At the same time a very creative and persistent student with years of clinical experience (Paula Rabidoux) convinced me to move into the area of literacy. She was a scholar of emerging literacy and saw many parallels between the communication approaches we had developed and the findings in early literacy. She saw literacy as one important form of early parent–child relationship that could inform us about how children learn language and literacy simultaneously. Paula's dissertation involved an ethological study of 20 parents and their socially limited children during storybook interactions (Rabidoux and MacDonald 2001). She found several styles of interaction but also found that certain parent strategies predicted whether the child would stay and participate. Those key strategies were:

1. responding to the child's nonverbal behaviors and point of interest

2. matching the child's behavior in terms of acting and communicating in ways the child could try

3. playing with emotional affect and making the interaction more play than work

4. balancing the interactions and allowing the child silent time to take his turns

5. sharing control by following the child's lead some of the time and taking the lead some of the time.

The study also involved a procedure in which Paula systematically used the five responsive strategies with the 20 preverbal children. The result was that, even though she was a stranger, she yielded much more interaction and communication from the children than did three-quarters of the parents. We concluded that storybook interactions are very effective ways to help children communicate when they are conducted in a reciprocal matched way rather than the directive and dominant ways that often prevail.

Our focus on parent–child interaction was the theme of the Ohio State University (OSU) programs. However, we realized that our children also spent several hours a day in classrooms and groups. We began to explore how these responsive approaches could extend to classrooms, where one-to-one interactions were more difficult. Monica Powell, Maria Dantas at OSU, Carolyn Glass in Pittsburgh, and the staff of the Discovery Center in Ohio spent several years applying the model to classrooms. The goal was to shift the classroom focus from a cognitive performance to social interaction. The process was interesting but not easy, since there is so much pressure to prepare the preschool child for later school that building a strong interaction base is often difficult. Powell and Dantas carefully prepared and tested a communication model for a classroom where the primary goal was to increase the children's interactions at any developmental level they were at (MacDonald and Mitchell 2002). We found that the critical feature was the teacher's commitment to social interaction as the key to generalizing learning to daily life.

In 1995, federal funding for the Nisonger Center was drastically cut and the Center was under massive reduction. I chose to take an early retirement and pursue the parent-based work on my own. As I say today, I am not retired but I am de-instutionalized. Being out of the university I have had more freedom to focus on the parent aspects of the work. Soon I developed the Communicating Partners Center to further the work. At about that time I joined Gerald Mahoney on a federal project to develop an early intervention program based on the responsive models he and I had been developing in parallel. I had been involved for years training his staff in the ECO program. We conducted a study with 20 families of autistic children and found that the model was very effective in making changes in the children's social and communicative development. We also found that the children changed to the degree that the parents were using the strategies of balancing, matching, responding, sharing control, and emotional playfulness (Mahoney and MacDonald 2003).

At the same time I have been applying Communicating Partners to several families of autistic children in my private practice and in a parent–school collaborative project at the Discovery Center in Logan County, Ohio. The program involved teaching all the staff of the school, and at least one family in each infant and preschool classroom, the basics of the Communicating Partners program. The school administrator, Susan Holycross, was very supportive and understood the need to making the entire school focus more on social and communicative goals than on the academic goals that had prevailed. It has been a real treat to work with the Discovery Center. Several of the staff and parents are now carrying out the program in both classrooms and homes. In fact, the theme of the preschool for over 100 students has become "Social Interaction," with the message to parents and staff that

The more a child interacts
with persons who act like him,
the more the child will learn.

2

Guiding Principles

Communicating Partners is guided by several principles that distinguish it from other approaches to communication disorders. The principles below will be reflected throughout the book in terms of what and how we propose that late-talking children can become social and communicative.

1. Each child is learning and learns best in his own way; when he fails to learn, the responsibility appears to be more with the adult's expectations than the child's actual capabilities.

2. Curing the child is not the issue; rather, the goal is teaching the child to interact within his current social and biological constraints.

3. Many environmental conditions at home and school interfere with becoming social and communicative.

4. When environmental interferences are removed, children begin to socialize and communicate more.

5. Communication disorders are primarily problems in asynchronicity in relationships with people; consequently, treatment needs to get the child and his life partners "in synch" in terms of cognition, communication, emotional functioning, and motivation.

6. Each child is learning either to communicate or not to communicate in each of his interactions.

7. Improving communication is a dynamic process that involves changing not the child alone but his daily partner's interactions with him. Thus, intervention requires two persons: the child and at least one durable life partner.

8. Late-talking children often live in incompatible and conflicting worlds: the child in a world of sensation and action and the adult in the world of thought and language. Successful treatment leads life partners into the child's world, both actively and perceptually.

9. Parent–child play is fundamental to developing effective communication.

10. Children need to become socially interactive before they will be regularly communicative.

11. Children need to be nonverbally communicative before their language is useful for relationships.

12. Language itself is not enough; regular communicative use of language is critical.

13. Certain adult interactive strategies have been identified as critical in supporting a child's communication development:

14. A responsive approach to children is superior to a directive approach in many significant and enduring ways.

15. Intervention programs that educate and clinically involve parents have more global effects than ones conducted by professionals alone.

16. While late-talking children can learn to be compliant students, academic and vocational performance is not sufficient to build socially effective communicative skills.

17. Children with communication disorders can often develop social and communicative relationships in society.

18. Parents are ideal in, and proven capable of, assisting late-talking children to become social and communicative.

3

Key Features of Communicating Partners and Contrasts with Traditional Approaches to Autism and Other Language Disorders

One mother describes her experiences with two vastly different views of autism. Peyton began to show many autistic features at about 18 to 22 months. His mother, Donna Jo, discusses moving from a negative to a positive approach with her son.

> The more I got into "traditional" therapies for Peyton, the more I realized and lamented how much we were focusing on what was "wrong" with him—"wrong" according to the professionals and normal development charts, that is. Professionals were focusing on making him compliant: reducing perceived "negative" behaviors, and teaching him skills for future schooling. They rarely saw the many positive things that we saw him do. Their goal seemed to be to make him into a new boy, to get rid of much of what he was. When Peyton was at the tender age of 13 months, I already had a laundry list of areas for us to make changes in him. I felt that everything he was was autistic and had to be replaced with "normal" behavior. The more I tried to change him, the more distant he grew from me and

the less I understood and connected with him. The more I tried to change him, the more difficult and isolated his behaviors became. He actually avoided me when he saw me coming. If there was one word to describe him, it was "resistant." With force and struggle I did get him to comply with a few activities for short times. But our relationship became tug of war and he now began avoiding people in general, except when he needed something.

Then the Communicating Partners program alerted me to many of Peyton's positive behaviors. I began to focus on the many positive behaviors I had not previously valued and I began to ignore his undesired behaviors. When I started copying him, studying him, caring about what he did, he began to open up to me like never before. It was only then that he made his first attempts to join our world. When I quit pressing him to do more and to be "normal," and when I accepted his unique course and time frame, he blossomed. I focused on what he could do, what he loved to do, and began to see more of what he could do than what he could not do. Now he colors, races cars, tries to help me cook and clean, feed him, etc. It is all coming in time—exasperating as that may be for me when I get too focused on "normal" development. But he also still likes to spin things and he hand flaps and toe walks when he is excited. Most people who meet Peyton today do not even realize that he has any problems beyond a speech delay. He looks at strangers in the eye and waves! He is now a far cry from the infant who could not stop screaming, the baby who could not hold himself up, and the toddler who avoided people completely.

This book is describing a new paradigm (as defined by Kuhn in the 1970s) for helping children with autism and other social delays become social and communicative. It is a new paradigm in that it differs from traditional approaches in the why, who, how, where, and when of intervention. A new paradigm is needed to replace or supplement the traditional "educational/therapeutic" approaches that were developed for children who already have the social and communicative skills to learn and generalize spontaneously in daily life. Traditional approaches have focused on the child's cognitive or knowledge base, on teaching information and skills that would be useful and develop further only if the children applied them in daily social and communicative life. The problem with traditional approaches for children with autism and other delays is that these children simply have little or no social and communicative life. Consequently, many children learn academic and behavior skills but rarely use them since they are not socializing and communicating. Communicating Partners addresses children's need to be social and communicative so that they learn in daily relationships.

Traditional approaches assume that the students have the social and communicative skills to use the educational and therapeutic effects in their daily lives. We have found in over 30 years of research that this simply is not the case. We have also found that the more a child socializes and communicates the more they learn and grow cognitively. This is not to say that traditional directive approaches are not effective or needed at times, but they are effective only to the degree that the students can use socially what they learn.

For children with autism and other language disorders, traditional education and therapy that focus primarily on instilling information and skills are fundamentally insufficient because these children are not actively in the social world where the information and skills would be further learned and established as life habits.

The Communicating Partners approach is a real paradigm shift from traditional education in that it finds traditional directive approaches are insufficient to provide late-talking persons with the basic skills to continue to learn on their own. This is not to say we are not interested in a child's cognitive development. But we see children's social relationships as the critical process for cognitive learning. Jerome Bruner, a prominent cognitive psychologist of the twentieth century, concluded after 40 years' work that social relationships that are responsive and balanced are the most important tool to enable children to develop cognitively. Jean Piaget, a pioneer in child psychology for over 50 years, concluded that the child has his own unique world of sensation and action and learns best when activities and life partners fit the child's possible world of perception and interest. Lev Vygotsky studied children in Russia at the same time as Piaget was studying children in Switzerland and reported very similar findings, but he found that children learn best when they are in relationships with people who match the child's capabilities and model behavior that the child can do and is interested in.

The central question this book addresses is: How can children with autism and other socially isolating conditions learn to learn in daily, natural social interactions? The answer requires a paradigm shift, needing not only answers in terms of what *children* need to do but, just as importantly, answers in terms of what the *child's life partners* need to do and the kinds of environments that will effectively support social development. Communicating Partners realizes that the bulk of a child's learning will not be accomplished by adults who are directly teaching them but rather with daily life partners in spontaneous interactions. Taking this view, critical lifelong learning is seen not in terms of information or skills but in terms of the quality and quantity of personal social relationships.

Another way Communicating Partners (CP) differs from traditional approaches in education and therapies is that it proposes that children learn to be social and communicative much more in relationships that are balanced and reciprocal and not directed teaching interactions. Consequently, a fundamental principle of CP is that changing a child requires changing the people in his daily relationships. To that end, CP focuses on teaching parents and other partners to use responsive strategies as much as it focuses on changing the child. Few educational and therapeutic approaches address the developmental needs of both partners in a relationship. However, the late-talking child's task in learning to socialize is much more like the task in marriage therapy or other efforts to address relationships. Few marriages in crisis will be genuinely repaired unless both partners exert effort that relates to the other partner's concerns, abilities, and efforts. Similarly children with autism and other developmental delays need to have stable and responsive relationships if they are going to learn how to learn in the world at large.

While traditional approaches assume the child will do the bulk of his learning with professionals in a classroom or therapy session, Communicating Partners predicts that the late-talking child will do the bulk of his social and communicative development in spontaneous daily interactions with persons with whom he is emotionally attached. CP supports the many views of child development that purport that children learn to learn in their natural daily environments doing activities that fit both their current abilities and their interests with persons who are responsive to their abilities and motivations and who provide natural models that they can learn from.

In the case study at the start of this chapter, Peyton's mother describes a confusing dilemma that many parents with late-talking children face, whether to change the child to act "normal" or to accept him and help him develop as the best unique person he can be. In 30 years we have found that children become much more social and communicative when parents play an active part in helping the child develop his unique strengths rather than trying to change his basic nature. The discussion below highlights some of the differences between the Communicating Partners approach to language delays and other traditional approaches. Communicating Partners views the child as developing signature strengths and needing to become social and communicative first. Traditional approaches, on the other hand, focus on making the child a compliant student first.

The issue of cure vs. development

Parents understandably are driven to "cure" as many of their child's ailments as possible. They treat a cold, fix a broken leg, and teach children to solve problems. Consequently, it is reasonable, when faced with autism and other language disorders, that they are immediately drawn to "fix" it or to seek a cure. This urge is natural and well intentioned. The problem with focusing on "curing" the "problem" is that it may lead to throwing the baby out with the bath water. What I mean is that, when we try to stop a child from acting in his own ways, we are often discouraging the abilities and interests every child has. Parents looking for a cure often think they need to wait until the child is "normal" before having a "real" relationship with him. In so doing, they miss many critical opportunities to relate in ways that help him develop.

Communicating Partners takes the approach of positive psychology (Seligman 1996) by addressing the child's "signature" strengths rather than his weaknesses. The goal is social development not cure, and the starting point is how the child is currently developing. This approach supports the child's interests and key abilities, so that he will develop more positively and less negatively. We see each child as having some "signature" strengths that can be built upon to form durable relationships. We are convinced that almost every child with autism or other delays can develop authentic relationships and that his total development depends on those relationships. While we have seen many persons diagnosed "autistic or PDD" become persons who no longer fit the diagnosis, our goal is not a cure. Rather our goal is to help children develop as many social relationships as they can. Consequently, an enduring goal of our approach is to help the child use his current strengths in becoming social and communicative.

What comes first: student or social partner?

Traditional education and Communicating Partners differ fundamentally in their beliefs about what children with autism or other delays need to learn. Traditional approaches focus on skills and information for becoming a competent student in cognitive learning and a competent worker. Spontaneous social behavior is rarely a primary focus of traditional education and yet, for late-talking children, it is the key to lasting relationships and the ability to use what they might learn academically.

Communicating Partners sees the child as first needing to learn to develop his current *signature strengths* within social relationships. CP views social learning as the key to spontaneous cognitive learning, in the sense of "social modeling" that Albert Bandura has proposed for many years. CP begins not by teaching new skills and behaviors but by learning to socialize with behaviors the child is already able and motivated to do. CP focuses on helping children learn and use skills that will help them *learn to learn socially*. As a social learner, the child then has many more opportunities to learn as a part of life and not be limited to learning what others choose to teach him. While traditional educational approaches often show successes in academic learning, they usually do not show spontaneous social changes.

How does a child best learn to communicate?

Traditional approaches often use directive approaches for teaching a child to be social and communicative. They assume children learn language and appropriate social behavior best by being told what to do and responding to questions, directives, and other external learning cues.

We have found children to be social and communicative most effectively when actively engaged in social relationships that have five characteristics:

1.   They are balanced in the sense of allowing the child to lead at times.

2.   They are matched in that the child's interests and abilities are supported.

3.   They are emotionally attached in that each partner is genuinely enjoying each other.

4.   They are responsive in that partners respond to the child's natural learning and signature strengths.

5.   They share control in that each person is having positive effects on the other.

What is the role of success and self-esteem?

Traditional approaches define success according to criteria that are external to the child and in terms of what is expected at the same chronological age. Children learn that they make mistakes and are often not supported for subtle gains they make if they are not up to the normative criteria. Traditional approaches usually do not evaluate progress by the child's feelings of competence and spontaneous motivation for learning. These approaches define success in comparison with chronologically age-matched children and not with their own recent performance.

CP defines success in terms of how the child is changing in comparison with his prior performance and not in terms of the performance of age-peers. Success is defined in terms of the child's "personal social best," which means that success occurs when the child does more of what he can do in social interactions. The child's own spontaneous interest in interacting and learning more is valued as the key to successful learning rather than measures external to the child's current competencies.

The child's role in his learning: passive versus interactive

Traditional approaches often place the child in the role of passive receiver of information, chosen and directed by others. Success is determined by performance in relation to directed cues and not in terms of spontaneous expressions of what is learned. The child's role in learning is limited to the activities that are being taught and do not extend into his daily life in spontaneous ways. The child's current learning process is often not taken as the base for future learning.

CP views the role of the child as primarily an active one that leads and shapes the learning process. His current strengths inform what he is to learn and his social interactions are seen as major ways he will continue learning. Valid social and communicative learning is viewed only in terms of the child's abilities and interests. The role of the child is to express his signature strengths in responsible social interactions. The child's role is to socialize his learning rather than to accumulate and store it. In fact the child's increased interactions are seem as inevitable signs of learning. Thus the child's role in learning is to become as interactive and communicative as possible, given that, since his primary limitation is social, his primary learning needs to be social as well.

What is the appropriate role of parents in communicative development?

In traditional approaches, parents usually play a peripheral role, other than delivering the child to school and therapy. The view is that professionals are the ones trained to teach children and parents have other responsibilities. When the child is delayed or autistic, traditional approaches occasionally encourage parents to replicate what happens at school or in therapy with the assumption that parents need to be teachers who extend school into the home.

CP takes an entirely different view of the parents' role. It views parents as the inevitable natural teachers and the indispensable source for helping late-talking children become social and communicative, since the child needs to become social and communicative before traditional education will have lasting effects. CP sees the child's daily living environments as critical to such learning. Social and communicative development, in fact, is seen as perhaps the key responsibility of parents. Consequently, CP takes the stand that rather than making parents into teachers, parents need to become natural play partners who insure the child becomes social within his time and limitations. In fact, CP strongly encourages professionals to play much more the role of a "parent," in the sense of a social and communicative partner, than the directive trainer that many feel they should be. This is not to say that there is not a time for directive teaching but that time is when the child is secure in becoming social and communicative.

Which teaching strategies are more effective: directive or responsive?

Traditional approaches often teach language in the same ways they teach other cognitive tasks. Language is taught as a skill to memorize and perform reactively. Rarely is language taught within conversational settings; hence children learn language without learning the critical social skills that allow language to contribute to building relationships. Furthermore, traditional approaches rarely focus on teaching children to communicate nonverbally, which is critical to successful social use of language. The need for control in traditional approaches does not allow for much spontaneous learning of the social interaction skills, such as imitation, turn-taking, and social play, that determine how much a child will become a communicator.

CP is based on over 30 years of research concerning which social strategies are effective in helping children interact habitually and then communicate. The findings from adult–child interactions with a wide variety of typical and delayed children clearly point to at least five classes of natural interactive strategies that impact on social and communicative development. A fundamental feature of CP is to help adults learn and use spontaneously in any interaction the following classes of interactive styles:

1. balance
2. match
3. responsiveness
4. sharing control
5. emotional attachment.

The value of this set of "responsive" (in contrast to directive) strategies is that they are effective at any developmental level and can thus be used with preverbal, nonverbal, and verbal children. They can also be used to help children communicate in any situations, such as teaching, play, care-giving, disciplining, and other natural events.

Several researchers have argued in favor of responsive versus directive teaching for communication development. Mahoney has conducted a series of studies that show that mothers who are more responsive than directive and controlling have children who interact and communicate more spontaneously and maturely. Several other child development researchers had made a powerful case for the superiority of being responsive over being directive when the goal is communication (Donnellan *et al.* 1984; Duchan 1995; Koschanska 2001; Sigman and Capps 1997).

The role of the professional: teacher or mentor?

The traditional role of the professional is one of teacher, behavior manager, and general regulator who focuses on external curricula with which the child is to comply. Whether a teacher or therapist, the professional by and large works only with the child in a controlled situation that greatly limits spontaneous activity. The professional's role is often seen as necessarily separate from the child's home environment and so rarely do parents even know what the goals and processes are for the child. The professional's role is often constrained by institutional goals of a school or clinic and so the professional is often compelled to teach skills for succeeding in school rather than in spontaneous social life.

CP provides for the professional a much more ecologically valid role in the sense that it views the professional as a valuable but not sufficient part of the child's development. CP recognizes that learning is not limited to school; consequently the CP professional teaches children in ways they will generalize to daily life. Traditional approaches place impossible demands on teachers and therapists who are expected to do the bulk of the job of helping children socialize and communicate. CP recognizes that professionals have the most impact as coaches and mentors to parents in helping parents create effective relationships with late-talking children. When professionals collaborate with parents rather than isolate them from the child's education, they are insuring their jobs are much more likely to succeed. The responsive strategies of the CP approach are just as effective as teaching strategies in the classroom and therapy session as they are in the home. When both professionals and parents have similar goals and strategies for the child, it is much more likely that the child will become more social and communicative.

CP also offers the teacher and therapist effective ways to make their relationship with late-talking children more social and communicative, and thus more successful. The responsive strategies have been successful in enhancing children's learning in classrooms and therapy sessions. Thus, while the ideal would be for professionals to work collaboratively with parents, when that is not feasible many professionals have shown that the CP model can increase communicative development when used in therapy or schools.

Which are the best contexts for learning to communicate: home, therapy, or school?

Traditional approaches have shown that children with autism and other delays can learn academic, vocational, and behavioral skills in controlled classrooms. What have not been demonstrated are spontaneous social and communicative relationships. Our work suggests that when the goal is to help children socialize and communicate, the physical context for learning must actively support that learning. In most traditional settings, children are rarely free to socialize and communicate spontaneously and the adults rarely respond to the child's natural social and communicative behavior in supportive ways. Rather, there is usually an external curriculum that dictates what and when the child should interact and communicate.

The CP model finds that children learn best to socialize and communicate in spontaneous one-to-one relationships in which they have at least half the control of the activity. Adults enter the child's world of sensation and action as much as they demand the child enters their adult world of thought and language. Thus the optimal context for learning to communicate will be relationships in which there is the opportunity for genuine reciprocal exchanges. These relationships can occur in classrooms, therapy sessions, or homes, but our work has focused on insuring that the children develop relationships in their homes where they have the strongest emotional attachments and the greatest opportunity to practice new learning. CP encourages concerned persons to seek out and create "natural therapy" environments that make spontaneous interaction highly likely.

Who is to be changed when communication is the goal?

In traditional approaches, the child is the primary, often the only, person to change. Educational and therapy programs expend most of their efforts changing the child's performance in the confines of the classroom or therapy setting. However, research into the effectiveness of early intervention programs has resoundingly concluded that children make cognitive and communicative gains to the degree that parents are actively involved in learning and changing their natural interactions at home (Mahoney and Powell 1988; Mahoney and MacDonald 2003).

For Communicating Partners, the primary goal is reciprocal relationships between adults and children. Consequently, effecting changes in any relationship involves helping both partners to change. One durable finding over 30 years is that when parents or other life partners change the ways they interact and communicate with their children, the children change as well. That is why so much of the CP model is devoted to teaching parents and other partners responsive strategies that match their child's development and motivation. Helping children to communicate may be analogous to the marriage counselor who is trying to assist a couple in their relationship. Very few experienced counselors would address the marriage by trying to change the behavior of only the husband or wife. It is only common sense that improving the relationship requires participation of both partners. So too with our children. If they are to build stronger relationships their life partners must be in on the learning as much as the children. Communicating Partners has found that helping parents change so they are intimately relating in their child's world changes the child in many ways and also reduces the parents' stress in raising the child.

The ultimate goals: compliant student vs. social partner

Often, the ultimate goal of traditional approaches to communication disorders including autism is to place the child successfully in an academic program and maintain adequate performance. Many current approaches suggest that they may have "cured" autism with the evidence that the child is maintaining age-appropriate academic behavior in school. Other approaches claim success when the child learns hundreds of words or when the child exhibits fewer "autistic" behaviors. While these goals, observations, language, and behavior are desirable, they will genuinely help the child only when they generalize to daily life and help develop relationships. Unfortunately, many traditional programs set goals for the autistic child very narrowly. Many professionals do not believe that autistic children can develop authentic relationships in society and so they limit goals to ones that can be made within a restrained life.

Two of the most well-known adult autistic persons are Temple Grandin and Donna Williams, each of whom have written and lectured about their lives extensively. While each has become a competent and successful adult, their individual stories differ in ways that apply to this discussion. Temple tells of years of rigorous academic and behavioral training and her success in restraining her life to many rules. She, long ago, accepted that she would not likely have intimate relationships with people and she has designed her personal and professional life so that she is usually in control over what happens in relationships. She describes eloquently how she prefers professional activity to social interactions. She learned early on that she was intelligent and she focused on honing her cognitive skills to become a very successful researcher.

Donna was also a very intelligent autistic child but one who was resistant to the rigors of academic life. She believed she needed to learn in her own ways, which were often unacceptable to her family and society. Rather than avoid social relationships as Temple did, Donna pursued them, frequently with disastrous consequences. In both social and academic worlds, Donna was not compliant and self-disciplined as Temple was. Unlike Temple, who had few if any intimate relationships, Donna has had and continues to have many relationships, which she relates vividly in a series of books. Donna has become a successful counselor and writer but she did it in a much less orderly way than Temple has. Temple settled, early on, for a successful autistic life in relative seclusion while Donna faced the social world and tackled it, becoming increasingly successful in having relationships.

Communicating Partners, on the other hand, does not focus on the autistic child's limitations. Rather it focuses on the child's "signature strengths," those skills and interests the child currently expresses when he is in supportive environments. This is not to say that every autistic child can do anything, but we have found a great many far exceed the predictions of highly trained professionals. Consequently, the ultimate goal of CP is for children to have communicative relationships and continue to develop social, cognitive, and adaptive abilities in those relationships. The goal of CP is not necessarily to rid the child of the label "autism," although we know many children for whom this has been the case. Rather, the goal is for each child to become more interactive and more successful in personal, and often professional, relationships.

Two ways of looking at children and language disorders: optimistic and pessimistic

Jeremy is five years old and generally non-communicative. He plays primarily alone, avoids people much of the time, and does many physical things that other children rarely do. He has had several diagnoses or labels, including autism, pervasive developmental disability, attention disorder, obsessive-compulsive disorder, auditory dysfunction, oppositional behavior, apraxia, depression, language disorder, anxiety disorder, and mentally retarded. He clearly shows certain signs of each of the disorders but does not fit one category. So, many people are asking: "What is he?"

There are two ways people generally look at Jeremy and other children: either the *what is he* approach (i.e. his diagnosis), and what are his weaknesses, or the *who is he* approach, and what are his strengths. A "what" is something viewed as an object, something you do something to. A "who" is someone you interact with. Pessimistic and optimistic people will interact very differently with the child, and these interactions will determine what they do together and how the child learns. A major goal of Communicating Partners is to help parents become more optimistic and less pessimistic about their child and their abilities to help him develop.

Let us apply these two approaches to Jeremy. He spends considerable time with Julie and Jack, his parents. Each parent is very concerned about Jeremy and they are having conflict about what to do. These conflicts relate to the fact that the parents see the boy from very different perspectives. Julie is the optimist and Jack is the pessimist in terms of Jeremy. Julie sees Jeremy as an enjoyable boy who plays and learns well at times. Jack sees the boy as "autistic," "handicapped," "disabled," and a "poor student." Jack has a much harder time enjoying Jeremy than Julie does.

Julie and Jack completed the Adult–Child Relationship Map (ARM) and we observed each parent play with the child a few times. We also interviewed them about their concerns and how they saw the boy. We asked about how the boy interacted, communicated, played, learned, and how he emotionally behaved. We also asked what each parent expected of Jeremy. They told us what they thought he needed to do next and what treatment they thought was called for.

We have often seen people approach a child very differently on the basis of whether they view the child as a "damaged child" versus a "growing child" or as a child "to fix" versus a child to "relate with."

Optimistic parents look for what the child can do while pessimistic parents look for what the child cannot do or is doing "wrong." Optimists are interested in helping the child to do more of what he can do while pessimists often focus on having the child stop doing things or getting him to do things that he cannot now do. When optimists look for the child's "signature" strengths they usually find something the child can and wants to do. They then learn to respond to the strengths and thus they encourage the child to continue developing. However, when pessimists focus on the child's weaknesses and inabilities, they often attend to weak behaviors and fail to support what the child can do.

Let's see how Julie and Jack view their son Jeremy from each special relationship with him.

Interaction

Julie sees Jeremy as beginning to enjoy being with her and others who play in ways he does. She sees him as playing mainly alone but willing to join people who play physically more than talk. Julie sees the boy imitate some of her actions and vocalizations when she does things he can do. She sees him acting like her after the fact, as in household chores. He stays interacting back and forth for up to a few minutes and takes turn with her when he chooses the activity.

Jack sees Jeremy as avoiding him and others much of the time. He feels the boy ignores him when he talks or tries to teach him things. He is surprised to hear that the boy imitates some people because Jeremy rarely tries to do things his dad does. He tries to keep the boy interacting back and forth by asking many questions and showing him how to do activities but the boy rarely stays more than briefly.

Communication

Julie sees Jeremy as communicating mainly with gestures and facial expressions, but she also sees him beginning to use more sounds to communicate and to make definite but unclear attempts at some words. She feels he understands much of what she says to him and that he communicates to show affection, to show her something as well as to get his needs met. He enjoys her reading to him but does it passively.

Jack is very concerned that the boy is five and still not talking. He has been told children do not begin to talk much after age five. Jack does not seem very aware of the many nonverbal and vocal ways that Jeremy does communicate. Words are Jack's only concern. Jack feels he should talk to the boy in adult ways but admits that his son rarely seems to understand what his father says.

Motivation and play life

Julie sees many changes in Jeremy in terms of wanting to play in new ways. When she plays with things as he does, he shows much more curiosity and exploration than when he is doing teaching tasks. She has recently been successful getting the boy to imitate her and to play in her ways some of the time.

Jack is very concerned that Jeremy does not play with regular "boy" things and that his play looks strange to others. He knows that the boy likes to be with him but he does not know how to play in ways that keep him there. Jack watches his wife play for long periods with the boy but is not sure he can act as silly as his wife. He thinks it is wrong to imitate Jeremy, which is much of what Julie does to get the boy interacting.

Civil and behavioral life

Julie has come to ignore Jeremy's stimulating behaviors and she has found that attending more to his positive behaviors gets him to do more of them and less of the less desirable ones. She has learned that he can interact and communicate with her even when he is making unrelated motions and when he gets distracted. When Jeremy gets agitated or physical, Julie successfully ignores him or silently restrains him. He is behaving much better with her now. She has learned that talking to behaviors she does not want backfired and increased them.

Jack has real difficulty allowing Jeremy to do the sensory behaviors that seem automatic, such as hand-shaking, looking around, and fighting. He is afraid others will make fun of him and has not yet learned that he can interact while doing these behaviors. Jack frequently gets into shouting matches when Jeremy "misbehaves" and he reports being tired of the constant war with his son.

4

Examples of Children Studied for this Book

You may find this book easier to read if you meet a few of the wide range of late-talking children we studied in the development of Communicating Partners. This chapter introduces the reader to a wide range of children we have studied. Each of the children was evaluated and diagnosed with the autistic spectrum, as PDD, autistic, or with Asperger's syndrome. Each child satisfied the characteristics of autism as described in the DSM-II, III, or IV manuals (depending on the year diagnosed) and exhibited the features on the Childhood Autism Rating Scale (Schopler, Reichler, and Renner 1986) that indicated evidence of moderately–severely autistic (scores from 30 to 60).

More case descriptions will be scattered throughout the book to illustrate individual topics. The descriptions below provide a view of the range of children involved in the development of this book.

Scott

At age three Scott would not be touched without screaming. The day I met him, he carried two real estate listing books and would not give them up for other activities. Cheryl, his mother, said, "Look at him. He won't let anyone near him or talk to them but he can read aloud most of the words in these books." She pointed to one page and he read, "Upper Arlington, three bedroom, two bath, 1800 square feet, two-car garage, walking distance from public and parochial schools."

Scott also impulsive-touched many things, rubbing them and waving them in the air. He rarely contacted people except when in need and with physical tugs and yells. He violently resisted most transitions and responded to personal intrusions with up to a half an hour of screaming. He apparently learned many skills by watching others but did not comply when others attempted to talk to or teach him. He appeared to be acutely socially aware but rarely responded when others spoke to him.

His signature strengths included his interest in books and his physical ability to read and say words, his physical and emotional attachment to his mother, and his ability to imitate others after the fact. His major limitations included his lack of spontaneous interactions, extreme anxiety when contacted, and his failure to use language to communicate.

Andrew

Andrew was four years old, nonverbal, and generally socially isolating. When I first worked with him, it was from across a large room. He stayed with his mother closely and went into a rage when I made any moves to be closer. I taught his mother, Pam, ways to act like him and responsive ways to play with him by coaching her from a safe distance. He resisted any directions and preferred to repeat many actions that seemed to calm him but did not appear to have other clear purposes.

Andrew's signature strength was that he showed enjoyment during physical contact with his mother. He responded to her touch and talk while he did not do so with anyone else. His mother appeared to enjoy him even when he was upset and acting in autistic ways. She stated, "I know there's a smart little boy in there and I'm going to find him." She appeared to be more interested in "finding" and then joining him than changing him. The program began by teaching Andrew's mother a few responsive strategies that led her into his world and kept him gradually interacting more with her.

Randy

I met Randy when he was six. He had been in a behavioral training program with one-to-one discrete trial instruction for two years, mainly in the home for about 20 hours a week with three to five different assistants. The parents reported considerable gains in academic learning and behavioral management. They were pleased that Randy changed from an isolated non-responsive and uncooperative child to one who was a compliant student and successfully learned many tasks and who adapted to a classroom with typically developing children.

While pleased with Randy's unexpected progress, given that at age three he was predicted to be nonverbal and referred to an institution, his parents were concerned that he still preferred to be alone and that, while he had some language, he rarely socialized with people or had genuine conversations. His language style was often rigid and he spoke more in monologues than in discourse with others. They wondered if he could ever become an easy conversationalist and build reciprocal relationships.

Randy's signature strengths were his rich bank of knowledge, his ability to cooperate with others, and his extensive vocabulary. His major limitations appeared to include his lack of spontaneous language, his passive role in interactions, and his apparent inability to take the perspective of others. His parents were eager to learn how to help the boy develop friendships and become more social. They had believed that their role should be one of a directive teacher and they enjoyed reducing the pressures and joining into his world. The program began by helping Randy's parents join into his activities and make simple conversations based on his motivations.

Molly

At age three Molly preferred to play alone in repetitive and apparently nonproductive ways. She resisted intrusions from people by withdrawing and occasionally striking out. While she said a few words to herself, she mainly communicated by physically manipulating others. She ignored people except when she was using them to satisfy her needs. She showed little emotional attachment with anyone. She rarely imitated other persons and appeared to be learning very little from observing others. Her mother and grandmother were concerned that Molly would hurt herself; consequently they were very protective and responded to her frequent demands and rages.

Molly's signature strengths were her persistence in activities that interested her and her occasional ability to charm others with smiles. Her family believed that she should be able to do many of the things that other three-year-olds could do, such as talking, toileting, and drawing, but they had developed a struggling relationship with Molly in activities that she was obviously not developmentally ready to do. The program began by helping the family have successful interactions with Molly in activities she both enjoyed and could do. The goal, at first, was not to teach her any new skills but to make social the behaviors she already chose to do.

Jacob

Jacob was five when I first saw him. He was nonverbal and made very few sounds other than to accompany his repeated behaviors such as spinning a string, rocking, and watching videos. Jacob's activity level was very low, perhaps in part due to his Down syndrome in addition to several autistic features. His mother had spent two years trying to teach him "age-appropriate" and school-related tasks, with considerable frustration on both sides. Once she realized that he was not ready for school, she began a program of sensory activities to help him relax and respond more to people. She found the sensory training helped him become more aware of people and he began to join spontaneously into parallel activities and imitate others. She felt he was more into the world of the family.

However, he was still not communicating much, except for basic needs. Additionally, he still did not use his sounds to communicate and he rarely interacted with others in any back and forth ways. His signature strengths included enjoying watching others play and beginning to imitate others' actions. The program began by having the family imitate his actions and sounds and keep him in interaction with any activities he enjoyed.

Serena

Serena was a 14-year-old girl with elaborate language but very little conversational skill. She repeated stories over and over and often responded to others' speech with unrelated language. She usually refused to talk about what others chose and she frequently turned a conversation into a silly game that appeared very immature.

Her mother reported that she had been a fairly cooperative student in the early grades and that she could learn many academic skills easily. At about age 12, though, she began to resist any directions from others and resumed many self-stimulatory behaviors, such as rocking and talking to herself, that had reduced since she was about five years old. Her mother was concerned that she did not know how to teach the girl any more after years of successes. We began the program by helping the mother and girl begin to enjoy each other by playing in silly ways and with no goal other than to enjoy each other. The goal was to make the interaction less work and more fun.

Colin

Colin appeared to be developing socially and cognitively in typical ways until he began to have seizures at age three. Diagnosed with epilepsy and subject to a series of medical treatments, Colin began showing several autistic features. He talked repetitively and mainly away from any social topics. Colin withdrew from social interactions when there was multiple stimulation, such as people talking at the same time as television programmes.

Colin's signature strengths were that he stayed interacting with people enjoyably in one-to-one situations and he was beginning to imitate others spontaneously. The program began building one-to-one interactions with the activities and language that he already demonstrated. His parents began to enter his world of sensation and action and came to understand more how he perceived the world. They also learned to "read" his learning availability and interacted with him more when he was accessible.

JP

JP at age four rarely stopped moving. He resisted staying in interactions even briefly. He played in very repetitive ways, such as twirling a toy as he ran around with little apparent purpose. While he made many speech sounds he rarely directed them to people and he seldom responded when others spoke to him. He did occasionally show he was learning by modeling others spontaneously.

His signature strengths included imitative skills, especially when others were doing things he could do and that were animated. The program began with the parents imitating his actions and sounds frequently, and in interactions doing things he clearly could do.

Delaware

One of three autistic children, at age four he appeared satisfied doing very little. If not bothered, he would sit alone motionless for hours. He was generally passive and somewhat cooperative but he rarely initiated contact with others. He would imitate some actions and sounds but with no enthusiasm. He occasionally showed considerable knowledge by solving life-problems, such as finding things he needed and taking care of his needs. But he did these on his own and not in interactions, where he seemed to shut down and allow others to do the doing. He was considered to be a "good" student in that he complied with directions in academic settings but rarely spontaneously participated in ongoing social situations.

The program began with the parents spending quiet time with Delaware where they made no demands but only responded to his actions imitatively.

5

Theoretical Foundations for Communicating Partners

The task of building communicative relationships with children with ASD and other language delays has required a multidisciplinary approach to our work. No one theory would suffice to address the issues that have faced us in the 30 years of development. While we refer to our model as Communicating Partners, that term reflects values and perspectives from several fields of child development, disabilities, education, and behavior change. Table 5.1 summarizes the theories and major proponents who have informed the development of Communicating Partners.

Table 5.1 The theories which have informed Communicating Partners

Domain	Principles and implications	Proponents
Parent–child relationship	Children develop in reciprocal relationships	Stern 1977 Bronfenbrenner 1979
Responsive education	Responsive approaches build social development more than directive ones	Mahoney and Powell 1988 Kohn 1993 Greenspan1985
Autistic spectrum disorders	Social relationships are the key to improvement	Prizant and Wetherby 1989 MacDonald 2002 Williams 1988 Koegel *et al.* 2001 Atwood 1998
Constructive child development	Children learn more by active participation than by directive teaching	Piaget 1963/Vygotsky 1978 Bandura 1986
Social cognition	Intelligence develops through social relationship more than direct teaching	Bruner 1977 Bandura 1986
Emotional intelligence	Children's social/communicative skills predicts life success more than intelligence measured in traditional IQ terms	Dalai Lama and Goleman 2003 Gardner 1983 Bandura 1986
Language development	Language develops in matched, responsive relationships, not directive teaching	Bloom 1993 Bates 1976 Wells 1986 Duchan 1995
Cognitive development	Cognition evolves from social interaction: the more children interact, the more they learn	Vygotsky 1978 Bandura 1986 Bruner 1983 Wetsch 1985
Communication theory	Improving communication requires changing both partners, not the child alone	Watslawick *et al.* 1967 Seligman 1990 Watslawick *et al.*1967
Family dynamics	A child is a function of his family, which must be involved in lasting interactions	Bronfenbrenner 1979 Greenspan 1985 Bornstein 1989
Positive psychology	Behavior change is more productive when signature strengths are supported than when negative behaviors are addressed	Seligman 1990, 1996 Goleman 1995
Developmental education	Education is most effective when matched to child developmental levels, not age in years	Elkind 1981 Goodman 1992 Kohn 1993 Sowell 1997

6

Basic Components of Communicating Partners

Five Developmental Stages and Five Relationship Strategies

Five stages of communication development

It could be said that we are learning to communicate anew in every interaction we have. The same is true with children: they develop communication in several stages. The stages are overlapping. For autistic and many late-talking children, these skills can be splintered in development; that is, they can develop the stages of some skills before or after the equivalent stages of other skills. We have found that it is critical to consider social and communication development on a long continuum from first interactions to complex conversations years later. Communicating Partners has found five stages in which our children have profound delays. These five stages are:

- interaction

- nonverbal communication

- social language

- conversation

- civil behavior.

This book will follow children along these five stages. Together the stages address the questions:

1. What do children need to do to become more social and communicative?

2. What are the key barriers and successes that face late-talking children?

Interaction

In the first stage, *interaction*, the late-talking child gradually begins to accept people into his world. He begins the habit of social play. He begins to initiate and respond to others and joins in their activities. He begins to prefer being with people to being alone and becomes more comfortable interacting for more social reasons than just getting his needs met. He also begins to have a reciprocal turn-taking relationship with people. He begins to play in a give-and-take manner with both actions and sound. He stays for longer interactions voluntarily.

He begins to act and communicate more in ways he sees others do. This development of imitation and modeling skills leads him to learn more and more as his interactions increase in number and length. This stage of interaction continues throughout the child's development of later communication and language skills.

This *interaction* stage addresses problems common to autism, such as ignoring and resisting people, preferring to be alone, acting in self-absorbed ways, and playing either a passive or dominant role in interactions. It is the stage at which the child becomes more accessible and responsive to people in general. This will happen to the degree that he has life partners who are responsive and matched to him in frequent, emotionally attached interactions.

Nonverbal communication

In the second stage, *nonverbal communication*, the child learns to send and receive messages in any physical way he can do. Learning to communicate for our children is a very complex process and involves much more than learning language per se. Communication requires our children to enter others' worlds in some way, often requiring a long period of communicating in nonverbal ways before using language socially. Here the child learns to genuinely connect with others' worlds in any way they can.

In the nonverbal communication stage, parents learn to support many of the child's nonvocal and vocal behaviors that they had previously not considered essential for communication. Not only does the child communicate first without words, he needs to communicate for many social reasons other than to satisfy his needs. Parents also help the child understand their communication by fine-tuning it to what the child can process and perform.

The nonverbal communication stage addresses several problems common in autism, such as a child's failure to communicate in any way, or communicating only with movements or sounds. The problem of communicating with the child is one that needs to be addressed long before focusing on teaching language, as does the problem of not responding when others communicate with him. Helping a child believe that his nonverbal behavior will successfully communicate is a major goal at this stage.

Social language

In the third stage, *social language*, the child learns to talk for several reasons that are personal, social, and instrumental. Too often, late-talking children learn language in rote or repetitive ways that are not really communicative much of the time. Here our child needs to learn that language is much more than words to perform; it means exchanging meanings with others in an authentic give and take where both persons are participating and are relating to what the other does and cares about.

Focusing on "social language" addresses the common problems in autism of talking that is bizarre or off the topic, rote and unresponsive talking, repeated talking, and self-absorbed language.

Conversation

In the fourth stage, *conversation*, the child is using language to have genuine relationships and to learn to take others' perspectives so that conversations are beneficial to both partners. Effective conversations are the culmination of the four previous developmental stages that a conversational life requires: regular joint activity routines, extended turn-taking, intentional communication, and a variety of uses of language other than speaking words per se. For many children, this conversational stage is long in coming, sometimes not until adolescence or adulthood. We have found that conversation can be hastened when careful attention is paid to helping the child become habitually interacting in social play and turn-taking and then to become a regular communicator with the child in any way possible. We have found that many children resist and refuse to become conversational if they do not believe that they will be accepted on who they are and what they can do, regardless of how unusual they may appear to others.

Developing the conversation stage involves addressing several common problems in autism, such as talking at, rather than with, others, insisting on their own topic, and interrupting others. This stage also addresses the concern when children shift topics rapidly, ignore what others say, either initiate or respond but not both, and dominate conversations with constant talking.

Civil behavior

The fifth stage, *civil behavior*, actually refers to skills that can be learned during each of the above stages. Civil behavior refers to the child learning to interact with others in empathic, respectful ways and reducing many common inappropriate or maladaptive behaviors. Becoming a civil communicator involves the child learning to cooperate with others and treat others with respect and kindness. He also learns emotionally appropriate behavior such as trusting and self-regulating as well as managing both positive and negative emotions with appropriate boundaries. The child also learns to take others' perspectives and to develop the empathy needed for successful relationships.

Focusing on a child's civil behavior addresses several problems common to autism, such as disregarding others' feelings, insensitive talking, and many forms of disrespecting others. Developing civil behavior is critical to the social success of autistic people, since even the greatest intellectual successes will not result in relationships if the person is not aware of what partners need in relationships.

Five relationship strategies

Anyone familiar with autistic persons understands that they have limited social and communicative skills, regardless of how many cognitive, technical, or physical abilities they have. We have found that their major problems lie in one or more of five levels of development:

1. playing with others
2. interacting spontaneously
3. communicating what they know
4. using language for conversations
5. sustaining socially acceptable relationships.

Regardless of the major concern, one fundamental problem is their lack of generalized social partnerships with others. The problem may be identified as a "speech," "language," or "communication" disorder or delay, but the underlying issue is often a need to develop relationships with people. Consequently, the major question is not "How do our children learn language?" but rather "How do they develop relationships that will support social use of language?"

Communicating Partners finds that, since social relationships are vital for authentic communication, we must consider broad changes in how we serve autistic children. These changes relate to the following questions we have addressed over the last 30 years:

- Can autistic children learn to have authentic communicative relationships?

- How do our children move from an isolated to an interactive world?

- What do children need to do before they speak?

- When is it time to help a child communicate?

- How do children develop language that is social and spontaneous?

- What is needed to help our children become civil and socially effective?

- Where and with whom do children best learn to communicate?

- What role can parents and other life partners play?

- And one core question underlies all of the preceding questions: What kinds of relationships are needed to become independently social and communicative?

Many clinical and educational programs appear to assume that the child has the social and communicative skills to use the academic knowledge that is taught. However, when we look at the education of "typical" children, schools usually expect children to be social and communicative before they make the child into a student. Before a child becomes a student, he needs to be a social person so that he will have a social world to use and practice the learning achieved as a student. Elkind (1987) alerts us to a rampant problem he calls "mis-education," which refers to the common practice of imposing academic and competitive goals on children before they have a stable base of social relationships. He finds that such children then learn a series of "circus tricks" that are not integrated into the fabric of the child's social learning. Elkind is referring to typically developing children. When the same notion is applied to autistic children, it is even more devastating. We are convinced that, regardless of how much knowledge and skills autistic children attain, their lives will be extremely limited without the social skills for authentic relationships.

Since the 1970s, research across several disciplines on social learning has reached surprisingly consistent findings regarding the key processes needed for social relationships. The research found a central core of child and adult competencies that contribute to stable social attachments. One key to successful relationships appears to be the reciprocal activity of partners—the child and adult partner—with each other. The point here is that children do not develop alone but in relationships where both child and adult are contributing to the child's development. Research now shows that successful relationships with children are characterized by a series of features that begin in infancy and proceed through the child's life span. Table 5.1 presents a list of some of these researchers and their findings regarding early relationships.

In our research we have found five major strategies that actively help children become social and communicative. Together we refer to these as "mutually responsive relationship" factors. The elegance and utility of the strategies is that they are effective all along the child's development, from initial nonverbal play to civil conversations. In fact, these basic strategies have been found consistently in the early mother–child interactions where later analyses have shown successful children in cognitive and communicative development (Mahoney and MacDonald 2003; Siller and Sigman 2002).

The following communication principles come directly from research into early adult–child interactions. As such, they are recommended to educators and families as instructive guides to help children become social and communicative with them. While these principles are in many ways counter to traditional approaches, keep in mind that the children in question are pre-conversational, not yet learning in, and generalizing to, social relationships. Most traditional teaching approaches were developed for and with children who already had social and communicative skills. The following principles address the question: How can adults interact so children become social and communicate with them?

Principle 1. The balance principle: communication develops within interactions that are balanced and reciprocal

Children learn to communicate to the degree they engage in frequent interactions that are balanced and allow the child to participate as much as the adult. In the 1980s our research found considerable imbalance in adult–child interactions where the adults did much more action and communication than the child, allowed the child little silent waiting time, and influenced the child to be a passive, not interactive, learner. Balancing involves waiting, taking turns, and inviting the child to share in the interaction.

Perhaps the most obvious fact about communicating is that the child cannot do it alone. However, autistic children spend much of their time actually alone or functionally alone. Being self-absorbed is often part and parcel of being autistic. Consequently, serious problems in communicating are to be expected. To become communicative, a child needs balanced and reciprocal partnerships (Bronfenbrenner 1979; Bruner 1983). The basic notion is that a child will learn from an adult to the degree the adult is an active partner in frequent give-and-take exchanges, where each person participates. One-sided interactions where a partner dominates the interaction will not enable children to communicate.

Several scholars in child development have shown that a child develops in the contexts of two-person relationships (Bronfenbrenner 1979). Your child will develop to the degree that he has frequent "joint activity routines" with persons who allow the child to interact as he can. Many view autism and suchlike as a disorder of relationships since there is often very little balance and reciprocity between the children and their partners. While many believe autistic children cannot have relationships until they reduce their condition greatly, our experiences strongly disagree. We have found that however removed a child is, he is capable of some kind of relationship when his partners enter his world and join in what he can do. This often requires major changes in how the adult acts and what he or she expects. We have also found the changes very possible and that little meaningful social and communicative development occurs unless adults become such partners.

In our work with children and parents, we encourage the parents to see their child as developing, not on his own, but in intimate relationships with them. Consequently, the task is not to teach the child but to enter the child's world and develop with the child. Communicating Partners is not just a convenient term; we are serious about helping parents become partners with their child in a very meaningful way.

As you enter your child's world and have a more balanced relationship with him, three things will happen: reciprocity, balance of power, and affective attachment.

You are reciprocal when each person influences the other in an interaction, unlike the common one-sided contacts where one partner is dominating. With autistic children, maintaining a back-and-forth flow can be a very long process. It requires that their partners accept at first many behaviors that may be unconventional, to say the least. The goal is to make an authentic connection, not to make the child act normal. In a reciprocal interaction, there is mutual feedback that informs each partner about how to connect. This may seem technical but it is essential for the relationships children need to learn with others. The learning here is spontaneous social learning, without which a child's learning may be limited to times he is taught and not throughout the social flow of life (Bruner 1983; Stern 1977).

The second feature of the principle of balance is turn-taking. When you and your child take turns, each has the opportunity to influence the other. Too often we see very little turn-taking in interactions with late-talking children. Either the adult takes most of the turns with the child playing a passive, nonresponsive role, or the child is dominating the interaction as the adult observes. When turn-taking is observed with our children it is often in a directive exchange, such as a series of questions and answers. Such an interaction may technically be turn-taking, but it is not reciprocal in the sense that each person is not both initiating and responding. Turn-taking allows a balance of power in interactions that allow the child both the active participation he needs and the regular access to the adult's feedback (Bronfenbrenner 1979).

Turn-taking can be a long-term goal for children if they do not learn early that it is essential for successful relationships. We have found that when children learn to take turns physically in play early on, they are generally more socially disciplined. It is as though they understand that social interactions, to be fair, need to be balanced where neither partner dominates the relationship. Children need to learn to take turns at every stage of social and communicative development. Nothing interferes with a conversation more than a partner dominating turns and preventing others from participating. Consequently, balanced turn-taking is a critical feature in all five stages: interaction, nonverbal communication, language, conversation, and civil behavior.

One value of balancing interactions is that it reduces the child's self-absorption that seriously delays his development. Turn-taking, while technical and superficial at first, is a key to convincing the child that interacting in a give-and-take way is not optional but necessary to his inclusion in society. When parents begin to balance interactions, at first they take a turn then wait for the child to respond in any way he can. When the parent waits, she is informing the child that she will accept what he can do. Too often when a child does not immediately respond, the parent takes more turns and virtually tells the child that she will handle the interactive load. Children often develop the appearance of learned helplessness, where they let their partners do all the social interaction. One of the most powerful ways to help children is to be very serious about turn-taking and to take your turn and wait for the child to do what he can so he learns that turn-taking is absolutely essential.

Principle 2. The developmental match principle: children learn to communicate to the degree they have frequent partners who act and communicate in ways that match the child's abilities and interests

Children with communication disorders often live mainly in a world of sensation and action while their life partners operate in a world of thought and language. This common "mismatch" results in a severe barrier to communicating. Children learn to communicate to the degree that their partners interact and communicate with them in ways the child is developmentally and emotionally able to perform. Our research revealed that adults frequently mismatch children by acting and communicating in ways that are too difficult for the child, or do not fit the child's interests (MacDonald and Carroll 1992). When adults match their children by being developmentally, emotionally, and motivationally within the child's receptivity, the children begin to interact more.

Matching requires that you enter your child's world and act in ways he can act and communicate. Several theories of child development support the strategy of matching. Piaget (1954) showed in a lifetime of experiments how children have a cognitive ("thinking") world distinct from adults. A core notion was that of the cognitive schema, which were general thought processes whereby the child perceived and understood the world. Children could learn to the degree that their world fitted their cognitive schema. Vygotsky (1978), a Russian contemporary of Piaget, extended Piaget's concepts beyond the child's learning alone to the child's learning within social interactions. Vygotsky and his many followers demonstrated the importance of the child's primary adults as mediators of the child's learning. They found that the child learned with adults to the degree the adults acted in ways that were slightly above, but not too far above, the child's abilities. Both of these powerful theories, substantiated by considerable amounts of research (Elkind 1987; Wertsch 1985; and many others), argue that a child has his own unique world of sensation and action and that he will learn to the degree that he has life partners who interact with him in ways that match his current abilities. The key strategy of matching is also supported by the lifelong work of Alfred Bandura, whose research into "social modeling" demonstrates that children learn from their life partners to the degree that they provide natural spontaneous models of behaviors the child is capable of doing (Bandura 1986). All three sizeable bodies of research and theory argue strongly that parents will be effective natural teachers to the degree that they act and communicate in ways the child can do.

Acting and communicating in ways close to your child's ways may seem unusual, even incorrect, at first. But if you watch parents with infants you see how natural and effective matching is. A growing body of research supports the conclusion that adults regularly change their communications to match their child's level with the result that the child interacts and communicates more with them (Lewis and Rosenblum 1977; Stern 1977; Trevarthen 1979). Matching provides the child with something that he can physically do and cognitively process and that motivates him through the successes it offers. With autistic and other late-talking children, success in communication is critical and not often an easy task. We have found matching to be a valuable strategy adults can use to make the communication task much more successful for the child. It is our experience that adults can give up and return to adult ways of communicating if a child fails to give them what they expect or does not regularly respond to them. Then we see a mutual standoff. The more the adult acts adult, the less the child communicates, and the less the child communicates, the more the adult expects the child cannot communicate and they proceed to act more adult-like. The outward spiral continues until the child and adult are rarely interacting except when absolutely necessary. We have seen this over and over again in the relationships with late-talking children. One of the major goals of Communicating Partners is to reverse this alienating trend and establish a communicative flow at the child's developmental level. Matching is one strategy that goes far in bridging this growing gap between adults and our children.

Principle 3. The mutual responsive principle: children learn to communicate to the degree that they and their life partners respond sensitively to each other

Children will learn to be social and communicative to the degree their life partners sensitively respond to the child's early preverbal and verbal behavior that is the building block to language. We have found a strong trend on adults' part to not respond to many of the important preverbal skills children need before language and communication. The major issue here is that human responses can be the most powerful reinforcers for a child's early communication. In fact, early language research shows that any behaviors can become communicative if adults respond to them "as if" they were communicating (Bates 1976). We also find that adults often respond more to the undesirable behaviors of the children than to the subtle productive behaviors. This responsive strategy is a pervasive one that requires careful fine-tuning to the child's world. Adults also assume that the child's learning will best generalize if it is based on what he can and wants to do at the moment.

Principle 4. The sharing control principle: children learn to communicate to the degree that they and their partners have effective but not excessive control over the other

Considerable child development research shows that children develop to the degree that they have control over their behavior and their effects on the environment. Our own and others' research shows that late-talking children often live in environments that they have little control over, or at least they perceive it that way. Our research also suggests that interactions with late-talking children show either the child dominating the interaction or the adult dominating it, with little reciprocal sharing of control. The adults frequently control interactions with children with questions and demands that fail to acknowledge and support the child's current experiences. Children learn to communicate to the degree that they have both the freedom to perform from their own motivation and experience and the finely tuned directions from sensitive partners.

Principle 5. The emotional playfulness principle: children learn to communicate to the degree that they and their partners interact in enjoyable, emotionally attached ways

Be emotionally attached and playful. Children will communicate to the degree that interactions are playful and enjoyable. Our research shows that many adults take more of a directive teaching role with late-talking children than that of a playful partner. The result is often children who are more passive and responsive than spontaneous and self-affirming. We find the joyful playfulness, even when it seems strange to the adult, results in a great deal more interactive learning than a task-oriented teaching atmosphere. We have also found that many late-talking children can enjoy contact with people but it needs to be sensitive to their emotional and physiological state at the moment. Stress-free playfulness often allows a distant child to interact. We find that teaching parents to be playful is much more difficult than it may seem on the surface.

Part 2

Five Stages of Communication

Martin Seligman, after studying optimistic approaches to child development for 30 years, summarizes his work by describing what he saw his daughter Nikki needed from him:

> More importantly, I realized that raising Nikki was not about correcting her shortcomings. She could do that herself. Rather, my purpose in raising her was to nurture her "social intelligence" and help her to mold her life around her strengths with people. Such strength, fully grown, would be a buffer against her weaknesses and against the storms of life. Raising a child, I know now, was far more than just fixing what was wrong with them. It was about identifying and amplifying their strengths and virtues and helping them find the niche where they can live these positive traits to the fullest. (Seligman 2002, p.28)

This part of the book will help you identify how your child's strengths can help him be more social and communicative. A basic notion of Communicating Partners is that when a child is autistic or similar, the most important task, as Seligman suggests, is not to "correct" the differences but to build the child's current strengths in social relationships so he finds his niche or special way of learning and developing. Each child has his own special way of relating to the world that will be the key to joining with the child.

Rather than making our children act like other children, we choose to help them find their own special "niche" where they can be the best "person" they can be. They do not need to relate as other children do, but they do need to relate. Your child will develop best when you join him in his unique ways of learning and relating to people. This part describes several developmental stages that children go through in becoming social and communicative:

- interactive play
- nonverbal communication
- social language
- conversation
- civil behavior.

Remember that being a social learner requires much more than language and that becoming a successful communicator requires developing stable relationships with people who enter the child's developmental world and respond to his immediate natural learning.

To build a relationship with your child, you will need to enter his mind and then slowly help him appreciate your thinking and emotions. For typically developing children, this process seems to come automatically. For children with autism and other developmental delays, the process can be long and arduous, but it often is possible. In contrast to early definitions of autism as an "innate inability for interpersonal contact" (Kanner 1943) or an inability to respond emotionally to others (Hobson 1993), we have found that while our children have "difficulties" in these areas, they can often be overcome in responsive relationships (MacDonald and Mitchell 2002; Mahoney and MacDonald 2003). Recent research has also found evidence that children with autism can indeed respond to others' emotions and are able to form affectionate attachments (Sigman and Capps 1997).

While many autistic children can be interactive, often they do not play with others or act like them, except in ritual ways. They may not readily seek an adult's attention and resist when forced to interact. Communication with an autistic child requires patient attention to how the child's interests and emotions change. These findings do suggest a difficulty in developing relationships but not an inability. We have found that parents are much more successful with their child when they see the child as having "difficulties" not "inabilities."

One notion that has helped us understand our children is the finding that autistic children lack a normally developed "theory of mind" (Baron-Cohen 1995; Leslie 1987). A main feature is an inability to attribute beliefs to others. The child may not form a mental image of how other people are thinking. This is seen as related to a failure to think of his own mental states or to realize that others have thoughts that are different from his own. In 30 years, we have come to realize that we will only connect with our children on a lasting basis when we realize that they and we live in very different worlds. We see children as living primarily in a world of sensation and action while adults live in a world of thought and language. This finding relates to the notion of "theory of mind"; that is, what goes on in our mind is not at all the same as what goes on in an autistic child's mind. Consequently the world as we see it will mean something very different to that child. Since we and they experience the world differently, we will need to enter the child's world if we hope to connect with what is really going on in there.

A primary feature of the Communicating Partners approach is that no matter where the child is developmentally, that is where we need to go. Until we enter the child's sensations and actions and build a relationship where he is, we are unlikely to have a relationship other than a superficial one. Consequently, you need first to determine where your child is now functioning socially, cognitively, and emotionally and then enter into his actual functioning just as you would enter into a theatrical role of a child. Pretend that you are an actor with the very important role of acting just like your child, actually using your child as your "coach." Once you become successful as your child, then and only then will you know how to bring him gradually into your world. But first you and he need to have a relationship with the cognitive, social, and emotional abilities that he currently has.

The following five chapters will guide you into your child's world of interactive play, and then lead you through his worlds of communication, language, conversation, and civil behavior. Settle in and enjoy the journey. We have watched many families take this journey and, once they have learned that entering their child's world works well, they do not wait for language before they cement a genuine reciprocal relationship with the child.

Over and over, we have listened to parents' questions such as:

- Will she ever talk?
- Will he always behave in these unusual ways?
- Will he ever be friendly and social?
- Will she ever be independent?
- Will he ever be normal?
- How can I help him talk?
- How can I help him play like other children?

In discussing these concerns with hundreds of parents, I have heard the same plea: "How can I connect with my child like a real person?" Many persons close to our children yearn for even the simplest social connections. They want to be in the same world as the child. However, many adults are unaware of what a child needs long before he will communicate with a partner. Our work has devoted years to alerting parents and professionals to the many things needed before their child is social and communicative.

A first critical step to connecting with a child "like a real person" is to become more like the "real" person that the child already is.

This part addresses three major questions:

1. What do children need to do to become habitually social and communicative?

2. How have late-talking children moved successfully through the early stages of social and communicative development?

3. What can parents and other life partners do to help children become more social and communicative?

In the next five chapters you will learn what you and your child can do to help him communicate. You will see that each of the stages may take a long time. It is critical to be patient and not push the child too fast and lose him. It is very important to state our repeated findings that many late-talking children do not begin to talk and socialize until they are much older than the expected ages. We know many children who have not talked and socialized regularly until they were five or six and even as late as ten or twelve years old. Regardless of our child's age he can become more social and communicative when his life partners enter his world and patiently have a social relationship based on any behaviors he can do. You will come to see that we are more concerned with having genuine social connections with late-talking children than merely achieving language, academic, or vocational successes. We strongly encourage you to establish many firm social connections with your child before you worry about language per se. Too often parents and professionals give up on interacting much with children when language is not forthcoming. Realize that it is precisely those natural interactions that will build language.

This part describes in detail how we have seen many children move slowly but surely through five major stages of social and communicative development (as discussed in Chapter 6).

7

Interaction

The First Stage in Learning to Communicate

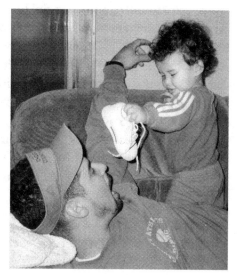

This chapter discusses many of the processes that can help your child become interactive in his spontaneous life. You may read the chapter once to see the wide range of things that are involved with what may seem a simple habit—interacting. However, for many autistic and late-talking children, interacting is neither easy nor natural and can be a lifelong task. You may stay with the ideas and goals in this chapter for months, even years. You also will need to return to the skills here when your child enters new developmental stages or new environments, like school. You can return to the information here when you follow the Interaction part of the Adult–Child Relationship Map (ARM) to identify goals and strategies to focus on next.

For many late-talking children, just being with people is difficult in many ways. While autism involves many features, one of the most common is that "being with people is very challenging." Consequently, a first critical step is to find ways your child will engage with people willingly. A second step is to find ways you can interact so your child enjoys being with you. We have worked very hard with our families on the deceptively simple-sounding goal of "staying with people." Many believe that "staying with someone" is not much of an accomplishment for their child. They often want more, even too much too soon. Then, the ensuing failures can drive them apart. We encourage you to realize that "staying with someone" is a very important and pivotal achievement for our children. Staying with people is pivotal because it sets the stage for much spontaneous learning. In this chapter we discuss several general skills needed to become a social play partner. Until a child is a frequent social partner with others, he will not have the opportunities to learn to communicate to his potential.

Social play: the first step in becoming interactive

Children must stay and play with adults to become social and communicative. While playing together is often automatic, it is usually difficult for our children. Many people do not believe that play with people is absolutely important for a child to develop fully. They often assume that playing alone or with peers is what children need most. It is true that playing alone can help a child think and learn in many ways, but only playing with people will help a child communicate. Children do not learn to be social and communicative by playing alone. Playing with peers can be very helpful, but first our children need to learn to be peers themselves, and that means being able and interested in staying in interactions. Children with autism and other language delays often find it very hard becoming peers since they have not learned to be social partners with adults at first. Sigman and Ungerer (1984) have studied late-talking children for many years and conclude that the responsive role of parents in contrast to directive teaching is critical in predicting a child's development of social competence.

What is social play? The kind of social play that helps children communicate is any interaction that has the interest and attention of both the child and adult and that involves little pressure to perform in specific ways. Social play is successful whenever you and your child stay in the same activity together. This may not seem like much when you are concerned about how "normal" your child can be, but hundreds of families agree that playing together is the most important thing you can do in the first instance and that without it little happens. For our children, learning to feel interested and safe with people is indispensable to learning to communicate.

Certainly social play cannot happen all the time. Children will not tolerate that and parents have much else to do. But daily joint activity routines can be made out of many natural events every day and are necessary for our children. When you and your child make daily routines into enjoyable social play, your child will learn much more with you than if you focus on just teaching him.

How to begin social play?

Begin social play by entering into a few of your child's daily routines, first by just being there and letting the child get used to your presence. Our children often resist people when they distract them from current pleasures or require difficult things of them. The first step is to convince your child that he can be himself with you. First, join your child by doing parallel activities and not making any demands. Take time to see where the child is in terms of his emotions, interests, and availability. Silent side-by-side activity often results in the child coming to you. Our children have difficulty with transitions and so it helps to contact them first by just being there, without intruding or demanding changes.

We have found that children who are not readily social, such as children with autism and other language delays, allow people into their world more readily when we approach them by doing four powerful things:

- BE STILL
- BE ALERT

- BE ACCEPTING

- BE RESPONSIVE.

When you first approach your child, BE STILL by being quiet in actions and talk. As we silently approach a child, we are more able to see him for who he is at the moment and what he is experiencing instead of seeing him in terms of what we want him to do. Second, we are then actively ALERT to the child's emotions, readiness, and interests so that we can fine-tune ourselves to fit the child's current state. The third step is to ACCEPT what the child is doing without judgment, and understand that whatever the child is doing there is good reason for it, even if we want to change it eventually. The fourth step is to RESPOND to what the child is doing with actions and communications that he can try to do. We use the acronym SAAR to refer to these four powerful things.

When you approach your child this way, he is more likely to accept and attend to you, and you are more likely to "read" him in ways that help you genuinely connect with him. Your approach will not be a shock to him and he will be able to prepare for your contact. Our children usually require more time than others to adjust to the presence of others. The more easily your child makes the transition from his activity and attention, the more open he will be to you entering his world.

Social play simply means two people interacting with no goal other than being together. Clearly, for many reasons, our children often do not enjoy being with people. Your first task is to build a relationship that your child enjoys so that he eventually seeks you out for more social time together. You may not think that "staying together" is much of an accomplishment. However, anyone who knows children who isolate themselves and resist contact will understand that "staying together" is a major accomplishment for these children.

Do not conclude that our emphasis on "play" is intended to make light of a serious need. As Jean Piaget, the great scholar of young children, demonstrated over years of careful and highly replicated research, "play is the most important work of the child." It is through play that children construct their reality and learn how they affect the world. Our children have a different reality to ours. Consequently, before they enter our reality, we must enter theirs. Piaget's influential contemporary Lev Vygotsky, and many followers, showed that children become social by interacting with adults who provide a bridge between the child's world of sensation and the adult world of language.

Like many adults, you may view play as something you do after work is done. However, play is the necessary work of the child and we can best help him develop by joining in his play, which is his developmental "job." Thus, when you enter your child's chosen play, you will be where he learns best. You need not play on the floor all day or abandon other skills children need. Rather it is to make regular contact with the child in his own world. This is often uncomfortable for adults but it is very fruitful. Many people believe late-talking children do not want to play with others. We have found that initially this seems to be the case. But then we often see that our children in fact do enjoy people but only when these people are doing things the child can do and is interested in.

One advantage of playing together is that it requires no specific skills of your child or training of you. Soon after birth, infants and mothers play elaborate give-and-take games. During these games the mothers fine-tune themselves to the child's nonverbal and verbal behaviors and to their pace and style (Bruner 1990; Stern 1977; Field 1980;) and the child actively reciprocates, showing he is changing "in synch" as his mother changes. Autism and other language disorders often interfere with this "in synch" relationship but the connections can be repaired.

Many parents of autistic children say that they played social games in infancy but then stopped in their second or third year. Whatever neurological changes occur at these times, we have found that most children can relearn social play when parents carefully join in the child's world. Children often return to socializing when people accept their current behavior, which may be less than "age-expected." It is vitally important to help a child become social with whatever behaviors he is able and interested in doing. Many adults conclude that children will not socialize or communicate after periods of forcing them to perform in ways that are not developmentally appropriate. Communicating Partners focuses on making the child competent and interested in a social play life before attempting to teach him directly. We have found that the more the child engages in natural social play the more he will learn spontaneously.

Imitation and modeling

Judith seemed to ignore everyone. At age four she rarely imitated what the other five in the family did and seemed to be learning very little from the many natural models in the family. Her family thought she understood adult speech so they talked to her in adult ways and tried to get her to play in four-year-old ways.

After your child accepts you in his world and begins to play with you, he needs to begin acting in ways that you act. This is *imitation and modeling* and it is a major step for our children to enter a social world (Rogers and Bennetto 2000). When I see a child spontaneously imitating people, I often find the child is soon ready to communicate. I take imitation as an important predictor of a social life. Learning to communicate means learning to act and communicate in ways others do. Your child needs to pay increasing attention to you and act like you without being told to. Once a child imitates, his world becomes a natural teacher for him. Parents are often unaware that they are already teaching their child when they act in ways the child can do and the child imitates them. Few parents seem aware that the more their child acts like them, the more the child will learn. It is important to realize that your child can learn from you in every interaction. For example, even very isolated children will know to put a telephone to their ear. Voila! This is one of many instances of something someone "taught" the child without "teaching" him. Becoming mindful that you can be teaching your child in every interaction will make you more attuned to your interactions with your child.

When your child begins to imitate spontaneously, consider it a very important breakthrough. For a child with a communication disorder, this is a sign he is ready to enter the confusing world of others. We need to make sure that the new world is simple and successful for him. We encourage parents to act and communicate in ways the child can do so he can imitate them even more. Your child's early imitations will not look or sound much like your behaviors, but that is as it should be. Be sure to accept any attempts to try to act like you. And be sure to accept and respond to his action imitations as well as ones with sounds and words.

A general rule your child needs to learn is to "do as others do," not only when told to do so but as a natural way of living with people. Once a child imitates, everyone becomes natural learning lessons for him. That is, your child will learn by imitating people even when they are not intending to teach him something. The imitation we encourage is not rote passive routines like "clap your hand," "say momma," or "draw a circle like this." No, the imitation that is important for social and communicative growth is the spontaneous modeling of people who are doing things the child finds interesting and is able to try to do. The child's behavior need not look like the adult's model; the point is that the child is beginning to be aware of others as having real effects on him.

One other value of imitating is the effect it has on the people around the child. They begin to see that they can have effects on the child and that they are not unimportant, as they may have thought. The traditional wisdom that "imitation is the sincerest form of flattery" applies to many adults who have long waited for their children to act like them. Imitation is a dependable tool for establishing social links when your child imitates you; he is doing something that you are both able and interested in doing. Thus, when your child imitates people, they are more likely to stay in social contact with him, and thus, naturally, help him to communicate.

> After a few months when Judith's family entered her play and imitated her actions and sounds, Judith began to do some of the things her brothers and parents did in daily life. She began sitting like one brother as he read, sweeping like her mother, and cleaning the car as her dad did. She also imitated their speech if only with beginning sounds. She was less in her own world and initiating more contacts with others. The family learned that the more they responded to whatever Judith did or said, the more she interacted with them. They also learned to reduce their actions to ones she could do and avoid trying to get her to do things she could not do. She was now no longer the loner she had been.

Reciprocal turn-taking

Once you and your child are staying together in play, it is time to begin the lifelong habit of taking turns. Turn-taking means many things to different people. For our purpose of helping children socialize and communicate, turn-taking means the habit of give and take. It means that effective interaction requires that each partner takes a turn with an action or communication and then waits for the other to take a turn back. The second partner then waits for the first to take another turn. Ideally, each person's turn related meaningfully to what the other did. Turn-taking is a fundamental skill for social learning and for effective communication. The failure to socially give and take is one of the most striking problems we have seen in our children. Turn-taking is one of the most important breakthroughs a child can make into the social world. Turn-taking allows a flow between two persons that is so missing in our children. Many children play alone, talk mainly in monologues, or only answer questions. There is little give and take in their lives.

Even infants and parents take turns regularly in the first months of life. When a mother responds to an infant's sounds or movements with similar sounds and movements and then silently waits for the child, the child often takes a turn then waits for the mother to interact again (Goldberg 1977; Mac-Donald and Mitchell 2002; Stern 1977). Such early interactions can continue for long periods when the mother keeps responding, waiting, and acting in ways the child can act. When the parent returns to acting like an adult, the interaction usually ends, as does the mutual learning.

> In our video-based studies, John and Debbie demonstrated turn-taking in several ways. John was five months old. We asked Debbie to do three things within a 15-minute period. First, we asked her to play with John on the floor in any way she liked. What we saw was a very friendly mother making constant motions and communications at the baby as if she were "bathing the child with language and stimulation." John watched for a while, did very little of his own, and then looked away. Second, we asked her to continue playing but now to respond with the movements he was making. The video showed a very different picture. Now when John wiggled or waved his hands, his mother did as well. The more she acted like him the more he attended to her and actively did the actions back. There was little sounding but a constant flow of interaction. John kept his eyes on his mother and responded to her movements with ones of his own. Third, we then asked her to continue playing but now to wait for him to make sounds and then make the sounds back to him. The difference was exciting in that the more she responded to his sounds the more sounds he made. Even when she waited a little longer, John enthusiastically got her back turn-taking with very animated sounding. This was a very instructive example of the power a parent has when she simply responds to her child with behaviors similar to his.
>
> In discussing this with John's mother, she learned that too much talking and stimulating could lose John's participation with her. She was surprised that when she did less, he did more. This was in contrast to the traditional recommendation to "bathe your baby with language and stimulation." She also learned that he stayed interacting

much longer than she had ever seen when she simply took turns doing what he was doing. She also was impressed and personally rewarded to see that when she changed so did he. She said it was exciting to see how much he enjoyed her and how much effect she could have on him.

Even the simplest turn-taking helps your child. A major first step is to convince parents they can help a child with even the most primitive turn-taking. After a child has been isolated and disconnected, it is a thrill and achievement for parents when the child finally gives them "something" back. Turn-taking shows parents that their children can socialize and opens a window into the child's life that has been closed. We encourage parents to appreciate any connection with the child and to consider it as a major achievement.

Many children show very little turn-taking. Interactions are often nonexistent or they are brief and fleeting. These children seem absorbed in their own experiences. In order to communicate, they need to respond to others. Turn-taking may seem simple and technical but it is a major and complicated accomplishment. Turn-taking requires changes in the traditional way children and adults relate, from the directive–passive pattern to a more reciprocal give-and-take approach. Turn-taking is a key component to the relationships we want for our children. Many parents get very little from their children to encourage the interactions they desperately need to develop. Suggesting to a mother that she takes turns with a child who regularly ignores or resists her seems unreasonable, even frightening at first. Who wants to go back to where they are rejected? Parents need to see turn-taking as a very effective way to regain connection with someone who might seem like a "lost" child.

One notion to help understand turn-taking is the comparison between the games of ping-pong and darts. Turn-taking is like a ping-pong game in which each partner takes a turn then waits for the other to take their turn. Ping-pong requires matching in that each person hits the ball in a way that the other can return. Success and enjoyment relates to the volleys or turns the players exchange. In a darts game, in contrast, only one person plays at a time and his performance is not directly related to what his partner just did. Often with persons with communication disorders, a conversation is more like a darts game where one partner takes most of the turns. The basic point of turn-taking is that a child will learn more and relationships will develop when partners relate more like they are playing ping-pong than darts.

Turn-taking is nothing new to adults. In successful relationships we see relatively easy give-and-take exchange in which each person does something and then waits for the other to respond. The partner does something back that is somehow related to what the first person did. The second person then waits for the first to take another turn. That is turn-taking. Look around and you will see it in most successful interactions. While one partner occasionally takes many turns at once, as when telling a story, these imbalances usually even out if the relationship is to continue satisfactorily for each partner. Imagine how limited your social life and natural learning would be if you did not regularly take turns with people.

Unfortunately, several investigations of children with autism and language delays show that reciprocal turn-taking is rare. One pervasive finding over 30 years is that children with autism and language delays interact much less than typical children and that, when they do interact, the exchanges are often one-sided with either the child or his partner taking most of the turns. In fact the lack of a reciprocal give and take has become one of the cardinal features of children with autism and other language delays.

When our children interact, it is usually for brief "dead-end" contacts that one partner dominates. It is very easy for adults to do most of the acting and communicating when a child rarely responds. If someone dominates interactions with you, preventing you from participating, you may well avoid that person and not develop much of a relationship with him. That is exactly what we see with our children. They interact mainly with persons who are doing much more than they can do and who give them little chance to participate. There is a circular dilemma here: your child is not responding…you do more and more…he resists and responds less…you reciprocate by anxiously doing more to get him to do something…he resists more and escapes…and any chance for learning is gone.

We regularly see such interactions with our children. It is very difficult to wait and allow a noninteractive child to do something and then to respond to whatever he can do. Yes, this is very difficult, but this is exactly what parents do when they successfully connect with late-talking children. It is not easy, but it is very possible, and the rewards are having a relationship with a child who used to be a stranger.

As we have clinically followed over 50 families of autistic and late-talking children for 2 to 15 years, we found turn-taking to be one of the most powerful skills children can learn. But turn-taking is not like riding a bicycle; once you learn it, you do not always have it. Turn-taking is a pervasive skill that needs to be relearned and strengthened as the child develops through many stages. While turn-taking in conversations is the ultimate goal, it is necessary to begin turn-taking with any behaviors the child can do. Just as the infant will take turns with his primitive coos and wiggles, a late-talking child needs to take turns with any behaviors he can tolerate. After following hundreds of late-talking children, we conclude that a major reason they interact so little is that their partners are not responding to what they can and want to do. Rather, their partners are often acting and communicating in ways the child cannot do or in ways that overstimulate them.

Just as life depends on breathing in and out in a regular turn-taking way, so do relationships depend on turn-taking between two partners. The more balanced the turn-taking between the two partners the smoother the relationship goes. Think of you and your child as "one relationship," then realize that your relationship will develop to the degree that each of you takes turns back and forth, similar to the turn-taking you do in breathing to stay alive. If one person does much more than the other, the relationship will falter, just as your breathing falters when you take many "in" breaths without taking "out" breaths.

Turn-taking creates a natural learning process that may be viewed as an interactive loop. That is, the adult takes a turn with any motion or communication then waits for the child to take a turn, then the adult reciprocates with feedback that relates in some way to what the child did. The interaction is kept going when the child takes another turn that also relates somehow to what the adult did. The interaction continues as long as each person responds to the partner's turns. Each turn is an opportunity for the child to learn from the adult and for the adult to learn more about the child and how to teach him spontaneously. Notice in your own conversations how this give-and-take turn-taking style defines the relationships you develop. Our ultimate goal is that children enjoy turn-taking with any behaviors they can do so that they have the freedom to build relationships when they wish. It is our conviction that many of our children want genuine relationships but do not have the basic skills that turn-taking affords them. To begin you will need to have frequent and little turn-taking interactions with your child in any way possible.

The really difficult part of turn-taking is not so much what the child can do, but for adults to learn to act like the child and continue interacting while accepting what the child can do and not demanding the impossible. Turn-taking makes teaching worthwhile.

Parents are frequently distressed to see that their child knows much more than others believe. Consider how hard parents and professionals work to teach their child many things. They know he has learned them, but then in social interactions he fails to show what he knows. To make matters worse, he avoids or fails in just those interactions he needs to continue learning. It is painful to see the child lose the benefits of learning because he does not regularly take turns with others in interactions.

For the child who avoids learning, turn-taking can be the key to showing and practicing what he knows. You may be aware of the often-devastating gap between a child's competence and his performance. Many of our children act as if they know much less than they actually do. Their success in the world will depend much less on what they know than on how they use that knowledge in interactions with others.

What can you do to get a social play habit going?

Getting started with a child who is not social or is actually isolated and resistant can be a daunting and frustrating task. It is natural to not want to intrude on someone who does not want you around. However, when you are responsible for a child, you know he needs to be with people in order to develop. We have learned that, while it may seem that our children do not want to be with people, this is often not the case. Most of the children we have known actually do want to connect with people but they can do so only under certain conditions. When many parents and professionals have learned to use a series of responsive strategies with children, the children show that they enjoy and learn from such daily interactions.

We will now discuss how five general responsive strategies can help children have a more interactive life by learning to play socially, imitate, and take turns. In our work with families we begin by teaching five basic rules of play with children:

- BE BALANCED

- BE MATCHED

- BE RESPONSIVE

- SHARE CONTROL

- BE EMOTIONALLY PLAYFUL.

Be balanced; do about as much as each other reciprocally

Once you and your child begin to interact, he will need many opportunities to practice what he can do. Much research shows that children learn best when they have some control over their activities and when they see they can have effects on their life partners. Even a little choice allows a child to explore and create in a spontaneous match between his skills and the opportunities of the moment.Our studies have consistently shown that adults often dominate interactions with late-talking children who, in turn, often do as little as 10 or 20 percent of the interaction. Many children with autism and developmental delay show many of the characteristics of "learned helplessness" that Seligman and others have found to be the result of adults doing more for children than they need. Clearly our children can be slow to respond and even slower to discover how to initiate social contacts. They need time and they need quiet time where their partners are not determining what happens next. Our work regularly shows considerable imbalance between late-talking children and their partners. Often it is the child who is dominating the interaction. In either case, the child is not learning to communicate effectively.

We encourage adults to make sure neither person does much more than the other. This applies to both actions and communications. Adults often find it very difficult to wait for the child because our children often take a long time. In fact many children seem to expect not to interact since they are seldom given quiet time to do something in an interaction. Adults often do *so* much that the child cannot show what *he* can do and so the spiral perpetuates where the child does less...and the adult expects less...and so the adult does more...and the child continues to do less...thus fulfilling the prophecy that the child cannot do much.

It is essential for children to have success interacting and for their partners to value simple interactions as hard-won successes for the child. They can do this by making a habit of not doing much more than the child. Many partners learn that when they do less the children will do more. This may seem like a simple prescription but it is definitely not easy. Why? Doing less is not easy for adults, who feel responsible for "helping" the child. They naturally think that helping the child means that they need to "do" something. Often what the child needs is for them to do nothing but wait and stay available in the interaction, and then accept and respond to whatever the child can do.

Clearly our children are often slow to respond and even slower to figure out how to initiate social contacts. They need time. We must give them that time and keep attending to them as they proceed. It is common to see adults dominate interactions where they do so much that the child cannot show what he can do. Instead, children become passive and do not bother to interact. They seem to refuse to compete with the faster and more competent adult. The consequence is that not only do they learn less but they also fail to learn the basics of being with people. To communicate children must participate, not just wait or have things done for them. When you and your child initiate and respond as much as the other, the child will learn more and appreciate social interactions.

When parents learn to wait for the child to interact, they often see many skills that were previously masked. This revelation is very motivating for parents when they discover that the child can do what they had not expected and they could facilitate this.

Be matched; act in ways your child can do

Your child will become more social when you act and communicate in ways he can do at the moment. While this may seem like common sense, it is not common behavior. Acting like a child may seem easy but it definitely is not. It is typical for adults to act adult-like and to interact with children by doing many things the child cannot attempt. Nevertheless, we adults often want and expect the child to do the things we do without realizing how impossible it is.

Widespread research with children demonstrates that children perform best on tasks that are at the child's performance level and slightly above (Deci 1975; Mahoney and Macdonald 2003; Vygotsky 1978; Winnicott 1965). When the goal is for the child to communicate, his task actually is to master what his partner is doing. Learning to communicate means learning to act in ways others do. Since children learn to communicate in daily interactions, it is important for their partners to act in ways the child can do. A child communicates more easily when his partners act and communicate in ways he can and wants to do. This is the major strategy of "matching" that we teach as an early and enduring tool for entering the child's world. Matching shows the child respect for what he can do. It supports him in continuing to do the activity but now socially. Another advantage of matching is that it helps you practice what the child can do so that you come to understand some of what the child is experiencing. Unless we match the child in many ways, we may well lose contact with him, fail to have lasting effects on him, and not understand his world.

Your child will learn more when you match the way he plays. If he is pushing cars, putting toys away, or having a snack, you can help by doing what he is doing. Try to get into little back-and-forth routines where each of you tries to act like the other, with you gradually showing him something new to do. The more you focus on what the child is doing, the more you will be matching both his abilities and interests, and the more he will find interacting tolerable and even enjoyable. We repeatedly find that having successes does wonders for a late-talking child in that they come to believe that interacting with people is worthwhile.

Sharing your child's focus will give you a clearer feel of what he knows, wants, and can do. Until you understand this, you may find yourself in a world the child cannot reach. Remember that what your child does in an interaction is less important than the fact that he interacts in any way at all. The more we understand that the simple act of interacting for our children is a real struggle, the more we will accept and be grateful for any kind of interacting. We need to appreciate that, for autistic and late-talking children, simple interactions are often difficult, frightening, and overwhelming. That is why we are so insistent on helping a child become social in any way before we focus on later academic or language goals.

Parents often tell us they are at a loss to play with a child when they do not understand him. Especially with resistant children, parents can be afraid of playing with them. They do not want to upset the child or be rejected. Some parents ask: "But what do I do with him? I don't know how to play any more." We usually show parents how to play by at first imitating what the child is doing in a parallel way. This usually catches the child's interest. Imitating a child has the advantage of doing what the child can and wants to do, thus insuring success. Our children are often told to do things that are impossible for them. Consequently, it is a relief for the child to be accepted for what he can do. He often avoids people with the expectation that he is going to fail. One of our primary responsibilities is to convince the child that he is competent. That can best happen by encouraging the child to do socially what he can already do on his own.

Remember that your first job is to convince your child that staying with people will be rewarding and successful. Do not expect the toys to keep him with you. If toys are keeping your child with you now, then he is probably not attending to you enough to learn from you. We encourage parents to practice being more interesting than the child's distractions so that gradually the child will pay more attention to people than to his distractions.

Be responsive to each other

The kind of play relationship your child needs is one in which each of you plays with the other, not only at or beside him. The goal is to attend to each other and respond sensitively to what the other is doing. With many of our children, this is easier said than done. You need to be very patient and to celebrate even the shortest times together at first. Realize that our children have many conditioned and neurological reasons for not interacting. Interacting clearly is very difficult, even painful, for them. For some children, it will take a while to just accept you playing parallel with them. The child will need time to realize you are not imposing changes on him but will allow him to be himself. The more you do what he does, the more you will share the same world of ideas. Sharing of a common world is essential for learning to communicate.

This common experience shows you the other's ideas and motivations. Learning what a late-talking child really cares about takes time and careful observation. Acting like your child enables you to "read" and connect with the child. For example, as you build a bridge of blocks, you could "play at" the child by stacking blocks and telling him what you are doing. Or you could "play beside" him by working on one side as the child works on the other. There is much more genuine connection and learning when both of you are actively together. You could place a block then wait silently for the child to place one, then each continue responding to what the other did. You can offer each other a block or in other ways insure that you are interacting back and forth.

Considerable research now shows that the more responsive parents are to what children are doing, the better they develop socially, emotionally, and cognitively (Koschanska and Murray 2000; Mahoney and MacDonald 2003). The value of responding is that it helps children have successes in interactions that have been frustrating sources of failure in the past. Another reason to respond to the child is that, in order to be a successful communicator, the child himself needs to learn to respond to what others do. Otherwise, others are not likely to stay with someone who ignores them.

Share control and decisions in play

Encouraging adults to play with children with autism and language disorders often falls on frustrated and deaf ears. Many parents are pushed away, screamed at, and otherwise rejected when they try to play with our children. Autistic children are known for resisting many typical kinds of play. We have often felt foolish recommending parents to play with children who clearly do not want to do so: "He doesn't want to and I can't stand trying any more."

After successfully interacting with many resistant children, I found that what I was doing did not look like regular child-play. We have found it necessary to redefine completely the idea of play with our children. For children unable to play in expected ways, we must come to accept any of their behaviors as candidates for social play. Many of our children can do a great deal but when others enter their world, they freeze.

An early goal in a relationship with a child is to let the child know that he can have some control over the activity when we are there with him. The child needs to know he can have some control in interactions. When you respond to a child's behavior, whatever it is, you are showing him he can have effects on you. Too often, the child has little or no control over his adult partner. We found that the more a child has effects on others, the more he will interact.

Be emotionally attached and playful

The fifth strategy for building social play is to be playful and express emotions effectively. It is easy to be serious and task-oriented when you are concerned about helping your child. We have found parents serious and to express little enjoyment when they are trying to get the child to do difficult or uncomfortable things.

When I first meet a child, I respond to anything he is doing in light, playful ways. Often I will observe the child's expressions and do more of what seems to make him smile. My goal at first is to let him know I will be someone he can enjoy and someone who will not make him do difficult things. My major goal is to make sure he enjoys being with me. But the enjoyment must be genuine.

And so, first I need to enjoy him by appreciating whatever he does. I see it as my job to be accepted by him and eventually to interact with him in any ways he can do. This requires finding out how I can act playfully so he attends to me more and stays with me. Often, my goal for quite a while is simply to have the child stay playing with me in any way at all. Staying with me is my early measure of success; without that all else will be lost. Frequently when parents watch me play with their child, they say to the child, "Dr. Jim is silly, isn't he?" Then they say, "I rarely see him stay with anyone that much." I often respond by saying, "Yes, I am silly, but developmentally effective." We try to convince parents that what they do with their child is not as important as whether the child stays interacting. And our children stay much more when we act child-like.

In Ohio many parents and I have had an informal group for many years. The group is called "SPEAK," which stands for the "Society for Parents who Enjoy Autistic Kids." After years working together, the parents decided that the most important factor for their child's progress was that they and the child learned to "enjoy" each other. I remember struggling with parents who were reluctant to act like their child. Ginny, a nurse-manager, was very uncomfortable imitating David. She was embarrassed watching me be silly with her son. She wanted her six-year-old to act polite and age-appropriate. I pointed out that, when he did, he was silent and alone. When she saw that he stayed and interacted with me more than he did with her, she began to lose her inhibitions.

When we do not visibly enjoy what a child does, we may be discouraging him from following his interests and being with people. Many of our children are very sensitive and vulnerable to adult judgments or lack of support. When we respond enjoyably to whatever the child does, he gains confidence and becomes more interactive. Consequently, doing something playful and enjoyable is often the best way to continue interactions and to insure the child comes to believe in social interaction. One of the most important developments for late-talking children is to believe they can interact successfully without being judged or told to change.

Considerations and problems in social play

It is easy to be in a hurry to help children communicate, play normally, and learn. We have found that when we do not spend enough time in social play with a child, we lose him and he does not become a social partner. We have found that developing a social relationship with children with autism and related disorders is an extremely challenging task but a possible one. What is so hard about playing in your child's world? Try it and, believe me, it is not easy. Think of this: you have been a successful adult for many years. Your daily rewards come from acting like an adult. These adult habits actually define who you are. Consequently, when we suggest that you enter your child's world by acting and communicating as he does, we are asking you to make a major shift in your thinking and self-concept, not to mention the physical changes that may strain a little at first.

We have watched hundreds of parents and professionals struggle to leave their world of thought and language and enter the child's world of sensation and action. They inevitably get stuck in their thought and language world that separates them from the child. But once they see that they begin connecting with the child, they begin to act like the child much more easily. The question is: Do you want to wait to have a relationship with your child until he is acting like you or are you willing to relate to him wherever he is? We have found repeatedly that children connect with us much more when we enter their world than when we try to have them enter ours. To do that you need to do less thinking and talking with your child and more acting and sensing, as he does.

How important do you really think playing with your child is?

Consider how important you believe that playing is for your child and how playful your child sees you. Several problems interfere with playfulness: the way you think, the way you act, and the way your child acts and sees you. If you think of play as only a vacation from "real learning," as golf may be for you, you may not see a constant need to play with your child. Many people believe that play is important for a child to learn to explore, manipulate, and master his environment, but that such play can be done alone or with other children. Rarely do we meet adults who believe that a child's communication will come from playing with them.

True, it may seem that typically developing children learn most through playing alone or with peers. This happens only after they have developed sensitive one-to-one relationships with adults who enter the child's world at least for a time. By the end of their first year children generally have a fairly stable interactive life in the sense that they have gotten into the habits of social play, imitation, and turn-taking that we have discussed in this chapter. Even some children with language disorders go through this stage, but then something happens. For many reasons the late-talking child is no longer neurologically and emotionally able to maintain interactions as he had. Just because a late-talking child stops interacting for a while does not mean he cannot do so again. But what is required is that his life partners join him at his social development level even if it has returned to a very primitive stage.

Another barrier to playing with children is parents' lack of confidence that their casual time contributes to their child's learning. Parents often fail to see how they have already helped their child learn many things in casual contacts. When parents realize that any daily activity can be an important interaction, they start thinking of play as critical to learning. Then, daily routines become interactive.

When a child has a developmental delay, parents feel pushed away and unsuccessful and come to believe their child does not want them there or cannot learn from them. This view can be very harmful to both the child and his parents. Playfulness can help spark or renew the valuable interactions that characterize contacts between parents and infant. Most children we have known do, in fact, want to be with people but they can only be with people when they are safely in the child's world.

Before parents can appreciate social play as valuable, they need to overcome another frequent barrier: expecting too much. When we are concerned with bigger goals like language, cognition, and school placement, we can ignore the little steps children need to make first. It is easy for parents to expect the child to do more than he can do at the moment. In our work with families, we stress the importance of not expecting anything in particular from a child in play other than "another turn." This means "staying interacting" by initiating or responding again. Parents often ask "What should we wait for?" or "What is he supposed to do next?"

Our answer may seem too simple but it is very effective. The answer is: "Something he can and wants to do." It takes a while to understand that interaction itself is the goal and not specific performance. In our rush to see progress, often we do not appreciate how difficult it is for late-talking children simply to stay interacting.

Another obstacle to social play is the adult's insistence on goal-orientation that raises stress and results in more failure than success. The notion that there is only a right or wrong way to do something often discourages the child who is not yet ready for the whole thing. Stephanie threw a ball halfway to her mother who responded, "No, throw all the way to me." The girl was just learning to throw but her mother did not accept little steps. After several such exchanges, the girl stopped interacting. Once her mother learned to accept any attempt from the girl to interact she had the chance to show her more mature ways to interact.

If your child was learning to climb stairs, you certainly would not place him on the bottom step and then go to the top step and say, "Come on up and get me!" No, you would be on the next step, coaching him to make the gains he could. The same applies when children are beginning to socialize; any attempt to interact is a success.

Parents and professionals regularly want their child to play with things in the "right" way. Often what is considered "right" to parents is actually "adult" behavior or at least not developmentally the next step for the child. In order to help parents appreciate the difference between their view of "right" and what is developmentally "right," I may whimsically ask them, "How well does he drive a car or balance his checkbook?" The point of this nonsense question is that we are often expecting of children behaviors that they are not ready to do, like driving or dealing with finances. This common desire for a child to do things "right," when right means doing it in the adult's way, highlights the fact that we adults often interpret a child's behavior in adult terms and not in terms of what is right developmentally for a child. Once you enter your child's world by actively participating in it, you will get to know intuitively what is a developmentally "right" next step for your child. You will no longer expect adult or other impossible behavior of him; rather you will expect him to do only three things: first, to do more of what he is doing; second, to do it socially with people; and third, to do just a little more that is possible.

Interaction: the bottom line

The key point is that each child, even if he has autism or a language disorder, has natural strengths and that the first step in development should be to build on his strengths rather than focus on his weaknesses. Most of our children interact much less frequently and maturely than other children. Communicating Partners focuses on helping you help your child do more of what he is doing now but to do it in social interactions. Our children have many bits of knowledge; what they need most is the social skills to share that knowledge and to learn spontaneously. By building a social play relationship with behaviors your child can and wants to do, you will help him become more optimistic and motivated. Parents have achieved this by making sure their child has successes in daily interactions. When a child's social successes outnumber his failures, children who are pessimistic and isolated become optimistic children who venture out and socialize more.

The beauty of seeing your child become more social is that you then become more optimistic that he can continue to socialize and eventually communicate. But these successes happen only when we allow children their own successes and not when we set them up for them. Often these successes are very subtle and so you must take care to support the little changes and not push for too much too soon. The best test of whether a child is progressing socially is to do two major things:

1.   Interact more frequently with any behaviors he can do.

2.   Stay interacting for increasingly longer turns.

As your child becomes more social in daily routines, you will find that he knows more than you expected. Once this happens, you will come to believe he can do more and no longer define him by what he cannot do or what he does that is unusual. Another benefit of having a social play life with your child is that you will get to know his "signature strengths," which are the only lasting source for his development. The ultimate goal of developing social play habits is to have a child who is optimistic about relationships with several persons who are optimistic about him.

Case example: Andrew (three years old with autistic features)

Andrew was diagnosed by a psychologist and pediatrician to be on the autistic spectrum. He was nonverbal, noninteractive, highly preservative in actions and sounds, and emotionally resistant to people touching or talking to him. He often screamed from two to ten hours a day. He resisted personal contact as if they were violent abuses. He was extremely sensitive to many sounds and most unexpected events. Most of the time, he allowed no one but his mother to contact him physically or verbally.

Andrew's parents tried to address many goals at once: speaking, reading, dressing, and academic goals like numbers and letters. He was resistant to most of these attempts, both at home and at preschool. His mother described life as a "nerve-racking struggle." However, she also said that occasionally, when they were alone, he was calm and responsive. She revealed hope when she said: "I know there is a little boy in there and I am going to find him."

Formal testing was not possible. Interviews and home observations revealed Andrew to be at about the six-month level in communication and social emotional functioning and the one-year level in some cognitive and adaptive skills. A major problem was that he had such a low rate of interaction with people and so few activities that he appeared locked in a world that kept him from learning. Clearly he lived in a world of sensation and actions that were extremely different from the ones his family experienced or understood.

His parents and we decided to focus on the pivotal goal of social play—that is, for Andrew to stay in any kind of interaction with others. A major emphasis was to simplify Andrew's life and to limit expectations of what he could do. We discussed several developmental topics with the family to help them understand the importance of Andrew playing with people who were acting in ways he could act and in ways that his nervous system could tolerate.

Since Andrew was resistant to strangers, we began by instructing his mother to use a few strategies slowly, one at a time. We encouraged her to become a play partner by imitating his sounds and movements and by waiting for him to respond in any way and then to try to keep the interaction going. She also learned to observe carefully his behavior and identify times he was more available to her. Then, she quietly acted in ways he was acting. This was neither a fast nor easy process since Andrew spent over 80 percent of his time secluded in self-directed movements. Andrew's mother said she was relieved to feel she did not have to teach him many things at once. We discussed that until he accepted people in his world and began interacting with them, any other learning would be short-lived. His mother agreed since he had learned many discrete behaviors but used them only in the teaching situation.

We also began to investigate which environmental stimuli set him off and shut him down. His family found that he participated more when there was little noise around and when he was not touched, unless he initiated the contact. The family began predictable daily routines at home where they would play with no goal other than to stay with him at first. They had not realized that, for Andrew, simply staying with someone was a major accomplishment. Interacting, even briefly, for the boy was very uncomfortable and perhaps even painful for him. These routines included times he occasionally enjoyed which were bath-time, rocking with his mother, parallel play with any object he selected, storybook times, bedtime, and riding in the car.

In about four months Andrew was staying and paying attention to his mother for more than a few minutes at a time. He then began initiating contact with her, which encouraged her considerably. Touching her, looking at her, and making faces were a huge reward for her. While maintaining parallel play, she gradually began to imitate the sounds and actions he made, and he began to attend to her when she acted like him.

Once he was staying in several daily routines without resistance, we taught her the important strategy of waiting with anticipation so that he would begin to learn a second pivotal goal, to initiate contacts with others. When he began initiating contacts, she learned two new strategies: responding to any behaviors he initiated and responding to all his sounds and actions "as if" they were intentional communications. We discussed and demonstrated several topics relating to how children learn to communicate and learn cognitively. We wanted the family to value many behaviors they had ignored or discouraged when they were expecting behaviors he was not ready to do, such as words.

After about two months, Andrew was showing more interest in playing with his parents and one brother. We then discussed how to begin to help Andrew communicate. We explained how communication develops from easy joint activities in which two partners take turns and neither dominates the interaction. Thus, we gradually added a new pivotal goal to the curriculum—joint activity—and spent several weeks discussing how language and conversation begin in social interactions without words and how joint activities with responsive and matched partners help the child communicate. We also stressed the idea that communication was not just a large vocabulary of words but an ability to interact with others meaningfully.

During this phase, Andrew's family learned new strategies, such as taking one turn and waiting, playing with sounds back and forth, imitating his actions and sounds, and matching his interests and immediate behavioral levels. His mother reported that she enjoyed this new kind of play with Andrew and that he was becoming much more calm and responsive when she played in his world without expecting behaviors he was not ready to do.

Once his mother realized that Andrew absolutely had to stay in interactions, she learned a few powerful strategies. She learned how to act like him, how to reduce her language and demands and to keep just one goal in focus, in order to keep him interacting more often and longer. The joint activities involved exchanging sounds, actions, and physical objects back and forth. These activities also taught him four new ideas: one, that he could survive interactions;

two, that there was no option to staying in interactions at least briefly; three, that he could have successes with other people; and four, that if he did just a bit more, he would be free to explore as he wished.

We discussed and practiced responses to several issues as they arose. One major issue was how to keep him interacting when he was easily distracted away from his mother. We taught her two valuable strategies: first, gently keeping him for one more turn exchange, and second, becoming more animated and more interesting than his distractions. She was eager to practice these strategies since she so enjoyed him staying with her and she had long waited to be silly and fun with him. She then reported that he was staying interacting much more at home and that he was just beginning to imitate her actions and communications. While he was still not communicating frequently, he was beginning to point and deliberately communicate with a few sounds at times. She was excited with the changes and she said she no longer saw limits for him.

Once Andrew was taking turns both imitatively and on his own, we encouraged her to hold out for more sounding to teach him that sounds would be more effective for communication than his current physical ways. He had apparently been making sounds more for self-stimulation than communication. Until then, he did not know the powerful positive effects sound would have on others and in his life. And sounds were not quick to come. It took much waiting and prompting as well as coaching the entire family into the habit of imitating all of Andrew's sounds even if he was out of sight. It took about two months to show Andrew that sounds got others' attention more than gestures and physical contacts. By now, he was choosing to play with his brothers and parents, of course briefly and often on his own terms. However, he was beginning to join the family at last.

At the end of a year in the program, Andrew showed gains in four areas:

1. *Motivation.* He now showed more interest in things and people than before. While he still played briefly, he was beginning to persist in a few activities at his developmental level. He now showed some enjoyment in play, whereas he showed none before the program.

2. *Cognition.* He was beginning to stay in social play and his behaviors were more meaningful and less for apparent self-stimulation. He still showed some self-stimulation when under stress but considerably less than before. His family was very pleased that he was now initiating contact with them rather than ignoring or resisting them as he had a year before. He was also exploring more toys and objects rather than just repeating physical movements with them as before. He was still not pursuing problem-solving much and he still needed to practice new cognitive skills in new situations.

3. *Communication.* He was now staying in joint activities with several people and sharing joint attention with them. His family reported that they felt he was finally and genuinely "with" them, especially when they acted like him in one-to-one situations without too many distractions. He was now vocalizing a wider range of speech sounds, and while it was only a beginning, he was starting to communicate intentionally with sounds. He had yet to begin to say words, but he was showing that he understood words as he began to understand what others were saying. Andrew was still not communicating frequently and communication would remain the major pivotal goal for a long time.

4. *Social emotional functioning.* While Andrew was still very sensitive to many sights, sounds, and touches, he was improving in his self-regulation. Whereas he still became agitated and upset, he calmed himself more quickly and his outbursts were much briefer. His mother reported that he might scream briefly several times a day but no longer did he go on for hours as he did a year earlier. He was showing more trust in others. It took almost nine months for Andrew to allow us to touch him, but when he did, he began initiating frequently as long as he was free to control the situation. This was a marked improvement. He also began cooperating with others when the activity involved tasks he could do. He was still cautious with people outside his family but he was venturing out much more.

Developmental guide: your child's interactive life

What your child needs to do to become interactive

Social play

1. Notices the presence of others
2. Allows people in his presence
3. Initiates contact with people
4. Responds to others' contacts
5. Joins in others' activities
6. Seeks out or invites others for contact
7. Prefers being with people than alone
8. Plays parallel with people
9. Plays reciprocally or back and forth with people
10. Stays voluntarily in interactions
11. Actively keeps others interacting with him

Imitation and modeling

1. Tries to act in ways others do
2. Imitates others immediately
3. Imitates others at a later time
4. Imitates others' emotions
5. Learns by observing others
6. Imitates actions
7. Imitates sounds or words
8. Imitates from media (e.g. TV, video, computer)
9. Plays alone in ways he has seen others play
10. Invites others to imitate him

Reciprocal turn-taking

1. Plays in a give-and-take manner
2. Takes turns with actions
3. Takes turns with sounds
4. Takes turns with words
5. Waits for other to take a turn
6. Stays in 2–4 turn exchanges
7. Stays in extended turn-taking (more than 4 turns)
8. Offers or signals others to take their turn
9. Responds appropriately to partner's turns
10. Stays interacting longer when requested

Possible problems

1. Ignores people
2. Avoids or resists people
3. Prefers being alone to being with people
4. Rarely acts in ways others act
5. Appears self-absorbed
6. Rarely takes turns with others
7. Dominates interactions with others
8. Plays a passive, nonresponsive role in interactions
9. Reacts emotionally when others interact with him

Developmental guide: five strategies to help your child be social

The following are ways you can help your child to interact more with people.

- Select first the ones that come most easily for you.
- Increase them and watch how your child responds.
- If certain ones seem uncomfortable, do not push yourself.
- There are many different ways to be effective.
- Try new strategies when little is happening with your child.
- Determine your success by observing your child interacting and enjoying people more.
- The goal is for your child to interact with you more frequently and for longer times in a gradual process.
- Be patient and feel energized by every new interaction.
- It may seem small for you but it can be a big step for your child.

Be balanced

1. Do about as much as your child in play together
2. Do one thing then wait for your child to respond
3. Take turns with actions
4. Take turns with sounds
5. Take turns with words
6. Allow silence so your child can respond
7. Act reciprocally; respond meaningfully to what your child does
8. Insist on taking your turn if your child dominates the time
9. Keep turn-taking exchanges going a little longer
10. Interact more like a ping-pong game than darts

Be matched

1. Act in ways your child can try to do
2. Communicate nonverbally in ways your child can do
3. Talk in ways your child can try to do
4. Communicate about your child's activity
5. Show your child a next developmental step
6. Expect behaviors your child can do
7. Avoid expecting the impossible

Be responsive

1. Accept your child's actions as meaningful to him
2. Physically join into your child's activity
3. Respond to your child's actions
4. Respond to your child's sounds and other nonverbal communications
5. Understand what is meaningful for your child
6. Respond without judgment or criticism
7. Act like your child, then wait for a response

Share control

1. Make sure your child has clear effects on you
2. Change your behavior until you have effects on your child
3. Share the agenda or direction of the interaction
4. Make the interaction more playful than task-oriented
5. Follow the child's lead about half the time
6. Take the lead about half the time
7. Limit directions and commands to less than 20 percent of your behavior
8. Limit questions to less than 20 percent of your talk

Be emotionally playful

1. Find ways to enjoy your child
2. Make sure your child has successes
3. Make interactions relaxed and unstressful
4. Accept what the child is doing and join his activity
5. Interact in flexible not rigid ways
6. Be animated
7. Be more interesting than the child's distractions
8. Play in the way your child plays
9. Do more of whatever behavior gets your child's attention
10. Show your child you genuinely enjoy playing
11. Express affection
12. Laugh and smile authentically
13. Touch your child warmly
14. Comfort your child during distress

Parents' experiences using Communicating Partners to help their children become more interactive

Mario is living less in his head now

"Whenever people tried to get Mario into their heads, he disappeared. We had to learn how to get into his 'head' and we learned that his 'head' was not ideas and words like ours, but rather his 'head' was his actions and sounds. Once we acted more like him and with him, he gradually interacted more and slowly began to act more in ways we did." (Elaine)

I had to get my priorities straight with Nick

"When Nick was four and not talking or playing with people, I thought my job was to teach him what he needed for school. I drilled him with numbers, colors, and picture cards, but he still stayed in his own world. Then you showed me how much more he did and happier he was when we joined him and took turns following his lead.

Then I realized that the things I thought were important— reading, counting, swimming, talking like me—were not what he needed. In fact, focusing on school-related skills drove him away. Even when he learned those school skills, I saw that he was still 'incomplete'; he still wasn't a person who enjoyed people. Once we changed to fit him, he became a much happier boy, and to this day at 18 he is a friendly and considerate young man with friends." (Ann)

I had to be more interesting than his distractions

"I always thought learning to communicate for Jon had to be serious work. Then I learned that the more fun I was, the more he stayed with me. One important thing I did was to be more interesting than his distractions. And for Jon that was challenging, especially since junk mail or a doorknob or any crazy thing could distract him. I found that imitating him got his attention as well as just acting silly. The trick was to convince him that people were more interesting than things." (Darlene)

Imitating his sounds may seem crazy but it works

"When I was told to imitate Jonathon's sounds, I thought it was silly, but I did it. I imitated him at home, in the car, anywhere. I know people thought I was crazy. I didn't care because it took only once and almost never happened, and the look on his face was like: 'Hey, she does hear me. She does get that I'm saying something!' That was the best feeling in the world, to see I could get his attention by just doing his sounds back." (Angelia)

Elizabeth came to me only when I really entered her world

"I remember when Elizabeth was about two and she would get scared and scream and scoot to a wall for refuge. She almost always shut down when professionals tried to test or engage her. In contrast, when I entered her world and did not force her into mine, we made amazing connections. One day Elizabeth, as usual, was down on all fours with her head glued to the baseboard of our bed, rubbing her head back and forth, deep in her own world. I decided to join her. I put my head on the baseboard next to hers and did what she was doing. I moved my head back and forth once, and then waited for her to do something, without making a sound. She looked at me out of the corner of her eyes and then moved her head like mine. Soon we were rubbing back and forth faster and faster, heads glued together, totally in tune, and soon she was giggling and in my arms. This was from a little girl who rarely made personal contacts with anyone. Moments like that stay with you! Elizabeth is much more interactive than that now, but still makes the very best contacts when others enter her world and do things that she can do and that she is interested in doing." (Carolyn)

8

Nonverbal Communication

The Second Stage in Learning to Communicate

This chapter explains how children communicate before they talk and how adults can help them build a communicative habit. It is the second stage in developing communicative relationships.

One of the major concerns in autism and related disorders is a language delay and problems in socially communicating the language a child has. Parents regularly ask:

- "Will my child ever talk?"

- "When will he talk?"

- "What does he need to do before talking?"

- "He makes a lot of sounds, are they important for language?"

- "We have our own special way of communicating, why won't he talk?"

- "Why does he talk more to himself than to us?"

- "What can I do to help him talk?"

It is understandable that parents focus on helping a child talk. After all, talking with words is the major way we learn and make our way in the world. But in order to connect authentically with children we need to appreciate the fact that our children do not by and large live in our world of thought and language. Rather, they live in a world of sensation and action. They do not begin to connect with people by talking. They do so with many possible behaviors, such as sounds, motions, expressions, touches, and postures.

We encourage you to understand the important differences between language and communication, especially for late-talking children. Language refers to words, signs, and other symbols that we use to stand for meanings. Communication, however, is a very different thing. Communication refers to sending and receiving messages between two or more persons. Those messages do not have to be words; they can be any behavior that effectively conveys a message. Long before a child talks, he will communicate in many ways with any behaviors he can do (Bates 1976; Bloom 1993). For our children, communication will emerge out of the interactive skills (discussed in Chapter 7), such as social play, imitation and modeling, and turn-taking. This chapter focuses on skills children need to develop before language can emerge and be useful in relationships. Notice that since our concern is developing relationships, we will be just as concerned about how you and others communicate with your child, nonverbally at first. For many late-talking children, nonverbal communication will be important for a long time, even after they begin to speak.

One of the most difficult but important responsibilities parents have is to enter their child's nonverbal communicative world. Since adults live primarily in a world of language and thought, they need to shift their focus deliberately to join children in the physical ways they first communicate. As soon as a child communicates with a word, adults often begin treating the child as a "talker." But communication begins long before words and it continues to be mainly nonverbal long after the first words. To help our children in the difficult task of communicating, we need to meet them where they are. It is critical that adults avoid interacting mainly with words, especially if the child has few words. Many adults report that they will have relationships with a child when he begins to talk. Unfortunately for late-talking children, we must force ourselves to have nonverbal relationships with them or they may never come to believe in relationships.

One important developmental fact to keep in mind is that *any* behavior can communicate. Late-talking children are often communicating nonverbally when others rarely notice. This means that any behavior a child does—movement, sound, gesture, expression—can become his first way to communicate. Most children will communicate in these ways long before they talk. The fact that developmentally delayed children talk later than expected does not mean they do not communicate nonverbally. You and your child are sending messages all the time, whether you realize it or not. This chapter is concerned with what you and your child need to do together so that your child becomes intentionally communicative. We need to stress again that by communicating we do not mean talking. Long before your child talks habitually, indeed in order for him to do so, he will need to be communicating with all sorts of movement, faces, sound, and expressions, too subtle and delicate to describe. This is especially true of children whose behaviors often confuse others. They will not at first stay interacting for your words but for the rewards of the give and take that comes from communicating with you.

A common but harmful myth about late-talking children is that they do not want to communicate with people. We have found that when we join into the child's world of sensation and action and respond nonjudgmentally, most children do enjoy the connection and will communicate with whatever behaviors they can do. It will not be easy and it will not be fast, but children with language disorders can communicate, especially when we accept the communications they can do and do not expect the impossible.

Although verbal communication is a major concern, very little attention has been given to "communication before speech" in research, education, or treatment programs. One of the most important tasks is to develop relationships with the child by communicating nonverbally at first. Often this stage is a very long one. We know many adults who wait, push, and hope for their child to talk while they are missing many available opportunities to communicate with the child nonverbally in ways he can do.

Often the child believes he cannot communicate when adults try to get him to communicate in ways he cannot do. Thinking that "speech is the only way," they miss hundreds of chances every day to build the preverbal communication each child needs before speech. These adults often act as though they cannot enjoy their child or have a relationship with him unless the child talks. It is important for parents to understand that it is very possible to have rich and enjoyable communicative relationships with children long before they are talking.

Parents and professionals need to shed themselves of the bias that language is the only way to communicate. Unless they do, they may believe that a relationship is not possible because they are demanding a relationship with words or not at all. Children with autism or other communication disorders, who live in a world of sensation and action more than we do, are more able to relate to you with nonverbal communications they can do than language they are not ready for.

Failing to interact with a late-talking child nonverbally is much like a gardener planting seeds but then only watering and fertilizing them when they sprout above ground. That gardener will get very few plants, just as adults ignoring the child's nonverbal behavior will get few words. This book is about many parents who have had rewarding relationships with children by focusing on whatever sounds and movements the child has available. These relationships have often lasted years but they usually resulted in children who, when they did talk, did so in conversational relationships and not only to answer questions or recite what they know. When a child learns to communicate early, he is more likely to communicate with the language he learns later than simply use it for school and survival.

Case example: be a "constant social sounder" before language

Jacob made very few sounds between two and five years of age. His family tried signing, picture communication, and computers but he preferred to communicate in his own ways within his family. Since he was interactive, I encouraged building a strong sound communication habit before pushing him to language per se. I had learned that insisting on words too early often drove the child away from just the interactions they needed to develop. Clearly, it was physically difficult for Jacob to make sounds. He was diagnosed as apraxic as well as autistic. His family began imitating all of his sounds until he began making conventional sounds. They incorporated sounds in everything they did. They made sure not to force him to try sounds that he could not do. Our first goal was to make him a "constant social sounder," which means a person who makes sounds whenever he is interacting regardless of how clear the sounds are. He needed a great deal of practice with speech sounds but his family was willing to enter his world of sounds and stay interacting there with him. While his family was told several times that children do not begin talking after age four, I encouraged them to continue the sound communication program because I saw that he had many ideas that were ready to become words if only he practiced his sounding enough in real communication. Progress was not fast, but his family was patient and when the first identifiable words came at age seven, the family knew they were on the right track. Now aged ten, Jacob is a constant communicator, mainly with words. He is still struggling with articulating, especially in sentences, but he is a social talker and beginning to make friendships.

We have seen many potentially rich and rewarding relationships wither when adults do not join into the child's nonverbal world. No matter how strange it feels to be nonverbal with a child, it is necessary to help your child into your communicative world. When parents communicate in their child's world they report less loneliness, greater effectiveness, and more interest in being with him. The child is also more interested in being with them. One advantage of communicating in your child's world is that you do not have to wait for "language" or "school" to feel successful with your child. You can both be successful at any time. For a nonverbal child, try to define success as communicating, not talking in ways adults want. If you hold out for words, your child may experience so much failure and so little enjoyment that he will avoid communicating except when he needs something.

How do late-talking children begin to communicate intentionally?

We define communication as any behavior that conveys information to another person. Thus, communication can occur even if the person did not intend to communicate; it occurs when one person has an effect on another. Consequently, we do not mean only speech and language. In autism and related disorders, there is often a wall between the child and others that prevents effective communication. That wall separates the two distinct worlds of the child and adult: the child's world of sensation and action and the adult's world of thought and language. To break this wall down, someone has to change and it is much easier for the adult to do so at first than the child. The first thing to understand is that your child will do many things that have effects on you while the child is not intentionally communicating with you. Your important task is to help the child intentionally communicate with any behaviors he can do. The story below shows how a mother helped a child move from being noncommunicative to communicative.

> Jenna, at 26 months, played mainly alone and rarely communicated. She regularly played in her crib with a mobile toy above her. Often when Jane, her mother, entered the girl's room, Jenna was waving her hands hitting the mobile playfully. Jane began responding to the waving by picking up the girl. Jane was treating the playful behavior as if the girl was communicating "get me up." She knew Jenna was not really communicating but only playing. But Jane had learned that responding to her child's play behaviors could turn them into communications. After a few days of this "pretend communication," the mother began an experiment. She entered the room and waited silently to see what Jenna would do. Voila! Jenna began to wave her arms in Jane's direction. She was now waving no longer to play with the mobile but to communicate intentionally with a message like "get me out of here!" Jane had successfully turned Jenna's self-absorbed play behavior into an intentional communication by responding "as if" the child was communicating. The child's behavior was having effects.

The story shows the power you have in your daily contacts to help your child communicate with any behaviors at all. Let us make it as easy as possible for a child to communicate, especially our children who find it hard to do so. Allow the child to begin to communicate with easy behaviors he already does. For many reasons it is difficult for autistic children to interact, let alone communicate. Let us help them communicate by accepting any of their behaviors (as long as they are not harmful). Elizabeth Bates was a pioneer in studying how mothers and children begin to communicate. She found that children begin to communicate when mothers respond to natural play behaviors then wait for a response. As in the case study above, Bates found that young children begin communicating "accidentally" when any movements and sounds have effects on others. Then the children perform those behaviors deliberately to have more effects on others. Many autistic and late-talking children seem not to believe that they can have many effects on others. The point of the story is to encourage you to respond to your child's spontaneous behaviors and then wait for them to respond so that you teach them that any behaviors can communicate. You may have your own ideas about how a child should communicate. You may want him to say his name, identify colors, and tell you what happened. Try to remember that your child will first communicate with his own experiences, not about your thoughts.

> Andrew, at five, insisted on playing alone. Pam had long ago tired of trying to get him to do things her way. She began playing side by side with him. She imitated the way he played and sounded by himself. The more she responded to him, the more he attended to her. This went on for months and Pam was just happy he was finally allowing her into his world and noticing she existed. She then began responding more to his sounds by repeating them or giving him a word for the sound. Gradually but clearly, Andrew began directing his sounds more to Pam than to his play. He began making sounds to communicate what he wanted her to do. This was not a rapid process and it took the conviction on Pam's part that he would communicate to her eventually if she responded to the behaviors he did alone. Pam even said, "I know there's a smart little boy in there, and I'm going to find him." She learned that finding that smart boy involved responding to many behaviors most persons would have ignored or tried to suppress. She was not concerned about what she wanted him to do but only that he connect with her in any way he could. She wanted a relationship with the "boy in there" and she was not interested in making him into a student or changing him for now.

To become an intentional communicator, a child needs certain beliefs and attitudes about himself and the world. Children who communicate regularly in social relationships appear to operate by the following beliefs:

- "I can have control over people as well as things."
- "People will accept what I can do, so I will not fail if I try to communicate."
- "People want me to communicate with them."
- "People will come into my world and show me how to communicate next."
- "Interacting with people will give me more freedom, not less."
- "Communicating is an enjoyable way to be with people."
- "The more I communicate, the more I learn."

To become a partner who helps your child communicate, you may find the following attitudes will support you on the journey:

- "I can help my child communicate better than anyone."
- "Professionals can help but cannot do the job alone."
- "In every contact we have, I am teaching my child to communicate or not to communicate, whether I realize it or not."
- "The ways I communicate have profound effects on how my child will communicate."
- "My child must communicate without words long before he speaks regularly."
- "The more I communicate like my child, the more he will communicate like me."
- "I can have a rewarding relationship with my child even if he is not communicating the way I want him to."
- "I realize that wanting more than my child can do can drive him away and result in him doing much less than he can do."

What are the major skills children need to become communicative?

Communication means constant exchanges, not just meeting needs. To help your child communicate, build an environment where you and he are in a constant flow of exchanges of sounds, looks, and movements. In this way, you will communicate not only to meet his needs but to make the social connections that build relationships. Often parents and children seem to lose the earlier connections they had before the parents started expecting language and not accepting what the child could do.

Compare this goal of "continuous exchange of messages" with the "brief, dead-end contacts" that characterize the lives of so many of our children. When adults define communication only as language, they miss vital opportunities to help the child communicate. In a continuous exchange, you and your child learn to be reciprocal, which means that each person responds sensitively and meaningfully to what the other does, however primitive it may be. The goal is to accept any behaviors as valuable ways to connect with your child. The critical issue is the connection, not a specific kind of communication. Since our children have a difficult enough time just connecting with us, we need to be very careful not to make the connection harder by requiring something difficult for our child to do.

It is important to stress that the goals in Chapter 7—social play, imitation, and turn-taking—will help greatly in getting your child to communicate. We stress this because we know many adults who used to play with their child when he was nonverbal but then reverted to dominating and directive ways when their child began to talk. The problem is that the loss of control, motivation, and fun of a turn-taking relationship seems to drive the child away from communicating.

When a child begins to communicate, it is easy to think he has now come into your world of thought and language, but he has not. He is still in his world of sensation and action. Consequently, for a long while communications must continue to be built with those sensations and actions in addition to emerging words.

Try to make your life with your child a continuous flow of exchanges between you. Do not be concerned about what you do as long as you do more back and forth with each other. You can be exchanging looks, sounds, laughs, touches, or anything that makes a connection between the two of you. It is essential with a late-talking child to find ways to have more and more interactions to convince both of you that interactions are possible, enjoyable, and developmentally necessary for your child. Consider these spontaneous exchanges as the seeds for communication. Often it will take considerable forbearance to remain satisfied with many kinds of nonverbal exchanges without pushing for words before your child is ready. Many parents have had to appreciate the value of a nonverbal relationship with their child for years.

Jon did not talk until he was five and then only faintly and rarely. At age two he was diagnosed at the severe end of the autistic spectrum. His social life was limited to clinging to his mother and crying when approached by others. He appeared satisfied being alone doing very little. For several months, his mother, Darlene, played alongside him and responded to his movements or sounds. We encouraged her to be persistent and she was.

He finally began responding by looking at her. She considered that a huge development. Darlene learned to appreciate any new behavior or any responses he made to her. Observing this, I personally wondered if he was ever going to communicate. Darlene wondered too but she decided that she was going to be energized by any changes, especially social ones. She remained optimistic and regularly came with reports of new little social behaviors. She had for so long felt alone with him that she felt like celebrating every time he responded in any way or showed her that he cared.

She still hoped he would talk some day but she had learned to support the many steps he needed before speech. She was now excited about any time he communicated with smiles, touches, or sounds. After about a year, Jon began to make more speech sounds and showed more expressions. We made sure that we responded to even the slightest behaviors as if he were intentionally communicating to us. Darlene became an expert in waiting for Jon to do something since he seemed so satisfied doing almost nothing. Silent waiting paid off and he began spontaneously making sounds and movements to communicate.

Changes were slow but steady. Finally after about 18 months he began imitating sounds and actions. Once he began acting in ways others did, he seemed to have a communicative surge. At first, he began responding more and then began to initiate with word approximations. In my view, the key to Jon's success was Darlene's enthusiastic support of any ways Jon could communicate and her genuine enjoyment in seeing anything new. Then, when he communicated with sounds and gestures, she would immediately say an appropriate word but not pressure him to say it.

They made this communication game a way of life. She tried to practice with about five routines a day, such as picture books, bath time, and car rides, but she believed it worked best when she "read" that he was "open" and then took advantage of the moment to make an exchange with whatever he was doing.

You and your child will become communicating partners when you see him as an authentic communicator and when you accept and expect him to communicate in any way he can. Communicate on sight: begin to see the mere presence of your child as your signal to communicate. It is virtually impossible to keep a highly social child from communicating at the sight of another human being. That should become a goal for your child—to communicate whenever he sees another person. He does not have to talk; he just needs to make some exchange to let the person know he is aware of them. We want your child to regard people as more than just tools to help him or direct his behavior. You child needs to contact and stay with people so that communicating becomes its own reward. Only when the social rewards of communication become motivating to the child will he develop social relationships.

So what do I do to get my child to be a habitual communicator?

Five responsive strategies to enable your child to be a habitual communicator

When parents ask "What can I do to help my child become a real communicator?" we know they hope for a magic bullet. They expect "it" is just going to happen. They are often looking in the wrong place and expect the professional will do "it" or the child will do "it" on his own. While we respect the serious concern parents have, we sometimes respond with a little humor by saying, "There is a magic bullet. Do you have a mirror?" The point, of course, is that we have found that the best answer is the parents themselves. We encourage parents to learn that they are the best routes for their child to become a communicator. Often parents feel they are supposed to be teachers who make the child a successful student, but we have found that children learn to communicate socially much more with parents who are responsive play partners than directive teachers. Parents rarely look to themselves as the answer since they feel that what they have already done has not worked well. We work hard to convince parents that while their child may not have been ready for their help before, or for the kind of help they thought they should provide, they can immediately connect with their child and begin to have a closer relationship with him.

Be balanced

Your child will communicate more when you allow him many opportunities to do so. However, the goal is not just to communicate nonstop. The goal is to communicate back and forth with people. Consequently, to do this your child needs you to balance your interactions with him. Balancing means that each of you does about as much as the other. This is the notion of turn-taking where you take a turn, then wait for your child to do anything he can do, and then he waits for you to take a turn again.

In our research we find adults taking many more turns than the child as they communicate with him. The child often has little opportunity to communicate. When children begin to communicate, they will be unsure and so it is essential that you wait and assure him that he will have enough time to communicate in any way he can. At first you will respond to even the simplest communications so he is successful and continues to communicate as he can.

Be matched

When you respond to your child, it is critical how you respond. We have found that when parents act and communicate in ways the child can do, the child stays and communicates more. We call this *matching*, which means that the closer our behavior is to the form, content, and intention of the child's behavior, the more likely he is to respond to and learn from us.

Considerable research supports the conclusion that when adults change to match their child's level, the child responds habitually by communicating with any behaviors available to him (Stern 1977; Trevarthen 1979). If the child's life partners do not match his level, the child will more likely play alone and not communicate. Matching is a very practical strategy for helping minimally communicative persons to be more willing to communicate. Matching provides the child with something he can do physically and process cognitively and that motivates him through the success it provides.

Adults often give up and retreat back to adult ways if a child fails to respond or to give back what they expect. Then we often see a mutual standoff. The more the adult acts adult-like the less the child communicates, and the less the child communicates the more the adult expects the child cannot communicate and proceeds to act more adult-like. The pattern continues this way and the gap between the two widens. It is a cycle that isolates the child and the adult from each other even more. We have applied one pervasive developmental finding to our work with late-talking children (Bates 1976; MacDonald 2002; Mahoney and Powell 1988; Wells 1986). That finding is that even young infants learn to communicate when adults carefully match their actions and communications to the child's immediate sensations and actions. Recent research with 20 children with autism (Mahoney and MacDonald 2003) supports the premise that the more the parents match their child the more the child communicates.

Be responsive

The first step is to value your child's current behaviors as developmentally important and build on them to help him communicate. Once you look for the positive things your child is doing, you will begin to support him and not focus on what unusual things he is doing or what he is not doing. The more you respond to your child's spontaneous behaviors the more likely he is to begin to use them to interact with you. That is the beginning of communication.

We have come to realize that formal teaching is not the way to learn to communicate. Once your child is habitually communicating, formal teaching can then be effective. Otherwise anything he learns in formal teaching is not likely to generalize to daily life and he will have few social opportunities to practice what he learns. Until then he needs you and other close people to support him in his first communications. Think of your responses to early communications as those of a gardener who must regularly fertilize the flowers and vegetables but not the weeds. Every time you respond, you are helping his communication grow. Every time you ignore his actions and sounds, they wither like an untended flower. Like the gardener, you do not have to fertilize every single behavior. But a regular habit of responding to your child's little sounds and actions will go a long way in helping him communicate.

What behaviors should you not respond to? Even casual attention seems to strengthen inappropriate or lazy communications. Adults frequently wonder: "Why does he keep acting that way when I keep telling him to stop?" Or they say, "I keep telling him to use his words and not just sounds. Why doesn't he?" Therefore, unless the child's behavior puts someone in danger, we try to ignore socially undesirable or clearly nonconstructive behaviors. You can safely ignore the child who says "don't" or "no" or answers only "uh, uh" when he can do more and wait for something better. Often your child can communicate more maturely but will stay with the old ways as long as they work for him. You will not hurt the child, as some parents fear; in fact you will help him by showing him that the world will only give him more if he gives a little more than he can do. We know that it is difficult not to respond to a child you have worried about, but we have found that truly ignoring inappropriate behaviors not only stops them but also allows the child to find more appropriate ways to do things.

Sharing control

Another prevailing observation is that when a late-talking child and adult are communicating, one of the partners is usually dominating the interaction, such as directing the topic and doing most of the communication. When this happens, there is little reciprocal communication and the partner in the passive role often ends the interaction. When parents wait and take turns with their children and insist that the child takes turns as well, the communicating is much more like the conventional give-and-take exchanges that are accepted in society.

Consequently we encourage parents to insure that both they and the child have equal chances to communicate their interests and that the "conversation" belongs to both of them. Too often we see in both the child and the adult the passive communication role interfere with learning to communicate. The child will be passive and get little practice communicating when the adult directs the interaction with questions or commands. On the other hand, the adult will be passive and provide little communicative modeling when he or she allows the child to make all the decisions and directs the interaction. Your child can learn to share control just as he is learning to communicate nonverbally. In fact, we believe that the sooner your child learns that communication is a give-and-take event, the sooner he will interact frequently enough to become a habitual communicator.

From ages two to four, Olivia resisted her mother's attempts to teach her to talk with picture cards and computer games. Olivia shut down with her mother and even made fewer sounds than she did playing alone. Her mother, Jenny, believed that since the girl was autistic she needed to drill her with many activities. At five, Olivia was becoming violent whenever anyone tried to teach her traditionally. Then I worked with Jenny to show her how much the girl would cooperate when we followed her lead and tried to get her to do more of the positive things she already did rather than pressuring for behaviors she could not do and was not interested in. It took considerable work on Jenny's part to sit back and share control with Olivia. But the more she played and communicated as the girl did, the more Olivia interacted with her and even began cooperating on the teaching tasks. Jenny made a "flip-chart" of the five responsive strategies that she referred to daily as brief reminders of how to play so Olivia would communicate more. Olivia is now nine and talking both in sentences and in back-and-forth conversations. Of equal importance, Olivia and Jenny are enjoying each other more with many fewer negative outbursts.

Be emotionally playful

In many video analyses, interactions with autistic children look more like stressful work than enjoyable play. The adult is often trying to get the child to do something he is either not interested in or is unable to do. It is not surprising that many of our children prefer being alone. Imagine yourself constantly being prodded to do something you simply cannot do. That is precisely what happens when we demand words from a child who can only communicate with sounds and gestures.

But the picture frequently changes when we treat communicating as enjoyable play and not a tedious task. When you treat early action and sounds playfully for no purpose other than to interact with the child, he stays with them and intentionally begins to communicate more. The job is to let your child know that all of his positive behavior can be playful and can become a form of communication. Here we mean that the child needs to learn that he can have effects on you by doing things he enjoys and can do.

Parents usually find it awkward at first to play with communicating. They suspect they are making light of a serious job or are being condescending to a child. We have found that since the job is to get the child to communicate more, it really does not matter at first how or what they are communicating. Communication is the goal and not the form or content of the communication. Make it easy for your child since communicating is already difficult for him as he does it so little. The first important job is to convince him that communications can be both successful and enjoyable. Realize that even what may seem a simple communication for you can be very intimidating, disturbing, and physically difficult for children with autism.

Considerations and problems

We often hear parents say that their child communicates but we then observe that he is far from having a communicative habit. Many late-talking children "have a lot of language" but rarely communicate with it except to answer, request, or perform. Try to understand the difference between "language" and communication. Even if your child has some language, he may still have much to learn about how to communicate. In fact many children still have to learn to communicate nonverbally even if they have some words, since they learned those words only in rote, noncommunicative ways.

Be mainly concerned that your child communicates *any* ways. Be less concerned with *how* he communicates until he is easily and readily communicating. Many parents become satisfied with a few words after waiting so long for any at all. This is understandable but it is also dangerous. There is much more to becoming a communicating person than having words. With the view that "something is better than nothing" parents easily accept too little and do not expect more. Many children who had not spoken by five, or later, have now become successful communicators because their life partners were willing to communicate in ways the child could.

Low frequency

Ask yourself if communicating is a natural part of your child's time with others. Build on just those times that your child is communicating. This recommendation comes from the finding that children develop best when we support their current positive behavior rather than focusing on their weaknesses. How much is your child communicating? When you estimate this, consider whether others are communicating regularly with him and allowing him to participate. When adults believe a child should be "seen and not heard," your child may not be encouraged to communicate much. For children for whom communication is difficult, this can be devastating. Some believe children have a right not to communicate if they do not want to. We agree, some of the time. But do we have the right not to allow them to learn? The more your child communicates the more he will learn and build relationships. Just as you do not let your child avoid school, you need to stop him avoiding communicating since communicating will be his most valuable source of learning.

Infrequent initiating

A child who communicates on his own is more motivated than one who mainly responds when others communicate. The child who initiates will also be seen as a "communicator." It is important not to assume that he does not want to communicate just because he does not initiate. Late-talking children often have little opportunity to initiate. We have found that adults initiate many more times than late-talking children do. The child may be learning that communication is "responding," not initiating. When parents wait for their child to start communicating, they are often surprised how much the child knows, and that indeed he did want to communicate if only he had the chance.

Infrequent responding

Late-talking children will drive others away simply by not responding to them. Be sure that you are doing a few things to increase your child's responses to you. First, do or say one thing, then wait silently with expectation for your child to do something. Second, do something that matches your child's interests and his abilities. Third, be sure to accept any responses at first. If you accept only responses that are difficult for the child, he will interact and communicate less.

Too much instrumental communication

After waiting for a child to communicate, we can become too satisfied when he communicates mainly to get his needs met. We know many children who communicate so well to meet their needs that they do not bother to communicate for social reasons. Many will describe a child as "communicating" when all they are doing is satisfying immediate needs.

Let us look at the problem of "instrumental communication." Consider the number of needs a child really has. Then consider the number of potential ideas you and your child can share. Ideas greatly outnumber needs. Nevertheless, a great many children communicate mainly to get needs met or to respond to others' questions and directions. Not only are these instances quite infrequent, but they usually require only brief communications, and consequently support very little natural learning. Thus, such communications will be insufficient in number to help a child build a communication habit.

Vocalization

Vocalization is the necessary but forgotten world of communication development. When a child begins to talk, people often see him as a "talker," as though the child had joined their adult club of talkers. What is wrong with that? The problem is that when late-talking children begin to talk they do so either very little or they use language to meet needs or to perform but not to communicate. The world acts as though their major way of relating with the world is linguistic, yet it definitely is not. The fact is that our children remain in a world of sensation and action for a long time and so will continue to communicate nonverbally for a long while.

Our research with late-talking children resulted in the following findings that provide a framework for thinking about your child's vocalizations. I stress the importance of these conclusions because few people seem to pay attention to a child's vocalization development and many rush to speech or give up on speech when a child is not speaking by three or four.

1. Many of our children have neurological delays that affect their speech development.

2. Many of these children need much more practice communicating with sounds than they usually get.

3. Many of these children live in a social world totally of words and few get much support for the sound practice they need.

4. Our children live in a world of sensations and actions, many of which are sounds.

5. Our children's life partners live in a world of thought and language and do not usually respond to their child's sounds with sounds or words the child can do.

6. Children develop speech in three stages: first sensory motor, second communicative, and then and only then linguistic.

7. Children need to become "constant social sounders" before they will be ready for effective social language.

8. With very few exceptions, most children, even with autism, can learn to speak habitually if they have frequent sounding interactions with matched playful partners.

9. Entering a child's world of sounds is often difficult and uncomfortable at first, but it is very successful in the longer term.

10. Children with autism and related disorders who stop speaking for a while can usually speak again.

11. For many children the hope for speech is abandoned far too soon in favor of alternative modes of communication that are usually not maintained. The child has then lost the indispensable practice for speech they needed.

Children with autism and language delays make many personal sounds that may not mean much to others. Their sounds relate to their world of sensation and not social interaction. Often these individualistic sounds will be used with people but not for clear communicative purposes. We find it helpful to look at these sounds as actions that are as natural for the child as the movements of his arms and legs. It is easy to think that any sounds a person makes are intended to communicate, but this is definitely not true with our children. In fact, children often make many sounds alone, only to quiet down when others enter their space. Our approach with a late-talking child is to treat his sounds as we treat his other behaviors, as signals to interact with him. While these sounds will be instrumental in building speech and language, they are not language and should not be interpreted as such. They are valuable in themselves, though, as interactions.

It is critical for parents to view sounds as the seeds that will grow into more speech sounds for talking. Parents often appreciate the importance of sounds when we describe them like seeds from which future plants will grow. They then realize that they must fertilize these seeds by supporting all of the child's sounds so they develop into words.

You will go a long way in helping your child speak when you actively support his spontaneous sounding. When parents exchange sounds playfully, children interact and communicate more, making their parents' sounds. But we must warn you that this will not happen overnight. It can take months or even years.

Vocalization develops in three stages. Too often we assume a child is communicating when he makes sounds. For late-talking children this is often not the case. We have observed over 1000 children emerge from the nonsocial to begin social sounding and have found three stages in the development of vocal behavior: sensorimotor sounding, communicative sounding, and linguistic sounding. Many children stay for long periods in the sensorimotor stage in which sounds are primarily sensory playthings. Then, if lucky, they will learn to communicate and use their sounds to do so. Third, they begin to use the sounds as meaningful linguistic behaviors, but these may or may not be communicative.

Sensorimotor sounding

Children will first vocalize with any sounds they can make. These sounds will differ among children but one thing in common is that they are not clear speech sounds and they are not used primarily to communicate. A child's first sounds will cover a wide range and only some will resemble speech. It is important to remember that they are not "speech"; they are playful sensory movements with no meaning than the stimulation they provide the child. While they are not speech sounds, we need to think of them as just what we need to respond to in order to help the child gradually build them into speech by our careful matched feedback.

Children appear to make their first sounds because they can and do so automatically as their oral motor muscles and respiratory system develop. They are kinesthetic experiences that provide enjoyable sensations. In other words vocalizing feels good and the child plays with vocalization for the sensory experience it provides in ways similar to playing with his toys.

Consequently try to see your child's spontaneous sounds as valuable toys for his communication development. Then you can help your child become a habitual sounder by responding to his sounds, even the automatic and noncommunicative ones. A first step in helping a child communicate is to play socially with his sounds. We can use sounds to build the child's most important kind of sound play, which is communication. The principles discussed in Chapter 7 of social play, imitation, and turn-taking apply here since by playing with sounds you will join his favorite and most frequent game of exploring his sounding. At the same time you will be teaching him that his sounds can also have another very important purpose: to communicate.

> Peyton, 29 months, visited us recently. He was diagnosed with autism at 24 months and was nonverbal and isolated at that time. Peyton seemed to enjoy making sounds to himself and attended to us more when we imitated his sounds then waited for more. His parents had been trying to figure out what the sounds meant and were frustrated that their adult translations did not seem to connect. I explained that he was not "speaking" with the sounds; he was "playing" with them. I also pointed out that since he was not

directing them at people, he was not really communicating. The parents were disappointed until they found they could help him communicate by responding and having communicative games. For three months they focused on imitating and playing with sounds in turn-taking games. They tried to treat most of Peyton's sounds as potential communication and they did not push words on the child. The first step was to get him to interact more with them than by himself. That, in itself, was a major breakthrough. After about two months, Peyton got the idea that sounds could get his parents' attention. When this happened he began initiating and demanding that they play with him with sounds. The next step was to respond to his sounds with single words that matched what he was doing. In those three months, he began to talk a little. The parents are still focusing on responding to sounds so he becomes a "constant social sounder" who regularly uses sounds to communicate and who continues to practice his sounds.

Communicative sounding

After a child vocalizes for sensorimotor reasons, he begins to direct sounds to others only accidentally. Then, as his family respond, he begins to communicate with sounds. Children may first communicate for attention but then they will begin to make sounds like their parents' sound as long as the parents make sounds they can attempt. It is at this time that parents, especially those with late-talking children, need to respond sensitively to all of the child's new sounds with acceptance and attention. Many of our children find communicating with sounds very difficult. For many, the task is a double problem. First, they are not comfortable socializing, and second, they may have developmental delays in their vocal abilities. Consequently communicating vocally for our children often means learning to do two new developmental skills at once. In the case of Peyton, above, we knew that he needed to begin directing his sounds to people if he was to became a communicator. His family needed to respond to whatever sounds he made just so he would get the idea that sounds can communicate and can have effects on others as well as being enjoyable playthings for himself.

Linguistic sounding

Once a child has many different sounds and is combining them, certain combinations are associated with events or objects and become words that are understood. For the late-talking person, the first use of sounds for words may be related to conventional meanings such as "eat" and "car," but may also be reflections of their own sensations and actions. Consequently there is often a mismatch between what the child's early words mean and the experiences of his partners. We encourage parents to pay less attention to what the early words mean than to the fact that the child uses them socially. Consequently, we discourage parents from correcting or questioning the child but rather encourage them to respond to any sounds so that the child learns the value of talking to people more than to himself. When we focus on building communication habits before specific language, the child will communicate more and get two kinds of necessary practice: practice at making sounds and practice at using sounds to communicate rather than to stay in his own sensations.

Keep a staircase in mind. Then do things that are on the child's developmental step and one step above. He will then learn to communicate more with you.

Nonverbal communication

The following case illustrates the importance of nonverbal communication in a late-talking child who was constantly moving, touching, and sounding, and resisting interacting with people.

Case example: JP

At two and a half years JP was nonverbal with many signs of attention disorder and autistic behaviors. He was in almost constant movement with little apparent purpose or persistence. He appeared motivated by movement itself as he sustained little interest in one action over another. He communicated with touches, cries, and loud sounds, but only rarely. He made a wide range of speech sounds but used them mainly when he played alone. He knew how many toys and objects worked but he practiced playing with them only briefly. He showed emotional attachment with his mother and is thus considered loving and social, but he rarely sustained interactions.

We estimated his developmental ages, through play observations and interviews, as follows:

- cognition—5 months
- motor—20 months
- communication—6 months
- adaptive behavior—14 months
- social emotional functioning—6 months.

In summary, he was learning some functional, adaptive, and play skills, but mainly alone. He had yet to have regular social and communicative interactions with people.

Stage one

JP's parents were mainly concerned that he talk and get ready for kindergarten. We explained that these goals were several developmental stages beyond where he was, and suggested to begin with that they focused on two more developmentally appropriate tasks: first, to interact with behaviors he could do, and second, to respond to where he was developmentally. Initially, we interacted with him in responsive ways for a few sessions to identify his strengths. His parents were so concerned about later goals that they overlooked several skills he had. We showed the family that he could do much more than expected when we interacted in a balanced and matched way. To do this, we waited for him, kept him interacting, and acted in ways he could try to do.

His parents made two realizations: first, that he could do much more than they expected, and second, that many of his little behaviors were more important than he had believed. For example, he began to show several pivotal skills—joint attention, joint activity, social play, and exploration. When we responded to whatever he did and imitated him, he attended to us more. When we gently kept him interacting longer, he began to vocalize and play appropriately. Our first task was to show JP's parents how much more he could do when they responded to him rather than direct him to do what they wanted.

Stage two

The second major task was to make the parents aware of where JP was developmentally and what he needed to do next. We introduced strategies such as matching and balancing turns to help him interact. We explained that the program would be gradual at first and would involve enjoyable activities that fitted into their lifestyle and would not take extra time.

Since the parents' major concerns were for their son to communicate and settle into activities to learn cognitively, we focused on the goal of joint activity, to address both outcomes. The program encouraged JP to stay engaged in back-and-forth ways with others.

We practiced with the family how to be responsive to his immediate interests, abilities, and behaviors. We explained that he would learn from his current activities more than activities imposed on him. We practiced matching, and the parents learned that the more they acted like him, the more he interacted. His parents found it difficult at first to play in JP's ways and not to lecture and teach him skills they wanted. However, when they learned to wait and take turns, he participated much more. He clearly enjoyed their responses as long as they were doing things he could do. He began initiating contact more with others, making an important breakthrough by preferring being with people to being alone. They began enjoying taking turns with any behavior, sounds, or actions the boy could do. They made turn-taking into animated games with no particular goal other than attending and interacting. Waiting was also difficult and so we demonstrated how much more he did when we waited silently for him. We discussed the fact that he needed more time than other children did.

For five months we focused on increasing family playtimes and adding new activities, such as sound play, picture books, and household tasks. We discussed the fact that learning to communicate does not require toys and that joint activities with just two persons was important. The family selected five daily routines to make it a regular lifestyle and not just occasional games.

Then JP began making more sounds. This was a striking change and encouraged his parents to push for real communication. Since they were now interacting in balanced, matched, playful ways that allowed him some control, we slowly shifted the goal to vocalization.

We discussed how important it was for him to vocalize socially for a long time before he would say many words. We began by making sounds the major focus of the joint activities. His parents learned to play with sounds back and forth as a natural lifestyle. We also played face-to-face games without toys to stress the importance of turn-taking with sounds. We explained that he currently made sounds mainly alone and that he needed to make sounds more with people since they would be his best long-term way of communicating. Our goal was to help JP become a "constant social sounder," so that he would get into the habit of making sounds more to other people than to himself.

Since it was so tempting to talk to him in adult ways, JP's parents spent some time practicing two strategies: communicating less so the child would do more, and responding to his little sounds so he would communicate more with sounds than movements. They learned to respond to all of his sounds, not only the ones directed to them. After about a month, JP was making many more sounds and, more importantly, he was directing them to others in meaningful ways. Before he was three and a half years, he was becoming a "constant social sounder" and learning that sounds were more effective than his more primitive ways.

Since he was staying more in play, we decided to focus on building his cognitive skills within the new social contexts. We continued to practice the joint activity routines and the vocalization but now focused on activities that were more meaningful. We focused on the goals of exploration and manipulation to discover and experiment with his abilities. His mother observed him learning new concepts in their play. We practiced responding to his play behaviors with a little more advanced behavior to show him how to do related things with his old routines.

JP's family now got into the habit of showing him a further step in an activity, either by changing it or by adding a sound to it. It was still difficult for his family to wait for him and not return to old habits of directing him. Consequently, we reviewed and practiced again the strategies of waiting and responding more than directing. They saw that he interacted more when they made the changes. We practiced several ways to follow his lead and help him explore by showing him how to do new things that made him more successful in achieving his goals. His family reported that he was now bringing them new objects to explore and they enjoyed showing him how things worked. He was now able to attend longer and he began to persist without being prompted to stay.

They also reported that he was beginning to imitate some words as they played. The words were rough approximations but we practiced accepting and responding to any attempts without judgment so he would continue. Soon after he began saying a few words, his parents were concerned that the words were not perfectly clear. We explained that any new motor skills, like speech, begin in small incomplete pieces and that they should not expect words before he made many changes in sounds.

After a year and a half, JP was much more social and communicative. He began to solve problems and habitually explore his environment. Rarely did he play alone any more, but usually demanded that others play with him. While he was still very active, he could now easily be brought into a social activity. He stayed with people back and forth for several minutes at a time when his partners waited, matched, and responded to his interests. Another important change was that he was beginning to imitate others and learn concepts by watching others as they played together. The key of the program remained having his parents and he play and communicate like partners.

The more he interacted, the more he communicated with sounds and then some words. During the year, he made clear gains in developmental domains that had not been directly addressed, especially in motivation and social–emotional functioning. JP was more motivated to be with people and he persisted more in social contacts. He now enjoyed people whereas he used to be agitated and unable to enjoy very much except movement. He appeared more competent as he tried new things and showed initiative and assertiveness with others rather than passive behavior, as had been the case. He was still chronologically delayed in language, cognition, and self-regulation, but he was clearly making gains in the direction of each.

Follow-up two years later (2003)

Now at age five and a half, JP has become very social and communicative. He generally prefers being with people than being alone. He makes appropriate eye contact and is very responsive to others when they act and communicate in ways he can do. He still moves very fast and needs to be kept interacting. While he understands turn-taking, he still needs considerable help to stay in longer turns since he is somewhat impulsive to leave at the sight of something new.

JP has a considerable vocabulary that he uses communicatively but sometimes too repetitively. He often says the first thing that comes into his head rather than responding to what his partner says. Generally he moves very fast, both in actions and thinking. He can stay in brief conversations when he is in a joint activity with someone, but not yet without concrete cues. He is still at times imitative in language but I feel this is a useful strategy to ground him in the social interaction.

His social–emotional functioning has been a concern to his family and his school but both have noted a marked improvement in the last year. Staying at a task and in social interactions seems physically difficult for him. His current emotional states fluctuate from calm to agitated. He learns well when he is calm and it is my judgment that he needs time to work out his agitation. He is sufficiently interested in people and functional play that I predict he will continue to learn communicatively and cognitively.

I recommend that future education includes his mother intimately in the program since she has become an expert in following and supporting his development. She has become finely tuned to what JP needs and can do. I am sure she can make his future education easier for teachers and for him. She has become a very responsive, matched, and enjoyable communicating partner and she is skilled enough to teach others to do the same. It is important that we do not assume that JP has finished developing. He still needs responsive partners to help him adapt to the social chaos of the world.

Developmental guide: your child's nonverbal communication

What your child needs to become communicative

Nonvocal communication

1. Communicates with facial movements
2. Communicates with hand movements
3. Communicates with body language
4. Communicates with natural signs, pointing, or gestures
5. Communicates with learned signs
6. Communicates with pictures or symbols
7. Communicates with touches

Vocal communication

1. Makes sounds to himself
2. Responds to others with sounds
3. Initiates communication with sounds
4. Makes nonspeech sounds
5. Makes conventional speech sounds
6. Takes turns with sounds
7. Makes strings of sounds
8. Imitates others' sounds
9. Makes unusual sounds
10. Yells or screams
11. Changes his sounds to be more like others' sounds

Reasons your child communicates

1. To get his needs met
2. To show affection
3. To express emotions
4. To protest
5. To get attention

6. To accompany play
7. To imitate
8. To get information

Receptive communication

1. Understands others' emotions
2. Understands single words
3. Understands sentences
4. Understands nonverbal communications
5. Understands others' intentions
6. Follows directions

Possible problems

1. Rarely communicates in any ways
2. Communicates only with movements
3. Communicates only with sounds
4. Communicates more to self than others
5. Communicates mainly to get needs met
6. Rarely responds to others' communications

Developmental guide: five strategies to help your child become communicative

The following are ways to help your child become a communicator with any behaviors he can do.

- Communication here does not mean talking; it means exchanging messages with people
- Start with the strategies below that come most easily for you
- Try one or two as you play with your child, then watch how he responds
- Keep doing the ones that work with your child
- If certain ones seem uncomfortable, do not push yourself. There are many different ways to be effective
- Try new strategies when little is happening with your child
- Determine success by what results in more communicating
- The goal is for your child to communicate more frequently and in new ways
- Be patient and feel energized by every new communication. However small it seems, it is important for your child

Be balanced

1. Communicate once then wait silently
2. Take turns back and forth with actions
3. Take turns back and forth with sounds
4. Avoid dominating the interaction
5. Do not allow the child to dominate the interaction
6. Get into the habit of give and take with your child

Be matched

1. Act in ways your child can act
2. Communicate nonverbally as your child does
3. Talk in ways your child can talk
4. Show your child a next step
5. Match his action with a sound
6. Match his sounds with a word
7. Imitate his sounds playfully

Be responsive

1. Respond to your child "as if" he were communicating
2. Respond to your child's spontaneous movements and wait
3. Respond to your child's sounds and wait
4. Respond to your child's play and wait
5. Respond more to positive than negative behavior
6. Respond with a behavior your child can do

Share control

1. Initiate as much as respond to the child
2. Respond as much as initiate to the child
3. Take the lead half the time
4. Let child take the lead half the time
5. Avoid being dominant or passive

Be emotionally playful

1. Play with sounds back and forth
2. Be animated and noticeable
3. Do the unexpected
4. Do more of what your child finds funny
5. Be physically playful
6. Play pretend
7. Do pantomime games
8. Be affectionate

Parents' experiences using Communicating Partners to help their children become more nonverbally communicative

Becoming a communicating partner instead of a teacher was like a wonderful light coming on

"I came to feel that it was not only okay, but imperative, to relax and play with Noah in a balanced, challenging fashion and enjoy these his childhood years. It was such a relief after following the myriad of stress-invoking traditions imposed on us. Most importantly, he now has a strong desire to communicate. This was definitely not the case before. Both of us live with less stress and we communicate much more." (Clover)

We entered his world of sounds and he flourished

"At first I thought all I wanted was for my son to talk. I soon realized that he wasn't even on the same planet as the rest of us. He had totally blocked us out of his world and no teaching or demanding could get him to enter our world. Then we began imitating all of his sounds and actions and getting into his world and matching him. We did a lot of turn-taking with anything he wanted to do. It was a lot of work sometimes, but a lot of it was also easy to fit right into our lives and it just became a natural part of our lives. It took over two years before Jon started to say words, but he was really communicating with us long before that." (Darlene)

I never believed silence could be so successful

"We have been doing an experiment you suggested, for me to play with Jacob silently unless he said something. I am truly amazed at what has been happening. Typically as we watch Sesame Street on TV, I would run a monologue of what's going on, talking all the time thinking that the more language he heard the more he would learn. Then I tried being quiet and I was surprised how much more Jacob vocalized. He even tried some words that I had no idea he knew. I realize now that I was drowning him out and making it impossible for him to practice the sounds and little wordlets that he could do. This doesn't mean I am silent all the time. When he makes sounds I respond with sounds or a word but I do not talk on and on. I wait again and let him do more. I guess I was actually making it impossible for him to talk with all my talking." (Kathy)

Learning this was not an instant pie you microwave in an oven

"Learning to communicate with a delayed child is a slow but enjoyable process. Learning this approach takes away the myth that we need to leave our children to professionals. That myth is very strong here, not only for speech but in mainstream education. We parents are often intimidated into thinking that we can't think when it comes to helping our children learn, we can't figure anything out, and that when a child has special needs it is totally outside our understanding. Our family is now finding that the myth is false and dangerous, and that we can remove that myth. We parents are definitely capable of being the ones who make the difference in our children's lives. Some parents in history have learned this naturally but here Dr. MacDonald is making this innovativeness available to all." (Jill)

Matching a nonverbal child gives him a rich interactive life

"We have nine children, including two with severe disabilities, one toddler beginning to talk, and lots of adolescents. So all kinds of communication goes on in this house at any time! The most important thing Michael and I do with all these children with diverse needs is 'matching.'

Matt has severe, multiple disabilities, and is in a world of his own filled with nonsense phrases, largely self-stimulatory, about 'nothing.' It is almost like his brain has tape-recorded everything he has heard, and every so often he puts in a new tape and plays back what he heard over.

Most of our children, from our nonverbal daughter to others who love to talk, make their needs known one way or another. What our children with limited communication are lacking are opportunities to communicate for the joy of connecting with human beings. We often get so caught up in helping our children communicate 'appropriately' that we lose sight of the need we all have to connect in ways that are meaningful to each of us.

That's why matching is such a beautiful thing. When we simply meet Matt in his world and join in his way of talking, we make amazing connections. We have long, hilarious conversations about all kinds of strange things, using nonsense words and phrases Matt has made up as well as song lyrics and other phrases. We don't worry about *what* we are saying. All that matters is that we are making a connection in a way that allows us to join Matt in a place that is meaningful to him. We all have a blast, and Matt has a very rich social life as a result." (Carolyn)

I found many bright little boys hiding in Lionel

"When I stopped demanding language and began communicating in the many nonverbal ways Lionel did, I found hidden inside my son was this delightful, engaging little boy. It was a thrill to discover the many layers of his personality. He reminded me of those colorful Russian dolls I think are called Matryoshka, that consist of a wooden doll, and nesting inside that one are more and more smaller ones. That is what I found when I peeled away the layers of my son's isolation. But that happened only when I joined his nonverbal world for quite a while." (Susan)

Communicating Partners opened my eyes to what my son needed

"Communicating Partners gave me a totally new way of thinking about my relationship with my son. It has transformed me into a communicating partner and my nonverbal son into a nonstop talker who initiates conversation with many people. The first time I matched my son's communication level there was an immediate relaxation and enthusiasm for verbal interaction that was never there before. As a parent I had been frustrated that therapy is so brief and therapists do not see parents as part of the answer. Dr. MacDonald gives parents tools they can understand and really connect with their children." (Barbara)

9

Social Language

The Third Stage in Learning to Communicate

Language is traditionally viewed as the system of rules that govern humans' use of symbols to represent their experiences. Language is often studied and taught in terms of one speaker alone. In Communicating Partners we view language as an interactive system of exchanging meanings between at least two persons. We do not want children only to "have" language; more importantly, we want them to "use" it in their social life. Consequently they need to learn language in real world situations in real relationships. Learning language has just as much to do with the language of a child's life partners as with the child's own language. In this chapter we explore how late-talking children learn social uses of language in their daily relationships.

Too often our children have considerable language but use it only to recite, repeat, or perform, and not to communicate. They use language only when necessary and in passive or self-absorbed ways. They rarely use it to communicate spontaneously. The ways late-talking children use language relate not only to many autistic features but also to the ways they have been taught language. Often they learn language primarily for academic or performance purposes and not for daily communication. Consequently it is not surprising when they use language to recite what they know and answer questions but not to talk spontaneously with others.

The following example may clarify the difference between "social language" and "academic or adult language."

Evelyn watched as Kenny played with toy fire-trucks. She asked many questions and talked as follows:

Mother: Kenny, what color is your fire-truck?

Kenny: Red.

Mother: Are you playing fireman?

Kenny: Uh-huh.

Mother: How many wheels does it have?

Kenny: What?

Mother: It says Chicago Fire Department. Can you say that?

Kenny pushes the truck away and plays alone.

Kenny's mother gave the boy many words but they were not words that children are likely to use in play. She wanted to prepare him for school and so she gave him more academic and adult words than "social" language. The next example illustrates more use of "social" language. The mother now joins Kenny in the activity so that she and he are having similar experiences. She pushes a truck as he does. She waits for him to say anything. Kenny pushes his truck into hers and says "crash!"

Mother: Ouch! You got me!

Kenny: I got you.

Mother: My fire truck's broke.

Kenny: Fix it.

Mother: (pretending to use a telephone) Call a mechanic.

Kenny: Mechanic?

Mother: Mechanics fix trucks.

Kenny: Call him now.

In this example, the mother uses language that fits the interaction and shows Kenny how to use language socially, rather than how to just expand a vocabulary. Her language is more "communicative" and less academic. Kenny talks more when his mother describes their interaction without question. This language is more for use than for storage. We are very concerned when we see late-talking children with considerable language and they do not use it socially with others. We encourage adults to talk to children in ways they would in casual conversations. When adults ask "What would a child likely say now?" they usually begin using more communicative than academic language.

Hundreds of surveys reveal that parents often believe that language just comes automatically, like hair and height, and not from how they talk to the child. They also expect that, if language does not come automatically, it will probably not develop. Few parents seem aware that their child's language comes, in great part, from daily interactions with them. Parents become more optimistic and involved when they learn, first, that language comes from their daily interactions with the child and, second, that language can develop later than many expect. These parents then no longer "wait" for language to come on its own, but actively participate in learning language in daily interactions.

Communicating Partners focuses on teaching parents to help their child have social language for authentic relationships. Since language does not emerge from a vacuum but from active relationships, parents need to understand the role they play. Once you understand that your child's language is a direct reflection of your language, you soon realize that you can help him talk in every interaction. The key, however, is still *interaction* since the more your child interacts the more he will talk to people more than to himself. This chapter discusses how you can use your language to help your child develop his.

Learning language requires that you and your child interact frequently in a partnership that is balanced, playful, and mutually responsive. Consequently, any effective treatment will involve your child and a life partner. It cannot be done with the child alone. This chapter addresses a few basic questions:

- What do children need to do to learn language in their daily interactions?

- What kinds of language are most useful to our children?

- How can the child's partners communicate with him to make language learning a natural process?

- Why is language more than just an accumulated vocabulary?

- Why is "social language" such a critical issue for our children?

- How will we know that our child is on his way to becoming a social language user?

It is often difficult for parents to see that a child can learn to communicate in every social contact and to see that the more social contacts the child has the more the child will communicate. Parents often say "I wasn't trained to teach" or "How can I know what language my child needs?" However, once parents build intimately matched and responsive relationships, they quickly realize that since they know their child best, they can easily see what language he needs and is ready for.

The critical activity for learning language is not directive drills or lessons but interactions you and your child can have at any time. These events do not require any extra time. The more you are actively together, the more you know your child, what he knows, cares about, and wants to communicate. This is when your easy, stress-free comments will help your child learn to talk. These interactions do not take you away from your life; they make your life more social with your child. The most effective interactions are not long ones, but brief contacts that genuinely link you and your child together.

How many joint activities do you have with your child on a daily basis? Picture yourself and your child as two circles. When the circles are totally apart, neither of you is doing anything with the other. When the circles are totally together, you are actively engaged in the same activity. When you are with your child, try to picture the two circles and try to get them closer together, by joining the other's activity, even if momentarily.

Try this now. Think about five daily activities you do together. Call to memory what they were like recently. Then rate them on a 1–9 scale for how engaged and responsive to each other you were in each routine (your "togetherness"), where 1 means totally apart and 9 means mutually engaged and responsive in the same activity:

Activity 1 _____

Activity 2 _____

Activity 3 _____

Activity 4 _____

Activity 5 _____

Case example: Peggy

Peggy is ten and her mother began to see how they were interacting or not when she used the scale to describe their time together:

> Breakfasts: 3
> Television: 3
> Car ride: 1
> Homework: 4
> Cooking: 7

Even when Peggy and her mother were physically together, they were not really interacting very much. There were few opportunities to learn to talk. Only in the cooking routine was there much interaction. We recommended that they do more joint activities like cooking where they were talking together a lot. Peggy's mother also learned that events like car rides were ideal opportunities to talk together. When her mother turned off the radio, she found car rides a good place to practice language. Her mother learned that anything she and Peggy did together (like television, homework, or breakfast) could become a conversation to help Peggy talk.

The difference between language and communication: a major developmental concern

Many people—teachers, testers, peers, etc.—will judge your child's intelligence and potential by how he communicates in unfamiliar situations. We often see children diagnosed on the basis of their communication in unfamiliar situations with unfamiliar people. A major problem, therefore, is what we call the language–communication gap. This occurs when a child communicates much less than he knows. It is common to hear: "I know that he knows a lot; why doesn't he say it?"

Parents are frustrated when their child is judged, educated, and rejected on the basis of the little knowledge he communicates when he actually knows much more than he communicates. We are concerned that children communicate more of what they know rather than learn new language that may only be stored for memory or performance tasks. Many children with autism and related disorders recite songs, answer questions, and conduct monologues. However, they are at a loss to talk about the things that build relationships.

> Paul talked about more than 40 different animals but did not respond to peers. It did not matter how much language he had about iguanas, Koala bears, and yaks when it came to making friends and day-to-day conversations. He was often rewarded on how much he knew in academic settings and show-and-tell situations. His family thought he was a successful language learner. They had not considered how little he was actually communicating. His academic language rated about an 8 on a 1–10 scale but his social language rated about a 2. While his parents were proud of how "intelligent" (in the academic sense) he was, they were extremely concerned about how alone and awkward he was in social situations.

Think of the language–communication gap as a useful way to identify the language your child needs. In the case of Paul, it would be easy to teach him even more about animals, but would that help him socially? We need to stop focusing on language that does not give children words for real experiences that others care about. We need to focus much more on "communicative language."

One practical way to help a child develop is to help him communicate what he already knows. Consequently, before teaching more words, help him take more turns back and forth with words he knows. A major goal is not so much for your child to increase his vocabulary or sentence length, it is more for him to increase the number of turn exchanges with the words he has. We are more concerned with improving his "communication of language" than his "quantity of language." The critical goal is not "more language per se" but more interactions, which are the tools for language. The goal is not to teach "language" but to teach the child how to communicate with the language he has. This may sound similar to the old wisdom: "Give him a fish and he will eat for a day, but teach him to fish and he will eat forever." We care less about specific words and more about how he uses them in relationships. When we show him how to learn language from personal interactions, he will learn more language through casual interactions. The goal is not learning more language but learning to communicate the language the child now has.

What do children need language for?

"Why does a child need language?" Although the answers seem obvious, analyses of several academic and therapy curricula for autism reveals that language is often taught for academic performance and rarely for daily communication. Consequently, many children "have" a lot of language but rarely use it in daily social life. We encourage you to help children learn language more for their own experiences with people than for use in school. We predict that time spent teaching language about school topics would be more effective if it were spent on language in daily conversations.

We have found that children become more social and communicative when they learn language that fulfills the following three critical needs.

To show what he knows

When a child begins to talk, he is expressing what he knows. He defines himself to the world as someone who is thinking. This gives him a new role in the world, informs others about him, and shows how they can relate to him. How do we know what a child knows? We know what a child knows by carefully observing what he is doing.

We are treating a child with respect when we respond to the child himself and not what we want him to know. The word "respect" is not often used with children. We think more of "respecting our elders." Communicating Partners takes respecting children seriously. The word "respect" comes from a Latin root, which means "to look again." When we look again at a child, we will be using language that fits his experiences and not our expectations. For late-talking children knowledge is closely tied to their sensations and actions. Once a child learns that language is a powerful tool to express his knowledge, he will soon use language creatively. For this to happen, you must give him words for things he does and knows. We encourage parents to think of themselves as a *living dictionary* that puts words on their child's experiences and actions just as they happen. This is not done in a questioning or directive way but by simply commenting and showing the child a word for his actions.

To communicate with others

The language we encourage should be useful in daily interactions. Is all language communicatively useful? Consider the usefulness of the following sets of words:

- "Academic" words: yellow, round, triangle, Dalmatian, fourteen, mathematics.

- "Social communicative" words: up, push, give, fall, help, love, crash, ouch.

Which set would help your child more in daily interactions? Much language teaching is related more to academic performance than practical communicative uses. Consider how much a child will communicate with the academic language we teach. While we want academic language for concepts like color, numbers, and letters, this is rarely used in communication. How often is a child likely to have a conversation about "red," "seven," "K," and other "school" words? If you were on a deserted island with a child and depended on him for your social life, which of the following set of words would you want him to say: "red," "circle," "Tuesday," and "Nintendo," or "hug," "wet," "eat," and "boat coming?"

How can we expect our child to communicate much if we focus on language rarely used in relationships? We are not arguing against academic concepts; the question is not how to be a good student but how to begin to be a social communicator. Once a child becomes an effective social communicator, he will learn more language in relationships and then he will use the language he learns in school. Unfortunately, late-talking children too often talk only to questions and commands, which may relate to how they were taught. Even worse, a child who sees language as only for questions and commands may see it only as a passive tool for being told what to do. Thus, this view of language may contribute to developing "learned helplessness" (Seligman 1990), which has been found to greatly depress the functioning of many children with considerable potential but little expectation from others. A child must successfully express his own interests and intentions to become interested in communicating with others. We know many children who clam up and act mute when they are asked constant questions. However, the same children show much more language when they are allowed to control the interaction as and when others respond in supportive and nonjudgmental ways.

Elizabeth and Serena are twins who at four have language for the alphabet, complex numbers, and even read words like watermelon and antifreeze, but appear lost when communicating about toileting, affection, and functional information sharing. Their parents have been more concerned with insuring that the girls learn a lot of language and less concerned with using it socially.

Once their parents gave them words for daily communications, the girls became more social.

To build relationships

The language a child needs for relationships depends on the joint activities he has with others. Every relationship has its own vocabulary. We encourage families not to focus on teaching one vocabulary but to help the child learn different vocabularies for the different relationships he has. Thus, he will have as many vocabularies as he has relationships—the more the better. Nicholas has very different vocabularies with his mother in the kitchen, his father in the garage, his brother when roughhousing, his teacher in school, and himself when he is playing pretend. Because an academic, adult-focused language can discourage a child from talking habitually, we encourage language for playful relationships long before language for school.

How to be a language partner with a child

Your child will talk more easily with people who talk in ways he can do. Language learning is not an isolated task to be taught like academic subjects but a natural extension of the social learning discussed in earlier chapters of this book. You will need to use the elements of social play, imitation, taking turns, and nonverbally communicating in language learning. Do not view those social skills as a stage that ends; social play is still an integral part of language learning. The goal of staying together in enjoyable play with no pressure for particular achievements also applies to language development.

Turn-taking is still important for language learning. Turn-taking is critical to language learning since it promotes longer interactions and allows practice and feedback to maintain a natural flow of learning. When we see turn-taking as a key to language, we will attend as much to what we say as to what the child says. Think of every turn you and your child take as an opportunity to communicate. When you take your turn you show your child how to talk best by commenting and waiting rather than questioning or testing him. Think of turn-taking more as an unfettered flow of communication than as a series of tests or drills. Children learn best in interactions where each person talks back and forth with neither dominating the contact.

Where do your child's first words come from?

When a child is not talking much or at all, a reasonable question is to ask what he should start talking about. In the 1970s considerable research explored the issue of a child's first language. Roger Brown, Lois Bloom, Gordon Wells, and others took a child-based semantic approach to early language and found that children's first language expressed a few common classes of meanings:

- agent (doer)
- action (accidental or deliberate movement)
- objects (something the child does something to)
- location (places of the child's actions)
- feelings (positive and negative emotions).

These meanings accounted for the majority of a child's language up to three-word phrases. In other words, children begin to talk about these five aspects of their own immediate experiences. While this may seem obvious, many educational and therapeutic approaches do not teach these natural early words. In fact, autistic and late-talking children often have language for colors, numbers, rote recitations, picture names, and other meanings that are unrelated to their daily experiences.

We conducted a series of studies at the Ohio State University in the 1970s and 1980s with parents and children who were two to four years delayed in language (MacDonald and Blott 1974; Owens and MacDonald 1982). We analyzed the child's language before and after parent education programs that taught parents to teach their children language for the child's own actions, objects, agents, and feelings. Before the program we found that much of the parents' language illustrated the following profile:

- Balance: parents used many more words on their turn than the child; there was little balanced turn-taking and parents rarely allowed silent pauses for the child to try to talk.

- Match: parents often acted and communicated in ways the child could not try to do and they rarely gave the child language for the child's interests.

- Responsiveness: parents often spoke from their agenda and not in response to what the child was immediately doing.

- Sharing control: parents frequently took total control with questions and commands, expecting the child to talk about academically oriented things.

- Emotional playfulness: parents often took a directive teaching stance rather than a playful and emotionally expressive one. Parents reported that they believed they should act like a teacher. Much of their language had little to do with the child's experience or was very useful in daily communication.

The parents participated in a series of treatment programs that taught them to enter their child's world of play and talk about what the child was doing in ways that the child could do. Using the five responsive strategies (balance, match, respond, share control, and emotionally play) parents generally had the effect of enhancing their children's language about their experiences. These preliminary studies suggested that nondirected play interactions were effective for learning a first language. These and related studies (Willems, MacDonald, and Lombardino1983) showed that even severely delayed children can talk when their parents direct their language to four factors: the child's interests, knowledge, nonverbal communication, and current language.

When parents now ask "Where does my child's language come from?" we respond: "From the two of you in daily interactions." Your child's language will come from his interests, knowledge, nonverbal communications, and current language. On your side, your child's language will come from your language about his interests, knowledge, and your responses to his nonverbal communication and his current language. In other words, when you and your child are interacting you will help him talk when you observe your child and translate his life into words he can use.

Problems and considerations

We have found several conditions that interfere with learning language. It may be easy to misinterpret these conditions as mistakes that adults make in interacting with children. We view these conditions definitely not as mistakes but as natural consequences of having a child who is not talking and for whom adults feel responsible for helping them talk.

Many of the conditions described below are the result of a number of factors: first, parents not understanding how children learn language; second, parents believing they need to be a directive teacher rather than a play partner;

third, the belief that only professionals and schools can help children talk; and fourth, the natural frustration and sense of failure that parents have in the face of having a child who is very resistant.

Dominating the interactions

It is very common in interactions with a late-talking child for one person to dominate the interaction. The adult may ask many questions or talk without waiting for the child to talk, or the child may do the nonstop talking in a monologue style. We rarely see a turn-taking balance where each person talks then waits for the partner to respond. What is missing is the give-and-take flow that makes conversation successful. It is difficult for many parents to tolerate silence with children, especially ones who are language-delayed. It feels natural and necessary to respond to a quiet child with a stream of talk. Many adults even believe that constant talking is what will work. Some professionals even encourage caregivers to "bathe your child in language," apparently unaware that children communicate more when partners talk in ways the child can talk and wait for the child to talk. It is not uncommon to see the following kind of exchange with a late-talking child:

Vanessa: Outside.

Parent: It's cold outside. You don't want to get sick. You had better get your coat. Here, let me get it for you. You know where it is. Why don't you get it?

Notice how the parent is dominating the interaction, without waiting for Vanessa to take a turn and practice her language. If Vanessa learns from how her parent talks, she will have a difficult time trying to get a word in and to learn language from her parent's massive language that is impossible for her to try.

Let me stress that we are not placing any blame on the parents. After 30 years with children, it is still difficult for me to say just a little to a child and then wait. Our research has consistently shown that when adults talk less and wait for the child, children talk increasingly more. Notice in the example how Vanessa was discouraged from talking. After all it is difficult for our children to talk to begin with, and so if the adult will do it all, why bother? Our children desperately need to have many successes talking before they have the confidence to talk regularly. With concerted practice many parents have learned that when they talk less their child talks more.

Expecting too much or too little

When we surveyed parents, we discovered that many were not sure what language their child was ready to do and they believed that talking to the child in adult ways was correct. They did not realize that too much talking could actually prevent the child from participating. When parents expect too little or too much of their child, the child often stays silent and loses the motivation to talk.

> Madeline was four and totally nonverbal. After a few sessions with her father, he asked how he could help the girl communicate. My answer alarmed him. I replied: "Sometimes I notice that you expect too much of Madeline and sometimes you expect too little of her." The father said, "That doesn't make sense; how can I expect both too much and too little from her?" I responded: "I see how that seems strange. But remember, a few minutes ago you did two things with her as you were feeding her. First you fed her the crackers that she was able to feed herself. Here you may have been expecting too little. And then you said to her: 'What kind of crackers are these, Ritz or Triskits?' In this case you were expecting too much of her since she does not talk."

So what should we expect? Expect your child to do just a little more than he or she is doing, understanding that it is less important in the beginning to do anything in particular; the important thing is to interact again successfully.

The academic language problem

Many times a child's potential entry into school can pose problems for language development. Parents and professionals may focus on teaching language for school more than language for daily communication. Far too many children recite paragraphs, answer questions, and show much school language but have little idea how to talk in a social situation. They have not learned language common to conversations or social skills, like turn-taking, for communicating effectively. The pressure parents feel for a child to succeed in school is understandable. They frequently say things like: "If only he can get into normal school, he will become like other children." Unfortunately, becoming like other children requires that he knows how to have conversations. Very little school language will help him do that. Here again is the language–communication dilemma that, as we push for more language, we may be decreasing communication, which is just what is needed to continue to learn language.

David Elkind, the renowned cognitive child psychologist with over 40 years' experience, identified a serious problem in education in that there was a high incidence of teaching children skills before they could use them. He found that we often teach children what he calls "circus tricks" to perform on call while they lack the social skills to use them in real life. Using Elkind's notion of "circus tricks," we encourage parents to help children learn language that can emerge regularly from their own activities, and not have the child learn language as a "show and tell" skill that is performance-bound and unlikely to become spontaneous.

The hidden language problem

One of the first questions to ask is: "To what extent are you talking about what your child knows?" If you could make a list of everything your child knows and then check off those things he communicates to others, you would see that he knows much more than he communicates. This task leads you to identify many words that could help him learn. Choosing meanings your child knows as the words to teach makes language learning more successful for him.

Think of your child's current knowledge like a submerged iceberg of his future language. Then when you ask "What should he be saying?" you have the answer; that is, those things that he knows and is interested in that are right under the "waterline."

Language is too instrumental and not social enough

Autistic children often do not seem to know they should be talking about their experiences. They are often in such a habit of talking mainly to satisfy needs that they do not appreciate the enjoyment of just sharing what they know. It is incumbent on parents to enter their child's activities and talk about what he is doing, not to accomplish anything but for the enjoyment of learning what he knows and communicating about it.

Talking with others about what a child knows may seem obvious but it is not common with many late-talking children. They often talk mainly in response to questions, to request needs, or to perform monologues, but rarely do they talk just for the social connection. Consider the developmental and social consequences when a child does not talk in situations where he knows a great deal.

> Kenny, a six-year-old boy, was often socially isolated. He shied away from people. His teachers were surprised to hear that he talked quite a bit at home. At school his teacher saw him as a model student, never talking unless he was questioned and always responding obediently. His independent play showed that he knew a great deal but he rarely talked about it. We found that most adults communicated mainly with questions and so, while they discovered he had language, he never let them know how much else he knew because he was mainly reactive and did not express himself. Once we showed his parents how to reduce their questions and comment on his experiences instead, Kenny talked much more and showed much more knowledge than they thought he had. They were surprised at how much more he talked when they stopped questioning him and waited for him to say what he was thinking. They had believed they should be teaching him new language, and then they learned that they could best teach him new language by commenting on his ideas and showing him new things to say about his ideas. When his parents supported his ideas and stopped testing him he also changed from a very passive, almost depressed child to one who was enthusiastic to show what he knew.

The cognitive mismatch problem

Thinking that they are supposed to be a teacher, many parents talk far above the child's cognitive development. When a child hugs a baby doll and his mother responds by pointing to the doll's body parts and saying "What's that?" or "Show me her eyes," the mother is not responding directly to what her child is doing. She is distracting the child from the "hugging" and not showing language for the girl's current action and interest. We find that children learn language readily when we give them words for what they are doing. In this case we would say something like "hug," "hug baby," or "love you baby." These language cues would give the child words for her current thoughts and actions.

Children will learn more when their parents use language that fits their actions than when parents talk about things they think the child needs to know. If children simply used words for what they already knew, they would have a strong start on becoming social communicators. Remember, we want our children to become constant social talkers, not just compliant students and obedient children.

> Consider three-year-old Jeff's father who believed he needed to teach his son a lot of language. He carefully explained to the minimally verbal child how trucks and dishwashers and elevators worked. He explained the electricity and mechanics so the child would know as much as possible. His father did not seem to notice the MEGO effect he had on the boy (MEGO meaning My Eyes Gloss Over). The boy was lost and did not respond to the lectures that were far beyond his ability to understand or to model. Once Jeff's father responded just to the child's actions or communications, such as by saying "up" or "wash" when the boy pointed to the elevator or washing machine, Jeff began to talk more and to be more interested in learning from his father.

The language as a job problem

Typically, children begin to talk as a natural extension of their play and interaction with partners who are not directly teaching. It is as though the play activities are just "sprouting" language as their partners are naturally giving them words for what they are doing. While this often does not work automatically for late-talking children, we have found it is still effective with our children when they have become interactive with us.

We are very concerned about children who talk mainly to answer questions or satisfy needs. When we put the child in these "talk-only" contacts, we remove him from the natural action-based contexts that language evolves from. It may be similar to judging how a child swims by observing him in a bathtub rather than in a pool. On a numerical basis alone, the child just does not have enough experiences with practice and feedback to learn language as a habit. Further, language is not self-motivating for children like these. Unless language becomes rewarding in itself, children are not likely to do the work to develop real social talking. Our children seem to be learning: "I'm supposed to talk about what others want, not what I care about, so why bother?"

Remember: language learning is a living, not a job. When you make a job out of your child's play, he is likely to leave you. Similarly we need to avoid making talking into a job the child fails, since he will leave and lose the partner he needs to learn language. We need to be realistic about how your child will learn to talk. He has hundreds of chances to talk about what he knows every day. How can we expect the few times that parents or professionals deliberately teach him language to compete with all the natural opportunities he has? They simply cannot. Once you see natural interactions as the best times to learn, you will see that the more he interacts, the more language he learns.

Is your autistic child "always" autistic?

Try to understand that just because your child is said to be "autistic," it does not mean that your child is "always" autistic. Most children with autistic features also have many typical developmental features. Communicating Partners encourages parents to interact with their children more when the child is not behaving "autistic" so that they build their relationship on his emerging positive behaviors and do not focus on the "autistic" behaviors. Parents become more optimistic about their child's development when they stop seeing their whole child as "autistic" and as something that must stop before he can be successful. Rather, we encourage parents to focus on interacting with their child when their child is acting positively.

How often does your child act "autistic"?

Score each of the following situations with: 0=never, 1=seldom, 2=occasionally, 3=frequently.

- With you in play
- With you when you act like a teacher
- With you during quiet time
- With others in the family:
- With strangers
- In groups
- In one-to-one contacts
- In teaching contexts outside the home
- When he is active
- When he is alone and inactive
- When he is tired
- When he is emotional (positive)
- When he is emotional (negative)

Five responsive relationship strategies for building social language

However frustrating you find conversations with late-talking children, we have found a consistent conclusion from our work. The first step in helping your child talk is to realize that he can learn language in every contact the two of you have. You may ask: "How can he be learning when I am not teaching him?" The answer is that your child will not learn social language from the directive approaches we often think of as teaching. It is often a surprise and a major eye-opener for parents when they realize that their child is learning best from them when they are "playing" and not "teaching." When parents shift their head set from teacher to play partner, exciting changes keep happening.

Before we discuss how to use the five responsive strategies (the core of the CP approach), consider four roles you can play to help your child talk. We have found these roles in parents who have been successful in helping children become language partners. We encourage you to take on each of these roles gradually on its own until it becomes a habit. Just as you assume the role of caregiver and nurturer with an infant and the role of a nurse with a sick child, you can assume these four roles so that your child learns language in your daily interactions. The more you play these roles with your child, the less you will have to deliberately teach language and the more your child will learn to talk with you. In fact, you may find that the least successful talking times occur when you do deliberately try to teach language.

BE A TRANSLATOR—A FIRST ROLE TO PLAY

When a child learns language, he is learning your symbols (words, signs, etc.) for experiences, perceptions, and nonverbal communications that he already has in some way. He is not learning something entirely new but rather he is learning how to express in words something he already knows. That is why it is more effective to teach a child language for things he already knows, cares about, and communicates about nonverbally than for concepts that are new to him. When we teach a new word and concept at once, as in teaching the word "horse" when he is unfamiliar with a horse, we are making the child learn two things at a time: the concept and the word.

Let us make learning to talk as easy as possible, especially for children who find it difficult. Our children have a difficult enough time just navigating the often chaotic world of people. They should not have to learn language in a more complicated way than we expect of typically developing children.

Parents have considerable success playing the role of "translator" with their child. First they see their child already has his own personal and idiosyncratic language. He communicates with sounds, movements, word attempts, and expressions that are unique to him. I recall when our son Larry began to talk, he said "elegant" for "elephant" for a while. That was "Larry" for elephant. I recall our disappointment when he began saying "elephant." We longed for "elegant." Just as we appreciated Larry's special language, we encourage you to be mindful of your child's own language and value it as important for his development. Then, after your child is secure in his own language for a while, you can begin to translate that language into yours. Be sure that, as you translate your child's language, you do it positively and not in a way that makes him feel he is doing something wrong, for example by saying "elegant" for "elephant."

Especially with late-talking children, we should celebrate any early attempts to talk and not discourage early attempts that may not seem "normal." Be happy when he says anything and do not discourage him by treating his attempts as mistakes. Remember, when a child says "ater" for "refrigerator" he is *not* making a mistake; he is simply not saying it in an "adult" way. Often when parents are bothered by the special ways their child says a word and think of it as a mistake, we remind them that the child is simply not doing it as an adult. Often I try to make the point humorously by asking parents: "What kind of car does he drive?" This nonsense question points out that language is only one of many adult things he (appropriately) is not yet doing.

Think of your job in language learning as one of inviting your child to replace his language with yours. But to do that effectively he must not feel he is doing anything wrong. Then, when you give him a word or two that he can try, he will often want to say it more like you because he is motivated to keep communicating with you.

BE A LIVING DICTIONARY—A SECOND ROLE TO PLAY

Once you realize that much of your child's new language comes from what he hears spontaneously, you can actively show him new language in every interaction. You already know what your child knows and cares about. This information is the key to his next words. We encourage you to play the role of a "living dictionary" that treats your child's actions, interests, and nonverbal communications as his next words. At the exact moment the child experiences or communicates something, be a "living dictionary" by immediately giving him a word for it. When your child falls down, say "fall," "hurt," or "up" to show him words appropriate for the situation. Be sure not to say too many words, just an amount he can try. Then be sure to wait, showing him that you anticipate him responding in some way. He need not say the word you gave him but he needs to stay in the interaction. Your child is more likely to learn and use language when you give him words that match his immediate experience. Then you are making language learning easier by giving him words for what he knows and wants to communicate about. Consequently, whenever you ask yourself "What language should I be helping him learn now?" simply say what you see.

BE A COMMUNICATION COACH—A THIRD ROLE TO PLAY

Many of our children know a considerable amount of language learned in school or from the media, like songs and answers to problems. However, in casual interactions we wonder where all their language has gone. When your child learns language by memory or as an academic task, he will not likely use that language in daily conversations. The problem is not with language per se, but with not learning language in practical communicative contexts. Your child may have a large vocabulary "in storage" but little available for communication. It may be that he was taught language to store in memory or that he did not learn the kind of language that people ordinarily communicate. Songs, elaborate explanations, and lists of facts are the kinds of language that work in school but rarely work in daily conversations. When coaching your child with new language ask yourself, "How practical will these words be in daily interactions and how often will he be able to practice them?" Then you will begin to see the kinds of words your child needs to be a "communicator" and not just a "student."

Your child needs you to be a "communication coach" who gives him words for immediate communication and language to build relationships. Be careful of becoming too satisfied with your child's large vocabulary or skills in reciting information if he is not using language common in casual conversations. Be less concerned with comparing your child's language with his peers' language. Rather, like an effective coach, compare him to his most recent performance and try to get him to communicate a little more than he did last time. This is the notion of "personal best" that many coaches in athletics use to encourage sportsmen to improve. Tiger Woods' father and coach constantly reminded Tiger of his recent performance and then coached him to take a feasible next step. Tiger competed against himself and has done fairly well at it.

You may say, "But I was not trained as a teacher so I'm not sure what language my child needs to learn." However, since you know your child more than professionals do, you know the words your child needs most. When you realize that your child's language needs to be words for what he is doing right now, what he knows, and what he communicates about, then you have at your fingertips just the language he needs.

Children often learn many words in response to pictures of objects, hundreds and more, but when they see the object in the real world they often do not use the word. Why? These children have learned to talk in response to questions and directions and not in terms of commenting and communicating about their world when it happens. We want your child to "communicate" his language, not just "perform" it or show what he knows in tests.

BE A STORY PARTNER—A FOURTH ROLE TO PLAY

Language is not enough by itself. For language to be developmentally useful, your child needs to "say something," to tell the many stories that are his life. We must help children develop topics and avoid dead-end contacts when they talk. Become your child's "story partner" by keeping your child in conversations; brief ones at first, then gradually longer. The turn-taking you learned in earlier chapters helps a great deal here. No matter how inconsequential they may seem, these little conversations teach the child that language is more than a tool to answer questions or do performance acts. Your child needs to see language as a tool for expressing ideas, creating stories, and building relationships. When a child sees language as conversation rather than a way to gratify needs, he will begin to use people as rich resources for further learning. And once you see in your child's contacts the potential for an enjoyable story, learning language becomes a major factor in your daily relationship with him.

Five responsive teaching strategies

A major focus of research in early language in the last 20 years has been the role of parent–child interactions in enhancing a child's development. One major finding is that a parent's style of talk and play has considerable influence on how the child becomes a social talker. The work of Jerome Bruner (1990) showed that a child learns language as his mother "fine-tunes" her interactions to fit the child's immediate experiences, interests, and abilities. Lois Bloom (1991) and Roger Brown (1973), and others, demonstrated that mothers were more effective with their children when they used language that coded the child's own meanings, such as actors, actions, objects, and other events in the child's active life. Wells (1986) argued that language is best learned in conversations that are real to both the child and his partners and that the parents' communicative styles influence the degree of language learning. Other researchers have shown that the more "semantically related" the parents' language is to the child's experiences, the more easily language learning proceeds. By "semantically related" they meant that the more adults talk to a child in direct response to his immediate activities and interests, the more the child begins to talk. This argues against teaching language from external curricula such as picture cards, academic books, or prepared lessons, but rather argues for helping children learn language for their current "meaning" and communication.

In our work with hundreds of nonverbal and minimally verbal children, we have investigated the kinds of adult communication strategies that relate to increasing children's social use of language (MacDonald and Carroll 1992; Owens and MacDonald 1982). Parallel studies by Gerald Mahoney demonstrate repeatedly that parents who use responsive, child-oriented strategies rather than directive teaching styles have children who develop more rapidly in cognitive, linguistic, and communicative ways (Mahoney and MacDonald 2003; Mahoney and Powell 1988; Mahoney, Finger, and Powell 1985; Mahoney *et al.* 1999). Together we have been developing an early intervention curriculum for children with disabilities—Responsive Teaching (Mahoney and MacDonald 2003)—that focuses on a series of responsive relationship strategies that parents learn to build developmentally effective learning relationships with their child. The curriculum has been developed and tested with two separate groups of children with autism as well as other language-delayed children.

You can use the five responsive teaching strategies below to help your child learn more language and to use it in habitual social interactions. The five responsive strategies can be utilized specifically to help children learn more language and to use that language in habitual social interactions.

BE BALANCED AND RECIPROCAL

When helping children develop language, the critical goal is not the accumulation of words but the social exchange of words between your child and others. When children begin to speak it is less important that they say many words than that they stay talking back and forth with others. This requires that there be a balance between how much each partner says. Our video research with late-talking children and their partners often showed a decided imbalance when either the adult or the child tended to dominate the interactions with words. There is often little reciprocity. The child and adult often talk more *at* each other than in response to what the other has said. Consequently dialogues often look more like a series of unrelated statements.

It is critical to take turns with words as early as possible rather than get in the habit of answering questions or having monologues. When a child is learning to talk, he will develop more social language when we focus less on how many words he says (the traditional mean length of utterance—mlu—measure) and more on how many turns he exchanges with words back and forth.

> John, at age six, had been talking for only two years. He talked primarily to accompany his playing alone or to tell others about his play in monologues in which he resisted any interruptions. A typical exchange was as follows:
>
> Jodi (mother):   How's your game going, John?
>
> John: The monsters are all over the house and the boy cannot get in so he's going to throw a stink bomb to get them out and his friends will be coming to help him in their batmobile but batman isn't coming because he has to help somebody else downtown...
>
> Jodi: Where did you get the stink bomb?
>
> John: Mom, let me tell the story. There's a break-in downtown so Batman is needed there but he is sending his friends to help out here so we can get into the house and get the money that the old lady hid there before she died.
>
> Jodi: How much money is there?
>
> John: Mom, let me talk.

With children like John, we encourage parents to spend some time every day talking back and forth in balanced turn-taking ways since a dominating style will isolate the child from developing relationships. While turn-taking may seem a superficial and technical aspect of language it is absolutely necessary for acceptable communication. In the above case, Jodi made a few changes. First, she joined in his playtime and actively participated with the toys, figures, and playhouse. She took a partnership role in the play so that turn-taking with words flowed from the activities they shared. She signaled when she would take a turn so that he learned that he was allowed only one or two sentences and then she would take her turn. This was upsetting to him at first but Jodi persisted since she realized that no one in society would want to talk with him if he continued to dominate in such a self-absorbed way.

BE MATCHED

Once you believe that your child learns language from the way you talk, it will become easier to match your language to your child. Matching means communicating with words that do a few things; first, your words will match your child's immediate actions; second, your words will be of a length that your child can try to do; and third, your words will show your child how to go the next step and add another relevant word. In other words, you will talk in ways that fit your child's experience and that show him how to communicate about it.

In our work at the Ohio State University we taught many teachers and students to match their children's language in preschool classes. Through several years, a group of teachers and students were interviewed about the most helpful way to get a young child to talk. The majority of professionals who had used the model reported that "matching and waiting" was the one combined strategy that resulted in children talking more than others they tried (MacDonald and Mitchell 2002). Note that they did not say just matching but *matching and waiting*. They felt that while talking in ways the child could try was critical, it was just as important to wait and give the child silent time to practice.

The primary reason for matching your child's actions and communications with language is so he has successes and learns that you will accept what he wants to talk about at least half the time. Many parents have resisted becoming like their children in this way. They felt it was uncomfortable, embarrassing, or even wrong. Then, as they saw their child talk much more when we matched them, the parents began to appreciate how much more influence they could have than we who were virtual strangers.

Matching your child's language is much more than imitating what he says. However, a very effective way to keep a child talking back and forth is to imitate what he has just said. We find that imitating affirms what the child has said, which is helpful, especially when he is not secure talking back and forth. We also find that imitating what he says often gets his attention and keeps him talking with us. We are not proposing imitation as a major way of communicating with children, but it is useful to keep an interaction going when the interaction may end or when we say new things that the child cannot handle.

However, the kind of matching that seems to help children talk more is the kind that responds to what they say and follows on their train of thought. This language matching can take two forms: horizontal and vertical. When we match *horizontally*, we use words at the child word-length level but we give the child an altered message for it. For example, when a child says "snow," we can match his meaning and show him another way to talk about snow by saying, "it's cold," "wet," or "winter," words which show him more ways of talking about the same thing. When we match *vertically*, we show the child how to say more about the same thing. Again, when the child says "snow," we might match this by saying "the snow is cold," "make a snowman," or "look how white the snow is." Not only does matching show a child a different meaning but also says more about his idea by combining those meanings into a bigger picture.

BE RESPONSIVE

Closely related to matching is "responding." While matching involves talking in ways the child can try to do, "responding" encourages you to see your child's life as the source for his language, not adult or academic language that you may think he needs. The point here is that when your language responds to your child's interests and experiences, he will more likely learn and use that language than when you teach language for school or for purposes other than communicating his experiences. Being responsive recognizes that your child's language will best flow from his knowledge, interests, and actual activities than from a curriculum selected to prepare children to be students and adults. We encourage you to help your child have "his own language" and not just language for school and tests.

For children with communication disorders, responding to their actions and interests with language may seem unusual, even bizarre, at times. We want you gradually to release yourself from judgements about how appropriate your child's language is. We want him to become successful talking about anything he wants, at first. Only when your child enjoys talking with you regularly will he be open to talking more in your ways than from his experiences. We know that you want your child's language to be "normal" but you will first have to accept that your child does not have "normal" experiences and so his first language will probably seem unusual compared to typical children. That does not matter. What matters is that you and your child get talking together all through the day, regardless of what you are talking about.

SHARE CONTROL

Children and adults stay in longer verbal interactions, and learn more, when each partner has some control over the topics and directions of the exchange. Susan Goldberg (1977) found that mothers and infants interacted longer when each person was able to initiate at times and when each was having visible effects on the other. We have found that allowing a child to have his say half the time encourages him to stay talking. However, it is important to not totally follow the child's lead because the child needs to learn to listen as well.

Turn-taking is often difficult for late-talking children but we have found that in time they can self-regulate themselves and learn that effective talking is the kind that goes back and forth. They also learn that waiting for a partner to talk is a necessary part of relationships. You can help your child talk regularly by "keeping the child for one or two more turns" when he begins to leave an interaction. Too often parents allow the child leave whenever he has finished talking. Unfortunately, children rarely stay very long if we do so. Consequently, one hallmark of our work is to encourage parents to keep their child in increasingly longer talking interactions. The issue is not to keep the children for painfully long exchanges but to let the child know that learning language means staying for "one more turn." We want you to help your child out of the common habit of "dead-end" contacts where the child darts in and out without staying on a topic for any length. The more your child stays talking, the more language he will learn.

The following story illustrates how an interesting language topic can be built when both adult and child control the ideas in an interaction.

> Maura is on the kitchen floor, talking about the puppet Oscar the Grouch. Her mother is busy cooking but is also keeping her talking. Notice that she is not using questions as she wants to show Maura new things to say about Oscar.
>
> | | |
> |---|---|
> | Maura: | Oscar was sick to his tummy. |
> | Mother: | I'm sorry he was sick. |
> | Maura: | Me too. He didn't cry. |
> | Mother: | Good. He should sleep. |
> | Maura: | In the spaghetti bowl? |
> | Mother: | It's too small. |
> | Maura: | My bed is bigger. |

Mother:	Sure, he can have your bed and you sleep with Katherine.
Maura:	Oh, yuk. I sleep with Oscar.
Mother:	He might get you sick.
Maura:	I don't want to get sick.
Mother:	Oscar can sleep on the couch.
Maura:	Is supper ready?

As with most children, Maura's concerns were easy to keep going just by translating them into her important people and objects. There was no stress or chance of failure, no job to get done, and each partner had freedom to have their say. Here, Maura is not unlike many children we know. If we simply comment about meanings that match the child's interest and that are communicatively useful, children will stay for your attention, for the success of talking, and for the little surprises that make talking self-sustaining.

BE EMOTIONALLY PLAYFUL

When your child is not talking as expected, teaching language can become stressful and serious, often so serious that learning to talk is not enjoyable for either parent or child. At the outset of this discussion, we want to emphasize a very powerful finding from our work: the more enjoyable your interactions are with your child, the more easily he will learn to talk and the more he will return for the critical practice he needs.

Parents often feel responsible for teaching their children language for school and so they can get into a tug-of-war, pushing for words that simply do not fit the child's life or give him much practice communicating. We find that when parents take the pressure off teaching particular language and make interactions playful, children stay and learn more.

Think of new words as new toys that should be played with in interactions, showing the child many new ways of using them. When children see talking as fun, they do more of it. Many of the verbal exchanges with late-talking children are not light and playful and parents often have a rigid notion of what the child should say. We find that any words are important when a child is beginning to talk. Even nonsense words will work. Dr. Seuss, the Teletubbies, and the Muppets encourage children to talk by playing with words. Why? Because early words are difficult to do and the easier they are the more the children will do.

Barbara was frustrated trying to teach Mark words for school. He balked and refused even to play with her for a while. We decided to redefine talking for Mark. Now it was a job with many failures. We turned talking into a game where Barbara and Mark learned to throw words back and forth the way a boy would learn to throw a ball back-and-forth with the throwing being the game not correct catching. So too with Mark, they exchanged words just for the fun and practice of it. Mark's teacher's name was Mrs. Pucket.

Mark: Mrs. Pucket.

Barbara: Mrs. Bucket?

Mark: No, Pucket, not Bucket.

Barbara: Mrs. Pucket lives in a bucket.

Mark: You live in a bucket.

Barbara: I got stuck in my bucket.

Mark: Get out of that bucket.

Barbara: Get Mrs. Pucket to help.

Mark: Mrs. Pucket, mom's in a bucket.

Barbara: Mrs. Pucket, fix my bucket.

Barbara began to make word games like this a part of their daily routines and, as he had more language, Mark would change the games and start having conversations about daily topics in playful routines where talking was the game and there were no failures but many chances to learn new language from his mother.

Case example: Nick—a five-year journey from chaos to partnership

At age three, Nick came to me with his mother, Ann, who was concerned that he was agitated, upset, and acting out much of the time. She also reported several habits, such as repeating actions, abnormal emotional responses, unconventional body motions, and generally inappropriate actions in social situations. He was still not talking to others. He had about 50 words but he used them in fast strings, intelligible to himself but rarely to others. He was usually quite agitated and insisted on things staying the same, resisting change vocally and physically. Rarely did he respond when others talked to him. When he did it was mainly imitative and not apparently with understanding. He preferred to play alone, mainly in repetitive and apparently nonfunctional ways that seemed "bizarre" to his parents.

When people approached him, Nick showed anxiety by jumping, avoiding, and retreating into repetitive routines, such as hand-flitting. While Nick usually ignored people, he was sensitive to changes in his mother's emotions. He did show some attachment to her, especially when she was not trying to change him. He resisted eye contact and kept so busy that any interactions were too brief for learning to communicate. Nick's parents did not know where to begin. They saw so many things to change that they were confused as to where to focus.

I observed Nick with Ann and with me in several situations. He certainly did many behaviors that kept him from interacting. Since he was so unpredictable, I carefully sought out the situations and activities that kept his interest. A major question I asked was: "What is happening in the environment when Nick is positive and interacting?" His parents and I worked backwards from his successes. We identified when he was successful and then recreated those situations so that he could be more successful with people.

In this exploration we found that Nick had some very different sensory reactions to the world to those his parents had. A normal life for his parents was a house of music, television, and house-cleaning. Ann pointed out that Nick "acted out" more when there were changes in the noises at home. The vacuum and his father's guitar might completely unhinge the boy at times but not at others. Unexpected changes also upset the boy, as did unexpected touches, especially on the head. Haircuts became warfare. Once his parents understood that some of his difficult behavior was due to natural nervous responses to sensory stimulation that he could not tolerate, they gradually began to redesign their life to eliminate many of the stimuli that were not critical to their lives. They also learned to involve him personally in an activity if it was going to be upsetting so that he could prepare and be comforted during inevitable events like traveling and shopping.

I observed Nick and Ann together. She was consistently warm and positive, regardless of whether he was social or isolated, appropriate or not, and agitated or calm. She had so wanted him to include her in his life that she responded to whatever he did, regardless of how unpleasant. We believe she was correct in doing this because he used to be so resistant that he would not interact at all. Parents have a real dilemma here. Thus they attend to behaviors they do not want so that the child feels safe and attends back in some way.

With Nick our first and foremost concern for over a year was to make him enjoy interacting with people so much that he would no longer isolate himself. Once he really wanted to be with and stay with people, we could then begin to ignore his undesired behaviors. We were careful to do this only when we saw that it did not send him into isolation.

Ann reported that she had taught him many school tasks that he could do but usually did not do. She felt he understood her speech and she talked to him in sentences and paragraphs without stopping. She believed he needed to hear all the adult language she could give him. She believed he was intelligent and so she focused on teaching him many tasks that would show his intelligence. He was able to perform some academic and verbal tasks on call, but he did them more as a performer than a partner. He still rarely communicated with others. Most of the tasks were not social but were in response to questions and commands. He answered some questions but rarely initiated talk or responded spontaneously. While his cognitive skills were apparent and could be retrieved, his emotional and social skills were very limited and often drove away just the people he needed for development.

We began by discussing what Nick needed to do to become a civil and cooperative person. Nick showed very little discipline in the sense of predictable and ordered behavior. We did not want Nick to become just passive and obedient. We wanted him to develop social discipline while at the same time expressing his obvious interests and knowledge. Our long-term goal at that time was to insure that Nick developed a solid sense of "social discipline." We were just as concerned about him learning to have positive give-and-take interactions as we were for him to eliminate the "undesired" behaviors.

Treatment began with me learning how to keep the boy interacting with me in any back-and-forth ways. I began by imitating many of his behaviors since he attended and stayed when I acted like him. A basic step in becoming socially disciplined is to learn to take turns, and to recognize that there are two persons in an interaction. In order to help Nick stay with me, I focused on three strategies: matching, waiting, and keeping him for one more turn. I found that the more I acted and communicated like him (matching), the more he attended to me, and the more I waited silently, the more he responded to me and did something on his own. I found it necessary to gently keep him with me a little longer, then give him freedom. He came to learn that all he needed to do with me was to stay interacting, doing anything he wanted to. The goal was to teach him the social discipline of turn-taking so that he learned the practical ethic of "give and take." He learned that I was not going to give him something impossible to do and that anything was a success as long as he did it with me. After years of failing in many interactions, it was critical that Nick came to believe he could succeed with people. For many children like Nick, this can be a long time in learning.

When Ann began practicing, she found it difficult at first not to dominate the interactions with considerable directive talking. She really believed she was supposed to be a teacher and stop him from acting in "autistic" ways. She was beginning to see that the more I interacted without trying to "teach" him something, the more Nick stayed with me and the more he enjoyed our time together. Once she found that he interacted more when she was matched and playful, she slowly but surely released her self from the pressure to be a teacher all the time. She came to realize that in her anxiety to "change" him she was making their time together little fun and full of failures.

She also learned the power of her attention when she began to ignore his undesired behaviors and he did them less. When she responded to his subtle playful behaviors, the more he did them with her. It was not enough to tell her or show her what to do; she had to experience the successes that I had with him.

Nick began interacting with us more when he learned that we were willing to do all sorts of things to keep his attention. No longer was he in a world that tried to change him but now his world was just trying to interact with him in any ways he could do. He began to initiate contact more with people when they had a history of interacting with him in matched and feasible ways.

For several weeks, Ann played with the boy several times a day with the single goal of keeping him interacting with her with

actions, sounds, words, or any other positive behaviors. While she
interacted with Nick much more frequently, she learned to talk less,
wait more, and join more in his activity. She learned to be more of a
play partner than a teacher or regulator. At first she reported that it
was difficult not to question him to show how smart he was. Playing
like him seemed embarrassing but she continued doing so when she
saw Nick interacting more with her and becoming more of a
companion. Waiting and not telling him how to do something was
difficult for her. But she found that he became much more
cooperative and showed fewer behavior problems when she joined
into his activities nonjudgmentally and reduced her directions and
questions.

Through several months, Ann learned how to fine-tune herself
to Nick and come to a deep conviction that staying with people was
much more important than teaching new things or showing off what
Nick knew. When Ann saw that Nick often stayed longer with me
than with her, she wanted the same and began to enter his world and
require only that he stay with her back and forth. We were interested
to find that the more he interacted in a disciplined but spontaneous
turn-taking manner, the less disruptive and unpredictable his
behavior became.

Ann and Nick integrated these social exchanges into their daily
routines, such as bathing, car-rides, playtimes, literacy activities, and
spontaneous contacts. At first, very simple games of exchange were
the main activity. Nick and his mother would exchange
anything—looks, pencils, shoes, etc.—and then make it into a
playful game where the major goal was to keep the interaction going,
and make it enjoyable for both. Ann learned not to feel the need for
"right" answers, but to learn that every little interaction was a chance
for Nick to learn to communicate. She learned that, contrary to her
prior beliefs, language was not just going to come like growing hair
and height. Rather, she learned it was going to come from their
interactions when she was doing things he could do. She also learned
that doing for him was not as important as having him give
something to her.

We noticed in these months a real increase in Nick's enjoyment
of people. While he still showed occasional autistic and
unconventional behaviors when he was alone or over-stimulated, he
now interacted several times a day without much resistance or

undesired behavior. Nick's parents commented that they had been told that since Nick was autistic they should not expect that he would ever enjoyably interact with people. It took about a year to relieve themselves of many expectations and preconceptions they had of autism. Clearly, Nick enjoyed people when they entered his world. We concluded that the more successes he had with people the more positive and less negative he acted with them.

A major breakthrough occurred when Nick began imitating his parents in routine interactions. Before this stage, he was mainly self-absorbed and rarely learned by observing others. We encouraged his parents to celebrate and really appreciate the importance of Nick's new imitation skills. He was now leaving his own world and beginning to enter others' worlds. The more he attended and imitated others, the more appropriately he behaved. A very positive side-effect was that both Ann and her husband Joe were elated when Nick began acting like them. They had been willing to "do anything" for the boy, but they became much more emotionally attached when they saw that he cared about them and would give back to them. Ann and Joe had discovered the kind of people that Nick could enjoy and learn with and they worked very hard to become those kinds of people.

At first, Ann felt guilty that she had been doing the wrong things for Nick. But we quickly convinced her that she had been responding in very reasonable ways to an isolated child who she has worried about. We also showed her the many successes she had already had with Nick when she was playful and responsive. She came to see that when she joined his world everything went more smoothly than when she tried to teach or change him in ways he was not ready. She also learned that her two major goals for Nick—communication and civil behavior—could be worked on at the same time. She found that the more he interacted with her the less negatively he behaved. As he learned the basic turn-taking rules of socializing, his behavior improved greatly.

In reviewing Nick's progress over two years, I interviewed his parents and analyzed their relationship with Nick through reviewing a series of videotapes. Ann and Joe reviewed the major strategies in the program and gave us their views about what was working. We then corroborated their views with the video record over time. A major change we found was the contrast between them first treating

Nick as a child who was not doing what he needed to do for his age and then later treating Nick as a child who could do many positive things that they could turn into genuine reciprocal relationships with him.

They learned the importance of balancing by insuring that Nick became a "turn-taker" who was responsive to others and no longer only in his world. They found that the more they waited for Nick in an interaction, the more he did and the better he behaved. They also learned that by matching Nick's actions and communications, they made interacting much easier for him and reduced the frustrations related to his negative behavior. When they matched what they said to his immediate behaviors, he began talking more about the real world than the things he had routinely memorized in the past. They learned to respond to many little developmental behaviors that they had previously not noticed or believed were important. In keeping with this, his parents became less verbal and more physically involved in Nick's activities. At first, they resisted acting with him in one- and two-year-old ways but then, when he interacted more at those times, they were happy to have any kind of relationship with him. They learned that his skills were at several developmental ages from one to six and that he interacted more when they met him at the developmental age of the moment.

Nick's father found it easier to be emotionally playful with the boy. Joe was a part-time musician and knew how much more Nick learned when he was having fun. Ann felt the pressure of Nick's survival on her shoulders and so it took considerable training and practice to get her comfortable playing in Nick's world. Mother and son learned the critical skill of sharing control. Ann had to learn that Nick was not going to learn best when she chose what he should learn. She found that allowing him control in their interactions kept him interacting longer and learning more. She had to stick to her guns at times to insist that he allow her to have her fair turns, but he began enjoying her with him so much that he began to follow her lead as well.

Ann became an expert in what Nick could do and what he needed to do next. By learning how he experienced the world, Ann and Joe no longer worried about dire consequences and began to focus on Nick's signature strengths, which included curiosity, warmth, creativity, and real affection for his parents. These strengths became a part of every day with Nick. His relationship with his parents became much more positive and less focused on "changing him out of his autism." He certainly became less autistic as we supported the many positive "non-autistic" skills he clearly had.

At age eight, Nick was included into regular academic school. After several adjustments for Nick's sensitivities, he came to do age-appropriate academic work. More importantly, he began to have a few one-to-one relationships with peers. He was not very interested in group activities but valued his special friends. He was still quite naïve, sensitive, and awkward in social situations and more interested in being at home than his parents hoped for. His father was concerned that he lacked street smartness as he still took others literally. His father enjoyed humor and was determined to discover how he could get Nick to enjoy some of the things he did. Ann was a little reluctant to let Joe "have" Nick on his own but gradually Nick sometimes preferred being with his father. By and large, they saw him as becoming more social and conversational all the time. Nick's mother, at this point, told me that the most important and difficult thing she had learned was to play in his world and not push him too fast or act like a teacher.

Nick is now 18 and very conversational but still rather shy in groups. He has become a musician, to his father's pride, and has done well academically in high school. In June 2003 he will graduate high school and has been accepted in two colleges where he can pursue his musical interests. He still worries more than many of his peers and his parents see him as sometimes overly sensitive to how people treat each other. Clearly, though, he has developed a sense of empathy. His parents are still concerned that he prefers to be with much older persons and that he still needs to learn some of the "street smarts" that concerned his father years earlier. Ann expects that he will "loosen up" when he no longer has her as his primary conversational partner. The last time I saw Nick, I asked him about what he and his peers did together. In keeping with his teenage years, he was reluctant to talk with his mother there. Alone he told me that his big worry was how he would make it with his friends who did many things his mother told him were wrong. I was amazed at Nick's sensitivity and appreciated his "normal" conflict between peer and family pressures. I look forward to seeing how he does away at college.

Developmental guide: your child's language

What your child needs to become a habitual social talker

Form: how a child talks

1. Single words
2. Two- to four-word combinations
3. Sentences
4. Appropriate grammar
5. Strings sentences together
6. Dialog—back and forth
7. Monologue—one way

Content: what a child talks about

1. Objects
2. Activities and events
3. People
4. Emotions
5. Concrete facts
6. Ideas (abstract)
7. Now
8. Past
9. Future

Use: why a child talks

1. To initiate talk with people
2. To respond to others' talk
3. To get needs met or help
4. To get attention
5. To self to accompany activity
6. To give information
7. To get information
8. To enjoy being with others

Speech clarity

1. Makes approximations to words
2. Individual words are clear
3. Strings of words are clear
4. Repeats when misunderstood
5. Imitates your speech with clearer speech
6. Makes up own words—jargon

Appropriateness of talking

1. Relevant to situation
2. Responsive to what others say
3. Knows when to talk and when not to talk
4. Waits his turn when others talk
5. Talk fits emotionally to the situation

Possible problems

1. Bizarre or inappropriate talk
2. Talk is off the topic
3. Interrupts others' talking
4. Rote or memorized talking
5. Talks *at* more than *with* people
6. Repeats words unnecessarily
7. Unclear or mumbled talking
8. Self-centered talking
9. Short, unelaborated talking

Developmental guide: five strategies to help your child talk socially

The following are ways to help your child become a habitual social talker.

- The goal is not more language but more communicating with language.
- Start with the strategy below that comes most easily for you
- Try one or two as you play with your child, then watch how he responds
- Keep doing the ones that work with your child
- If certain ones seem uncomfortable, do not push yourself. There are many different ways to be effective
- Try new strategies when little is happening with your child
- Determine success by what results in more communicating
- The goal is for your child to talk more frequently and in new ways
- Be patient and feel energized by every new word. However small it seems, it is important for your child

Be balanced and reciprocal

1. Say one thing then wait for your child to respond
2. Talk in a give-and-take turn-taking style
3. Wait with anticipation for your child to respond
4. Allow your child to initiate talking; silent waiting helps
5. Avoid dominating turns with your child
6. Prevent your child from talking in monologues
7. Make sure you and your child talk about the same topic
8. Communicate more like a game of ping-pong than darts

Be matched

1. Communicate in ways your child can try to do
2. Talk about what your child is immediately doing
3. Act like a "living dictionary," i.e. put a word on what your child sees and does
4. Talk about your child's interests

5. Avoid using more words than your child can say

6. Talk not only to be understood but also to show your child what to say

7. "Match up" by giving your child one or two more words to say

8. Show your child new words to say about current things he talks about

9. Show your child how to extend a topic

10. Show your child how his words can become sentences

Be responsive

1. Understand that each of your child's actions can become a word

2. Give your child a word for his actions and experiences

3. Treat your child's experiences as his most important first words

4. Focus on teaching words for what your child already communicates nonverbally

5. Translate your child's actions into words

6. Translate your child's sounds into a word

7. Respond more to positive than negative talking

8. Avoid criticizing your child's language; show him what to say instead

9. Respond to a word with a short sentence

10. Return your child to the topic when he strays

11. Do not respond to inappropriate or undesired talk

Share control

1. Follow your child's topic lead about half the time

2. Encourage your child to stay on your topic about half the time

3. Keep your questions to less than 20 percent of your talking

4. Keep directions and commands to less than 20 percent of your talking

5. Make more comments than questions and commands

6. Silently prevent your child from interrupting

7. Discourage your child from dominating the talking

Be emotionally playful

1. Play with words in enjoyable ways
2. Make talking a part of your child's play
3. Accept any words your child says without criticism
4. Show your child a new way to talk playfully
5. Practice turn-taking games with words
6. Pretend play with words
7. Make talking more like fun than a job
8. Avoid pressuring your child for a certain word
9. Avoid making talking a test for your child
10. Be animated in your talk
11. Act out the words you use

Parents' experiences using Communicative Partners to help their children to use language more socially

First things first

"I always thought Therese's language would come by itself. Then you taught me all the things that both she and I needed to do before she would talk much on her own. The most important for her was to just stay interacting with me in any way she could and then to start making some of the sounds I made. And for me the key seemed to be responding to her actions and sound with a word that fitted the situation, then give her time to talk back." (Carlita)

Words are just the tip of the language "iceberg"

"My twin boys, Alex and Sean, are delayed with many autistic features. I wanted them to talk more than anything and so I responded whenever they said a word. But then you taught me how to respond to everything they did, not just words. I had been missing seeing many things they were doing. I responded to their words but words were a tiny part of what they did. One thing that really helped them come alive was my imitating each of the boys. Not only did they attend to me more, but I also got to know exactly what they were interested in and what they could succeed at doing. I had been pushing for things they could not do. By imitating, they stayed with me so much longer. The most exciting thing was that they responded to me: I was finally a person to them. They had rarely done that before. Now the twins are 19. Alex is independent and in junior college and Sean is still at home with a part-time job." (Maureen)

I kept the developmental staircase in mind

"One notion that helped me with Jenna was to visualize both of us on her developmental staircase. When she was on the first step, just playing, I learned to be on that step with her. Then, when she developed more, I made sure I was keeping one step ahead of her. The image of a staircase helped me see when I was doing things that were impossible for her. When I would change my talking or acting to be more like her, she stayed and communicated much more." (Jane)

A good parent and a communicating partner can be different things

"My son, Eric, is eight years old. At five he was only making sounds and mainly to himself. He rarely played with people and preferred being alone. We've been working with Dr. MacDonald for about three years. He has taught us that being a good parent is not the same thing as being a good communicating partner. We had to learn how to play in our child's world, which may sound easy—but was actually quite difficult. Some of the strategies that have been most effective for us are:

- *Using sound play to engage Eric and increase his interactions and turn-taking with us.* Sound play is a great way for Eric to be a successful communicator, which really makes him proud.

- *Being a "living dictionary" to give him the words he didn't have.* It's been exciting to see that our speech input often becomes Eric's speech output!

- *Being more interesting than his distractions.* This was quite literally a life-altering lesson for us. Eric had become increasingly lost in a world of self-stimulating behavior that didn't include any people. By learning to be more interesting than his distractions, he now only self-stims when he's tired or over-stimulated. While the desire and/or need to self-stim are still present, it doesn't rule his life anymore. We also know how to engage him and interrupt this behavior when we need to.

- *Above all, making sure that he felt successful in his interactions with us.*

Our goal for Eric is to become a social and conversational person. I truly believe that he will achieve this goal because the strategies have become a way of life for us." (Valerie)

I needed permission to play with my son

"I am grateful for Communicating Partners for giving me the 'permission,' that I apparently needed, to freely play with Noah, one of the most delightful playmates I've ever had. I thought I needed to be his teacher since he did not talk but that clearly had not worked. Oh! I almost forgot the *pièce de résistance*! We were going through photo cards, and I was pleasantly surprised to learn how many he knew without my actually ever teaching them to him. But the clincher was this: I held up a card I had never seen before. It showed a Barbie doll with lots of long blonde hair in a swimsuit. And guess what he said? He said: 'MOMMA!' Needless to say he made my day, and I had to advertise it all over the house! That's my boy!" (Clover)

10

Conversation

The Fourth Stage in Learning to Communicate

Case example: the consequences of not becoming conversational: the story of Pam and Marvin

This story is presented as an alert to anyone who is satisfied when his or her child finally has a great deal of language. The story illustrates what can happen when a person with considerable intelligence does not learn to have reciprocal conversations.

Marvin was considered cognitively bright but socially awkward around age five. He was rewarded for learning and reciting many things. He apparently never learned the importance of taking turns with others and taking others' perspectives. His odd behavior was often excused because he was "so intelligent." He grew up in the

1950s before autistic features were identified much and when cognitive intelligence could cover many social differences.

Marvin met Pam at a university abroad. She was young and impressed with his intelligence. She herself was an intellectual who found men her age uninteresting. They married rather quickly and then returned to the United States where Pam knew no one except Marvin. Soon she discovered that he lived a very isolated life. In the beginning Pam was astounded at how much Marvin knew and she enjoyed learning from him since she herself was hungry for knowledge and they spent considerable time devouring books together. Then Pam began to realize that Marvin wanted to talk but did not want to listen.

Hear the story now in Pam's words. "He talks so fast I can't get a word in edgewise. If I try to interrupt or respond when he ends a sentence, he rushes into another burst of ranting and raving and ignores me. I barely get one word out of my mouth before he barrages me with more talk. If I walk away he follows, talking endlessly. He even follows me into the bathroom, sits on the edge of the bathtub, and continues the monologue regardless of what I'm doing. Sometimes I feel that he is driving me crazy."

Clearly Marvin had many issues but two profound problems were that he had not learned to take turns with people and to see or appreciate the consequences of his lack of boundaries in conversation. Pam, on the other hand, experienced Marvin's communication style as extremely abusive and oppressive.

Beyond Marvin's habit of dominating the talk, he also had not learned to observe the effects of his self-absorbed style on others, often to his own detriment. Pam continues the story.

"Marvin got fired from several jobs because he spoke inappropriately with his bosses. In one situation, he constantly 'talked at' a boss whose personality demanded compliant 'yes-men' as his subordinates. Marvin argued with the man, often dominating him in meetings with other people. When he boasted to me about meetings in which he thought he had 'won' an argument, I suggested that he might be wise not to confront his boss in that way, in public at least. Marvin did not understand the concept of a boss wanting 'yes-men' subordinates and the concept of embarrassing his boss in public and he did not understand that he was being confrontational at all. He thought he was having a good time. Then he got fired."

Pam continued to work and support Marvin during his frequent unemployment periods. Another interesting situation was that Marvin had some money from inheritance, which he considered only his, not joint property with Pam. He often refused to use his savings when he was out of a job and thought it was perfectly fine for Pam to support him even though it meant that she could no longer pursue her educational dreams.

Pam always believed that she could survive by burying herself in her studies. Marvin also held out a faint promise that they could have a child, which she wanted very much. So she stayed, and stayed and stayed until…

"Marvin spoke inappropriately with respect to death and funerals. He clearly did not understand grief. He made jokes, loudly, at funerals and disrupted the solemnity of the occasion. People looked at him oddly and walked away from him. They were embarrassed and so was I. He bullied me with endless monologues about airline schedules when I was shocked and grief struck after the death of my brother and was having a hard time arranging a flight abroad for the funeral. The totally insensitive way he treated me when my brother died was a big part of my decision to leave him."

At considerable expense, Pam finally left Marvin after many years of tolerating his considerable uncivil behavior. It is unclear as to whether, early on, Marvin could have learned the basic skills of turn-taking and responding to others and could have appreciated the serious consequences of his behavior. From family reports, there had been no attempts to teach him social skills. In fact, he was regularly rewarded for his intellectual achievements. He was raised to believe that the most important thing was to have the facts and to be "right." Being right was more important than having relationships.

I have known many children who have learned to take turns and take others' perspectives, when their parents understood that it was absolutely necessary. Civil behavior should not be considered an "extra" in development. Clearly for Marvin, his lack of civil behavior had disastrous effects on other people and on him. He now lives alone without a job and with no one to talk at but his computer.

Certainly, parents need to understand that helping a child become intelligent in the traditional sense will not guarantee that a person will be accepted in society. This story is told to encourage parents to make sure that, regardless of how "good" a student their child is (Marvin excelled in school, but he was often isolated for correcting teachers when they made "mistakes"), all of that intelligence will not help him make others happy or build successful relationships. Consequently, when parents frequently tell me how "intelligent" their child is, I immediately respond by asking, "Do you and others enjoy being with him?" If the answer is "no" or equivocal, our work focuses on making sure the child learns to be an enjoyable social partner before the focus is on making him a more intelligent student.

Parents need to look carefully at their child's life and do what they can to insure that they are not inadvertently training him to be an inconsiderate nonsocial person. I have found that some environments do very little to encourage and teach civil behavior. Teaching a child to be a passive, compliant student, as some educational approaches do, does not help him learn how to be a social partner. And one of the most obvious facts of life is that people who know how to communicate and build relationships are in the long run much better off than people who have a great deal of knowledge but very little social and emotional intelligence. While autistic children often excel alone in cognitive tasks, we should not give up on their potential to be social and communicative. Many children have succeeded in this way.

Language is not enough. Parents are often surprised, relieved, and satisfied when their child finally talks in any way. They are surprised if professionals had predicted the child would never talk. They are relieved after spending considerable energy, time, and expense to help the child talk. And understandably but unfortunately, they are satisfied too often with language of any kind. It is fine to celebrate when a child begins to talk, but it is also important to understand that language itself will not be enough.

Often the language children learn includes a large vocabulary, long monologues, answers to questions, and schoolwork, which they seldom use for genuine conversations. After the first surge of achievement passes, parents are dismayed to see that their child is not really talking with people much. So many children learn language to answer questions, recite by memory, store facts, and perform academic tasks, but they do not learn to communicate with it. Little attention is paid to teaching how to use language for relationships. The fundamental tool for relationships is *conversation* and few approaches to autism and related disorders focus on conversation skills in the sense of spontaneous contact with people.

It is discouraging to see children spend years learning language for academic topics but then use that language only when questioned, tested, or in monologues. True, many of our children become successful students and employees, but they are at a loss for how to talk in social situations. Many believe that this is an inevitable consequence of "being autistic" but our experiences show that conversations are possible for these children. In 30 years, I find that language success has usually been defined in terms of school performance and not social use in relationships. In short, they have learned language but not conversation or even the basics of how to communicate, such as social play, turn-taking, reciprocating, responding sensitively, and related social skills. Many educational approaches to autism, in fact, define their success in terms of language performed on tests and in directive teaching contexts and not in using language to have a social life.

Children with autism and related disorders, unlike typical students, have few interactions to practice and apply language, and so in social situations they rarely show the language that took so much effort to learn. This is not to say that academic language is not useful, but consider how more useful it would be if children had the social skills to build relationships with the language. We need to believe that our children are very capable of conversational lives and we need not be satisfied when a child uses language mainly as a compliant student or a monologue artist.

We have clinically monitored the communication development of many late-talking children for as long as 14 years. Our goal from the beginning has been for the children to be social and communicative before they learned language as a performance or academic skill. A fundamental goal of Communicating Partners was to insure that late-talking children would become social persons before they became compliant students. We have encouraged parents to help children be interactive and communicative before focusing on language that they may not use socially. In fact, as the previous chapters describe, we encourage parents to make sure their children learn the basic tools for conversation long before language. We have insisted that the child becomes social before he becomes linguistic so that, when he does acquire language, he uses it socially and not only for cognitive learning. We are concerned that traditionally directive ways of teaching language actually convince children that the function of language is not to communicate but to store and perform for instrumental purposes.

It is understandable for parents to want their child to have language for school and vocational purposes when they have waited so long for any language at all. We are now finding, however, that many parents are alarmed to discover that the language their children learn does not improve their social lives. In fact, the children have often learned language that is not useful in relationships. How often will a child build a relationship on school-like language? We must understand two major kinds of language: language for intellectual purposes and language for communication. Parents are often saddened to realize that success in school does not automatically carry over to success in relationships. In fact we find that the reverse is true. The more social a child becomes the better he will learn cognitively in school and in life since he will have more natural practice talking.

Dysfunctional conversations

We have observed over 300 children in conversations with parents and strangers and interviewed over 100 parents about conversations with their late-talking children. Parents look at "conversation" in many ways and their children carry conversations out in many ways as well, some superficial and some more authentic. We are concerned that children learn to have *reciprocal* conversations where both partners contribute and respond and where the conversation is matched, balanced, and enjoyable. Many of the kinds of conversations below seem to limit a child's natural flow in building relationships. While each of the following conversation types may be appropriate at times, we find that when one or a few dominate the child's communicative life, he is unlikely to build satisfactory social relationships. Some common types of conversations we find with late-talking children follow.

The monologue

"John tells me all the details of his computer game and he balks when I try to talk. He wants me to listen to the whole story and it can take a half-hour if I can tolerate it." John had learned to talk and he wanted people to sit and pay attention but not participate and he was often compulsive about telling the whole story. At school, he was rewarded for his advanced language but his family was concerned that few people enjoyed talking with him and he was almost as socially isolated as when he did not talk.

The literacy drill

Storybooks are often one of the most enjoyable parent–child times together. They can go far, teaching the child to have conversations, or they can do the opposite. Three frequent patterns of "conversation" children have with books include: *reading*, where either the parent or child does most of the reading with the partner observing quietly; *testing*, where one person asks a series of questions and the other answers; and *partnering*, where both persons talk to each other about the book in a relatively balanced and responsive way. We have found that the main interaction style with books is either one in which the reader dominates the talking or one in which there is a rote drill of questions with little back and forth conversation (Rabidoux and MacDonald 2000).

The machine gun

Mario enjoys asking a rapid-fire list of questions but does not wait for answers or tells the people the answers he wants. Entering the office, he said, "Are those your old or new glasses? They're the old ones. Aren't they your old ones? I remember when you had the new ones. Where are they? Go find them. I want to see the new ones. I like the new ones better. Go find them."

Mario's family used to think this kind of talk was humorous but then it became irritating and his brother and peers avoided talking with him since they said, "He never listens to me." They had waited so long for him to talk by age five that they accepted any language at all, until they saw how unacceptable it had become.

The good student

Kenny answered almost any question. However, he could go hours with people without ever talking on his own. Some believed he could not talk. His mother's idea of typical "good" conversation follows:

Mom:	Kenny, are you pushing your truck?
Kenny:	Uh, huh.
Mom:	What color is it?
Kenny:	Yellow.
Mom:	Good, yellow and what else?
Kenny:	Black and blue.
Mom:	Who gave you that car?
Kenny:	Grandpa.
Mom:	Which one?

Kenny: Grandpa Joe.

Kenny's mother was satisfied with this kind of conversation since she had once worried if he would ever talk. We were concerned because Kenny rarely talked about his own ideas and showed little enthusiasm for talking. He was obedient but not interested. Once his mother learned to reduce her questions, comment about Kenny's experiences, and wait for him to talk, he began to use considerable language socially that many did not realize he had.

The commander

Scott mainly talked to people to tell them what to do. They served more as tools to get his needs met than as conversation partners. He would talk with me briefly if he could get to see my magazines.

Scott: Where are your magazines?

Jim: In the basket.

Scott: I don't like them; where are the other ones?

Jim: I threw them out.

Scott: Why did you do that? I wanted them.

Jim: You should have told me to keep them.

Scott: Go find one. Look in the wastebasket.

Jim: I tossed them out.

Scott: No, try to look for them.

Unfortunately Scott's longest conversations were ones where he was making a series of demands, often not stopping until he was satisfied or the other person left the room. His parents were concerned that he talked to people mainly when he wanted something from them. Consequently, his social life was very limited.

The moralist

John knew right from wrong and let everyone else know when they were wrong. He was very concerned that things were done "right" and there was usually only one "right way," i.e. his way. At the grocery store one day, John was in another aisle and called his mother over.

John: Mom, come over here.

Mom:	What's going on?
John:	Look, they are selling beer!
Mom:	I know.
John:	Beer makes people drunk and they get accidents.
Mom:	Don't worry. You don't drink beer, do you?
John:	(Loud) They shouldn't sell things that kill people.
Mom:	Quieten down.
John:	Go get the manager.
Mom:	That's okay John.
John:	No, we have to stop this. People will die.
Mom:	Your dad drinks beer and he doesn't have accidents.
John:	This is wrong. We have to do something.
Mom:	You're right. Let's go home.

John's rigid ideas of right and wrong were hard to reason with. His conversations often focused on making the world the way he needed it to be. People often felt that it did not matter what they said once he had his head set on message.

The detail man

Martin was in his late forties and highly educated. I met him one evening as the sun was going down. I casually said: "That's a beautiful sunset." For 15 minutes nonstop, Martin lectured me about why it was a beautiful sunset. He described the effects of the weather, wind, pollution, industries, seasons, and the humidity as we watched the sunset go down. Since he looked away all the time, it was difficult to signal him that I wanted to talk. He pursued several topics on the theme. He was clearly having a good time and I was late for dinner.

The self-absorbed

Joe is very outgoing and friendly. Many consider him "quite a conversationalist." However, upon close observation he is an expert at focusing the conversation back to him, no matter how others try to tell their story.

Joe: How ya' doing, Randy? Where have you been?

Randy: I was in Chicago last weekend.

Joe: Boy did I have a busy weekend. Georgia was out of town.

Randy: I had an accident in Chicago.

Joe: Did I tell you about the fall I had?

Randy: Were you hurt?

Joe: No but I could have been. It was during that ice storm.

Joe sometimes wonders why people walk away from him when he's talking. He seems not to understand or care that others want to tell their story too. Once an acquaintance experimented to see how much Joe was actually listening.

Joe: How've you been?

Sam: My brother died.

Joe: Oh, did you hear about the game yesterday?

Such a conversation style will surely limit intimate relationships.

The memorizer

Paul had a photographic memory but had not learned that most listeners are not interested in every detail of a story.

Frank: Glad to see you. How was the trip?

Paul: It took too long. I went east on 70 instead of west.

Frank: Sorry to hear that.

Paul: Then I got to Grove City and tried to get around the city.

Frank: Well, I'm glad you're here.

Paul: And then I hit 270 and wondered if it would take me around to 70 again.

Frank: Would you like a drink?

Paul: I almost gave up on finding 70 but then, there it was.

Frank: What kind of drink?

Paul: I knew how to get here once I saw 70.

Frank had lived in the city for many years and clearly was not interested in the "wrong" directions to his house. Paul seemed to need to tell everything that was in his head at the moment.

The performer

Elizabeth began to talk at four. Her parents happily responded to anything she said for over a year. Now they were concerned because she talked mainly like a performer, reciting things and directing others what to do and ignoring what others had to say.

> Elizabeth: Super-cali-fragi-listic-expi-ali-docious. If you say it fast enough you always sound precocious. Daddy, now say: Umdidilidy, umdidilidy.
>
> Father: Umdidily.
>
> Elizabeth: No, say it twice.
>
> Father: Umdidily, umdidily.
>
> Elizabeth: Now say super cali fragi listic.
>
> Father: Why don't you just sing the song?

The girl's father clearly was not enjoying the contrived "conversation" and wished that Elizabeth would just talk with him and not perform so much. They learned to take turns by letting Elizabeth know that they would obey her on two turns if she would respond to them on two turns. Her father realized that turn-taking and responding were more important for her than learning more language. He persisted by insisting that he take a turn with his own ideas. Then they both began to enjoy their conversations.

The pretender

Lorenzo had elaborate conversations with his action figures as he played alone but rarely had conversations with people. He enacted many adventures and intrigues between his toy figures. Listening to him, his parents realized that he knew much more than he showed with them or at school. When his parents became part of his conversations with his toys, he gradually began to have more conversations with them.

Just the facts, madam

Many of our children with autism seem to talk about facts more than feelings. If something is "true" our children might feel they must talk about it, regardless of whether their partner is interested.

> Conversations with Rico made his parents feel lonely. All he talked about were facts, not feelings. If they said anything that was not an observable fact, Rico would ignore them or reprimand them with something like "Say it right."
>
> | | |
> |---|---|
> | Mother: | Looks like you're having fun! |
> | Rico: | This is a big tower. |
> | Mother: | You did a good job. |
> | Rico: | It's a tower, I told you. |
> | Mother: | Can I play too? |
> | Rico: | Don't break it. |
> | Mother: | I won't break it. |
> | Rico: | Make your own tower. |
>
> There is little wonder the mother feels unwanted and that facts are more important than feelings for the boy. His mother knows she should play with him more to help him but it is difficult. She continues to play and tolerate the resistance since she knows that he must become a better conversationalist.

Emotional mismatch

A concrete approach to conversation was brilliantly illustrated in the 1930s movie *Ninotchka*. Dapper Melvin Douglas was trying to romance Greta Garbo, playing a Russian engineer. They were in Paris and he proposed that they see the view from atop the Eiffel Tower. Ninotchka's response reminds me of children who respond more to the concrete content of a statement than to the spirit of the partner's intention:

Melvin:	Madam, I would love to show you the beautiful view from the Eiffel Tower.
Ninotchka:	How long would it take for a man to fall to the ground?

Often our children respond in concrete terms that totally miss the point of their partner. This emotional mismatch certainly discourages people from relating to the child and further isolates him.

What kind of conversations do we want?

The conversations above obviously leave a lot to be desired if we want our children to have balanced, enjoyable relationships with people. There is no fixed answer to the question: What is a good conversation? Think about the kinds of conversation that make you want to know a person better and learn with them. Once you understand the kind of conversation partner you enjoy, then you can become that kind of partner with your child. In that way you will be showing him how to have conversations that will be appreciated in society at large.

Interviews with a number of people revealed that they do have preferences for the kind of conversation partner they seek out (MacDonald and Mitchell 2002). Some of the types identified are as follows:

1.   They take turns with you.
2.   They wait silently in anticipation for your turn.
3.   They listen and respond meaningfully to what you meant.
4.   They keep you with them if the conversation falters.
5.   They respond meaningfully to both your words and your feelings.
6.   They stay with the topics that you start for a few exchanges.
7.   They encourage you to stay on topics they start.
8.   They are seldom concerned about getting something from you.
9.   They communicate with you mainly for the pleasure of your company.
10.   They do not compete with you for a "right" answer.
11.   They clearly show that they enjoy conversations with you.
12.   They feel they learn from you without being taught.
13.   They seldom direct or control the conversation.
14.   They do not allow you to direct or control the conversation.
15.   They do not dominate with continuous questions.

16. They make you want to return for more conversations.

17. They disagree without aggression.

Consider this list a rough guide to see what kind of conversation partners you and your child are. You will be able to identify the strengths of your partnership and we encourage you to work on these first. Build your conversations with your child by building more and more of the good conversations you have. Do not focus on fixing the major problems you have. Some of them may not be fixable now and may diminish when you have more and more positive conversations.

Why should you and your child have conversations?

This question may strike you as strange or nonsensical. You might wonder: Is it not obvious? After all, conversations are the way people live in society. Everyone has conversations. They just happen. But is that true with your child?

The many examples of dysfunctional conversations provided above show that positive, balanced conversations do not often happen readily with late-talking children, who generally have difficulties in reciprocal conversations. Consequently, since conversations are the "way people live in society" and late-talking persons have difficulty with them, then it follows that conversations should be a major goal for our children. As we will see, not only are conversations not easy for our children, they are often actively discouraged by the kinds of settings children are expected to learn in.

Common barriers to having conversations

Successful conversations require two persons to be meaningfully connecting with each other. Clearly, this relates to the major "intersubjectivity" problem found in persons along the autistic spectrum (Trevarthen 1979). Intersubjectivity refers to the ability to see that others have thoughts of their own. This involves developing empathy and moving out of seeing the world only from one's own point of view. When a late-talking person begins to show he appreciates how his partners experience the world, his partners will be prepared to have effective conversational relationships. One of the most limiting barriers in autism and related disorders is the difficulty in "reading" others' ideas and recognizing that other people have feelings, ideas, and reactions different from their own. Trevarthen *et al.* (1998); Baron-Cohen (1995), and others have described this problem in terms of difficulty with a personal "theory of mind." Autistic persons often do not register or appreciate what others think or feel. The example of "Ninotchka" above shows how the lady completely missed the gentleman's intention; she responded to his words in a technical way but did not acknowledge his personal feelings. Often parents think their child is ignoring them when, in fact, he simply does not understand what the adults are really meaning in a conversational way.

While this problem of a "theory of mind" is often resistant to change in children on the autistic spectrum, we have found that fine-tuned conversational practice over considerable time can show children how to appreciate and respond to their partner's personal meanings. Often we find our children staying in verbal "autistic" habits after they actually do understand what others are saying. The point here is that the inability to "read" others' minds and to enter their interests and perspectives is not necessarily fixed forever. Many autistic children have learned to have conversations that respond to others' perspectives. While this is often difficult, it is possible. It requires that parents and others see authentic "conversations" as an absolute necessity and do not accept self-absorption as inevitable with autistic children. We are concerned that when people define "autism" as the innate inability to read others' minds, a case of self-fulfilling prophesy occurs and people do not try to help the child to learn their perspective.

> Scott, for many years, talked as though he were the only person in the world. He regularly ignored what others said or responded with his ideas, however unrelated to theirs. When he was eight his mother Cheryl said she never remembered him taking her point of view or really responding to what she was interested in. His father, Dale, agreed. With a few years of devoted persistence, encouraging him to respond to her intentions, through stopping and telling him what was on her mind, Scott paid more attention to others and showed that he actually did understand much of what was in others' minds when he knew it was necessary. Cheryl and her husband Dale did not want to live with someone who did not know either of them and both of them made sure Scott did. They knew he would stay alone in the world if he did not learn to read others' minds.

Both you and your child share the responsibility for developing conversations. It is your child's responsibility to stay and give back something. Almost any child can do that. No less will be expected of him in society. As you gently keep him in conversations, he will learn that brief contacts are not acceptable most of the time. You need to give him something in conversations that he cares about and can respond to. While many of our children may not develop the rich conversations we hope for them, most can do much more than we expect. The critical factor is having parents who accept and stay interacting with them no matter what. Sometimes this will require conversations that may not make much sense at first.

As soon as your child talks, he can have little conversations with you. Many adults do not believe that conversations are either possible or valuable for late-talking children. Some feel that conversations will come only when a child has a large vocabulary. Once parents realize that conversations are critical to a child's future in many ways, they will be as committed to helping him learn conversations as they were in learning language. We have found that many families can learn to develop genuine conversations with their children who had been very isolated. To do this, parents have found that they often have to overcome several natural barriers to conversation. Some of the barriers follow.

Lack of communicative responding between parent and child

Children communicate more when adults respond sensitively to their child's nonverbal and verbal behaviors than when they direct and control the children (Girolometto, Verbey and Tannock 1994; Greenspan 1985; Mahoney and Powell 1988; Mahoney and MacDonald 2003; Prizant and Wetherby1989). Nevertheless, many adults are unaware that the way they respond actually helps the child become conversational. Nor are they aware that ignoring the child's little communicative attempts will discourage him from being conversational. In discussing the issue with parents, we found that they also stop interacting when the child does not respond. When parents discover that responding to anything the child does, at first, will get the child interacting, they realize that they have been caught in a dangerous cycle of ignoring each other, a cycle that makes conversations impossible.

Communicating in a directive and controlling style

It is not surprising to see adults in the habit of directing children with questions, commands, and other controlling approaches. They genuinely believe that directing is the only way our children learn. A directive approach can teach some facts and skills but it will not teach the spontaneous habit of conversation, which is a child's bridge to the outside world. After 30 years, we have reached a conclusion that may surprise you. The conclusion is:

> Children will learn to communicate and learn with adults to the degree that the adults are responsive to the child's current development and interests and are noncontrolling much of the time in ways that allow the child successes in natural interactions.

Based on years of research with parent–child interactions, Gerald Mahoney found with more than 60 families that "research suggests that a directive, non-responsive style of interaction is relatively ineffective at promoting development of handicapped children" (1988). In a recent study with autistic children Mahoney found that a one-year responsive teaching program with parents and their autistic children showed significant changes in cognitive, communicative, and emotional development of the children (Mahoney and MacDonald 2003).

Children are motivated to interact when they are successful in getting others to respond and stay interacting with them. Many parents and professionals feel a responsibility to direct and control our children, thinking that questions and commands are the best ways to engage a child. They often define success in terms of some goal in their adult heads and not simple improvements in the child's interactions.

These adults are genuinely amazed when their child interacts more when they stop being directive and simply respond to what the child says with comments that show him a next step. They find that responding to the child keeps him longer in conversations. Once parents focus on staying in conversations, regardless of the content, then both are more successful.

Minimal topic sharing

Having a shared activity is as critical for conversations as it was for fostering your child's first interactions with you. While in the past the "something" may have been toys or other forms of play, the "something" now is ideas or topics. Our children are easily distracted in interactions and so they often flit from topic to topic in conversations. You need to realize that your child absolutely needs to stay in conversations if they are to fit into society. If adults do not recognize this need they will allow the child to leave the topic or ignore their ideas.

Often, when an adult and child are not on the same topic, they are also not engaged in a joint activity. The more adults and children are doing the same things, the more they will share ideas that maintain the conversation. We frequently find that, once our children begin to talk, adults tend to interact physically less with them. This can limit conversations. We find that the more you join into the play activity of your child, the more likely he will learn to stay on topics of conversation with you.

Failure to follow each other's lead

When you talk about your partner's ideas, he is more likely to stay in a conversation with you. The same is true of our children. When you follow your child's ideas, you enter his thinking and his interests. When you do not, you are likely to lose his interest and the conversation itself. Even when your child is motivated to be with you, he will be unable to follow you unless you talk within his frame of reference. Be careful of the message you may inadvertently be giving him; if you frequently take the lead, you may, in effect, be convincing him that his ideas are not worth a conversation. Late-talking children will learn to have conversations if their partners allow the conversations to focus on the child's interests, however unusual or bizarre they seem at first. We find that it is much better for a child to learn to have conversations from his idiosyncratic thinking than not to learn to have conversations at all. Having conversations with you personally rewards your child, and only then will you be able to have conversations that are more relevant and appropriate.

Academic or instrumental focus: conversation for school or meeting needs

When conversations seem like work, neither the adult nor the child will make conversation the habit it must become. We often see "academic" conversations in which the adult tries to teach the child something she believes he needs to learn. In an instrumental conversation, one or both partners are trying to get something done or get something from each other. The problem is that these tasks are too often approached with directive and controlling styles that tend to limit rather than foster participation. This is not to say you cannot meet these goals through conversations in which the child shares the control and choices with the adult. In fact, we find that responsive, nondirective conversations give the child valuable practice in academic and instrumental tasks. One reason is that children will stay longer.

How can adults and children use responsive strategies to build conversational relationships?

There is a colloquial phrase, "Let's get our heads together," that people use when they want to collaborate and build a relationship that is more than the sum of each of their ideas. They often want to come up with a conversation that reflects both persons' views into one united event. When "getting heads together" is successful, both partners feel they are included and that the result is something more valuable than their separate ideas by themselves.

"Getting your head together" with a child with autism or a language disorder is a considerable challenge, but it is exactly what your child needs to do with you if he is to enter your world and put his knowledge to use. Recently, I have reconnected with several persons diagnosed as autistic as young children who are now quite verbal in adolescence and early adulthood. The major concern for these children remains having conversations that are successful enough to support a relationship and to function in education and vocations. Whether these individuals are considered as having Asperger's syndrome or are no longer autistic, they clearly look and sound different from their peers, mainly in terms of the lack of ease and reciprocity in conversations.

One key factor in these conversations is that the two persons participating simply do not "have their heads together." The following profile describes many verbal autistic spectrum children I know in terms of the five major responsive strategies central to Communicating Partners:

- *Unbalanced.* There is little give and take and neither person waits much for the other to talk. One partner is often doing most of the talking with little chance for the other to talk.

- *Mismatched.* Often the two persons are not really talking about the same thing, or one person is doing much more of the talking than the other.

- *Unresponsive.* One person often feels that the other is not responding genuinely to them but is just talking at them. The person may be ignoring the other or just not responding to what the other is saying or meaning.

- *Lack of sharing control.* One partner makes most of the decisions and directions as the other plays a passive or resistant role. The conversation often seems stuck and there is no apparent development of a topic.

- *Lack of playfulness.* The conversation is usually more tense and task-oriented than relaxed and seldom reflects much humor.

While this profile does not fit all interactions we see in verbal autistic children, it does occur frequently. The profile highlights concerns in five areas of responsive strategies that help children become more conversational. The discussion below addresses how you can interact on a daily basis to help your child become conversational and negotiate the social world. The five strategies are ways many parents have learned to "get their heads together" with their child. Not only are these strategies skills for parents to use but they are also skills the children need for relationships with others. Thus, the five strategies are also an answer to the question: What do autistic children need to do to have successful conversations and build stable relationships?

Balance

The notion of balancing turns relates to the finding that relationships go better when there is a give-and-take flow with neither partner doing much more than the other. We do not mean turn-taking that is restricted to talking in alternating speeches. We mean balanced turn-taking where each partner takes about as many turns as the other and waits sufficiently to give the other a chance to have his say. If your child has learned to balance turns in play with you, he has learned the basic rule of give and take that is central to satisfying relationships. We have found that some parents and children balance turns in play but then seem to forget taking turns in communication. Parents are so used to their own adult style of talking and not waiting that they often need to learn to take turns with their children.

Pay very careful attention to monitoring your conversations and strive to talk less so that your child will talk more. Take your turn, saying one thing, and then wait expectantly and silently for him to take his turn. The more you do, the more your child will play an active role in communicating. He will gradually become less passive or less dominating. Turn-taking gives your child excellent practice in social discipline in the sense that it teaches him the basic rule of social fairness; that is, that you do not deserve more than you give. The more you respond sensitively to your child when it is your turn, the more he will learn how to communicate with others. He will also believe that he can get much more satisfaction in communication than getting his needs met. Ask yourself: "Would others stay in conversations with my child if he acted the way I act toward him?"

An example of a mother and child baking together illustrates low and high balance in a conversation:

Low balancing

Mother:	I think we'll make cookies today. We haven't had any for quite a while. Should we make chocolate or lemon?
Celia:	I want…
Mother:	Oh, I know. You like lemon best. But Buddy likes chocolate.
Celia:	Lemon, lemon.
Mother:	Here's some dough to play with.
Celia:	Lemon cookie.
Mother:	Make the dough nice and flat.
Celia:	Cookie.
Mother:	Look at all the cookies we have.

Higher balance

Mother:	Cookie time.
Celia:	Lemon cookies.
Mother:	Get the lemon.
Celia:	I squeeze it.
Mother:	In the bowl.
Celia:	Tastes yuckie.
Mother:	Lemons are sour.
Celia:	Sour lemons. I get it.

Notice the increased sense of participation Celia has in the second exchange. Ask yourself, which of these conversations would you want to return to if you were the child? Then try to understand how you feel when a partner takes many more turns than you and does not wait for you to have your say.

We two major benefits when conversations are balanced. First, children talk much more when their partners talk less and wait for them to talk. Second, when conversations are balanced, the child shows that he knows more than his partner expected. Thus, balancing conversations will also change the attitudes of both child and adult to be more optimistic of the child, which in turn encourages more conversations.

Match

The more you communicate in ways your child can try to do and about his interests, the more your child is likely to stay in conversations with you. Matching means insuring that how you talk, and what you talk about, will match your child's immediate world. A child is more likely to have conversations about his immediate sensations and actions and he is more likely to talk when you give him language he can do. One effective way parents become more matched is actually to join the child's activities so that the conversation comes directly from the child's sensations and actions rather than from the adult's head. Remember, many autistic spectrum children have very different minds to us and the more we match the child's experiences, the more we will be getting into his mind.

In the first of the two examples with Celia, above, her mother mismatched by talking in ways the child could not attempt. In the second, the mother sensitively matched her language to the child's language, actions, and interests. By matching, the mother was both keeping the child in a conversation and teaching language that fitted the child's mind. If we are to show a child how we think, we must first enter their thinking so we know the kind of bridge to make to our experiences.

Respond

One critical strategy for becoming conversational is to respond to what the child is doing and saying. The goal here is for a child automatically to enter conversations on the sight of another person. Children learn this when you respond with feasible language to whatever they are doing at the moment. Too often, our children engage in one-shot interactions that will not build relationships or teach the child more about a topic.

By responding to the child rather than directing him, you make the contacts reciprocal; that is, you make them go back and forth about the concerns of each partner. In other words, the child directs the contact to the adult and the adult responds in a way meaningful to what the child said. The reverse occurs as well: the adult starts some contacts and the child responds to what the adult said. As soon as reciprocal exchanges begin, the adult keeps the child a little longer and builds a conversation out of any exchange.

We always try to follow the general rule of "giving the child one more idea." This builds the conversation slowly, at the child's pace, with an idea that clearly relates to his interest and to ideas he has expressed during his turn. Children often act as if nothing more can be said on a topic, even when we know from their actions that they know much more about it. Watch your child and you will find it easy to add new ideas. Simply say what you see that he knows. A second rule is not to wait for a word to be perfectly clear before we get talk about new ideas. The more a child stays in conversation, the more practice and feedback he has to strengthen his sounds and the more motivating and successful conversation becomes for him.

See this example of how responding keeps the conversation going:

Arjuna:	Look at the boat.
Teacher:	Two boys in the boat.
Arjuna:	No. One boy, one man.
Teacher:	Maybe that's his daddy.
Arjuna:	Dad took him fishing.
Teacher:	I don't see a fishing pole.
Arjuna:	They have a net.
Teacher:	Nets get more fish.
Arjuna:	They got a million.
Teacher:	A million fish in that small boat?
Arjuna:	Maybe ten.

The conversation was clearly back and forth and reciprocal; each person offered his ideas then waited for the other's turns. Note that the teacher took the responsibility of feeding the child with a new idea that both taught new language and helped him stay longer in the conversation. The new ideas related directly to what the child said and motivated the child to follow with another comment. Notice that this conversation flow occurred without many questions.

Share control

Conversations are longer and more frequent when both persons are sharing their ideas. If we always have to initiate the topic and keep the conversation going, we soon withdraw, sometimes even from the relationship. On the other hand, if the other person regularly controls the topic and ignores our ideas, we are likely to go to someone who shows us more respect. You too should follow your child's ideas at times and at other times see to it that he follows yours. While it is sometimes acceptable to do most of the talking, as when relating a story or giving directions, it is important that each partner listens and responds to the other. Adults and children stay in conversations more when they expect their ideas will be heard. Therefore, we encourage you to have several brief conversations with your child every day, conversations where you have no job to get done or lesson to teach. Simply tell yourself that the goal is to listen to his ideas and make sure he listens to some of yours on the same topic. This will take very little time, less than a minute in most cases. It will require that you make sure each of you has a say on the topic.

In the example below, Calvin and his dad build a conversation on a topic that each partner contributes to:

Dad:	Hey, your bike looks broken.
Calvin:	It wiggles.
Dad:	Let me see. What wiggles?
Calvin:	The wheel. It wiggled and I fell and got hurt.
Dad:	Let's have a look. You have a scratch.
Calvin:	Ouch, don't touch.
Dad:	It's a wiggle owie. You need a wiggle doctor.
Calvin:	You're silly. Fix my bike.
Dad:	What?
Calvin:	Please.
Dad:	Look, the spokes are loose.
Calvin:	What's a poke?
Dad:	Spoke, ssspoke—these wire sticks. They make the wheel strong.
Calvin:	I found a loose one.
Dad:	Let's check them all.

Notice how the conversation flowed from the activity they did together and how each person had his say and responded meaningfully to what the other said. Here they shared control and respected what each person said. Each person led the topic at times and at other times followed the other's topic. If the father simply fixed the bike, Calvin would have missed a valuable opportunity to learn how to have an easy conversation and also to learn how to think and talk about a new topic. Calvin could practice his old ideas and get some new ones from his father.

Think of conversation turns as pendulum swings. I think of an old friend, Vern, when I remember the following story:

> "Before I learned to take turns with Sally and realized how important conversations were for her, I thought my job was to tell her as much as I could. Now I feel much of that was wasted time and I recall Sally not liking it at all. I found that waiting for Sally to say something was very hard at first. I had so many ideas about what she should be saying that I had to slow down, be quiet, and find out what she really wanted to talk about. I tried your ping-pong idea and then I came up with an idea of my own. I kept the image of a pendulum in my mind. When I talked, the pendulum ball was with me, and then when I waited, the ball went to Sally, then it came back to me. With the idea that the pendulum keeps moving, I tried not to hold onto it by saying too much and I came to encourage. Whenever the pendulum in my mind was stuck on my side, I stopped talking and let it go. When the pendulum was stuck on Sally's side I silently signaled to her to give me a turn or gently took a turn. Trying to keep the pendulum swings in mind, I could more easily see how important it was that each of us do our share then move on." (Vern)

Emotional playfulness

The fifth strategy to build conversations is genuinely to enjoy the interaction, not for external goals like information but for the social contact. Look around and listen to conversations between friends. What keeps them talking? It is usually not the information but the connection itself. Recently I spoke to my son, a physicist, who lives far away and is in the habit of e-mailing me instead of telephoning. I asked him to call more. He argued that the computer is a much more efficient way to convey information. I agreed but informed him that it was not information I wanted, it was "connection." I wanted to hear his voice and to enjoy his company. I really did not care what we talked about.

So too with our children, it is the social connection, not the information, that is key to relationships. A conversation can be built on anything you and your child do and say together as long as each person feels successful and enjoys the connection. Often parents do not enjoy simple conversations when they believe their job is to teach the child things and get him to act "right."

> Andrew began to talk to others at five but mainly imitatively. He started conversations at nine when his parents, Pam and Rick, joined in his play and talked in a relaxed way about what he was doing. They did not question or direct his behavior and they did not try to get him to say anything in particular. Their goal was for him to be comfortable and successful talking with people. They just superimposed their words on the playful interactions. The words were part of the play and any words were allowed. The goal at first was to get Andrew to let them in and to enjoy talking without any pressure to get anything done. Soon Andrew initiated a conversation game. He gave nicknames to each person in his family and pretended he was another person. In this routine he began to have conversations but required that each person play the new name role he gave them.
>
> Andrew: (making a talking movement with his hand) Ralphie wants to know when we're going to the store.
>
> Mom: (also doing the hand play) Trickster (her new name) says at ten o'clock.
>
> Andrew: Ralphie wants to go now.
>
> Mom: Trickster has to finish the dishes.
>
> Andrew: Ralphie wants to help you.
>
> Mom: Trickster says "go get the blue towel and dry the dishes."
>
> Andrew: Ralphie will dry so we can go.

Admittedly this conversation is unusual and not the kind we want in the long run. But we found that, when we permitted the distance that the roles allowed, Andrew would stay for long exchanges whereas his prior conversations had been very brief or nonexistent. Clearly Andrew enjoyed this game and it seemed to add just the fun he needed to relax into conversations. Gradually, his family began to have conversations directly with the real "Andrew," dropping the pretend names. The whole family enjoyed the game until his teenage brothers began to insist on "normal" conversations. By that time Andrew had learned to be comfortable in conversations and began to have more normal conversations because he wanted to be with his brothers.

Why should conversations be fun or enjoyable? Don't our children need to have age-appropriate serious conversations? We hear these questions when we try to have light, enjoyable conversations with late-talking children. We find that many of our children have a long and painful history of communicating with people who convinced them in many ways that they are not talking "right." It takes considerable work to repair the damage that has been done by convincing late-talking children they are "wrong" in the way they are talking. Our approach is to join into the child's activities and talk with him in any way he can tolerate. Often we find that conversations that may seem "nonsense" to outsiders are just what the child needs to discover that he can be successful talking with others. Once you understand that your child has a long history of failure in conversation, you will lighten up and show him that any kind of verbal connection is important and enjoyable to you. It may take some time for your child to trust that it is all right for him to say whatever he wants in a playful way. Remember that it is the personal connection that is more important than the information.

Expect your child to talk

Beyond using the five responsive strategies above, we often find that what you expect from your child can influence the conversation habits he develops. Do you ever feel that someone is talking at you without caring about, expecting, or allowing a response from you? Do you ever feel that way with your child? We have regularly seen this pattern on both the adult and child's sides with our children. Each may be communicating at the other but not really for a response. One partner says one thing after another, neither waiting nor signaling that she intends to get something from the other. It is not uncommon to hear an adult say something like: "Oh, you found the truck, where was it? I bet it was under the bed. I wonder if there are more toys under there?"

Similarly, it is common to hear our children talk like the following: "This is my tow-truck and it picks up cars that crash because people drink too much and don't pay attention and then get into accidents and sometimes they get hurt and go to the hospital and have to get stitches and that can hurt a lot and then they miss school and their teacher does not know where they are."

Clearly in both examples the speaker was not expecting the partner to say anything back. When either adults or children get into these "rhetorical" habits, they may in fact be teaching their partners not to have conversations with them. Two basic skills are missing here: taking turns and taking the other person's perspective. Children with considerable language can seem very intelligent and successful in cognitive and language terms but clearly they are missing a great deal in terms of emotional and social intelligence. Conversations that involve reciprocal turn-taking are crucial practical tools for moving our children from language storage units to conversational partners.

Of course, there are times when adults need to just talk, such as "Watch out, that's a big dog" or "Up we go, let's get your coat on." Sometimes a job has to be done and conversations just get in the way. However, if your child is constantly exposed to talk that does not expect or allow him to respond, he may learn that it is acceptable to let others do all the talking.

To develop the habit of communicating "for a response," think of your conversations more like a game of "ping-pong" or tennis than a game of darts or curling. In ping-pong or tennis the game depends on two persons taking turns and responding sensitively to what their partner just did on her turn. If one partner is not taking the other partner's perspective the game will not continue. On the other hand, in darts or curling, the game depends on one person performing alone in a series of actions that are not in immediate response to what their partner just did, other than conceptually.

For our children, perhaps the most important game of life to learn is *conversation not language*, and yet so much more education and therapy is directed at insuring that our children "have language" rather than using it in social conversations. Much education and therapy approaches act as if the child already had the interactive conversation skills for using language in the world. For children with autism and many other conditions such as Down syndrome, attention and neurological disorders, and emotional problems, conversation is the missing link to success in society, not language or knowledge.

Adults and children often act as if their job is to "talk at" or give information to their partner, the way a player throws darts at a board, rather than to get back a response to what you gave as the players do in a ping-pong game. You will help your child have conversation when you follow the same rules of turn-taking and matching that help children become interactive and communicative. Say something the child can both do and understand and then wait silently with a clear look of expectation on your face and a tone in your voice that says you definitely expect a response and that you will wait for it.

If your child has not been responding to you much, you may have to wait a while at first. Then be sure to accept any kind of response he makes. Children often respond first with a change of face, a gesture, or a sound that you may not consider important. Accept it. If he is pressured to say something that you think is "right" he may withdraw. You may have actually taught him that he need not respond to you and that you will do all the talking for him. Be sure to give him successes for any response at first, and then you can gradually begin cueing him to give you more of what he can do.

The question of questions

In surveys of over 2000 parents and professionals at workshops, I have asked them to describe how they usually talk to children. Over 80 percent reported that they would usually ask a series of questions. In our video-based studies of over 50 families (MacDonald and Mitchell 2002) we found that questions are the predominant way adults communicate with children across situations such as care-giving, teaching, and play. However, we have also found that when adults ask questions the children usually stay in conversation only briefly and do not express their own ideas. On the other hand, when adults reduce their questions and comment instead on the child's experiences, the child stays for longer conversations and expresses more of himself.

When we encourage adults to reduce their questions, commands, and directives, the adult is usually surprised. Many even say this makes no sense to them. Their position can be described in these words: "I have a child who is not communicating much, so I have to teach him. How else do you teach other than with questions and commands? Who is going to do it if I don't?" We find this attitude deeply ingrained, not just in parents but also in many therapists and teachers. Understandably, this attitude is an almost natural reaction to someone in need. It can be changed if you come to see that such an attitude often turns a child off and quiets him. Once you see that your child stays and communicates more without pressure to perform, you will reduce your questions and get more from the child. Parents have found that conversations do not require the work of questions but rather the enjoyable practice of responding to what the child says and does.

Another reason to limit your questions is that you may not want to get from your child what you give him. Consider the possibility that your child is likely to become the kind of person that you are to him. You need to decide which of your images you want him to mirror. Many of our children interact mainly with questions, commands, and other controlling communications that pay little attention to their partner's interests. They often look and sound like their parents and teachers. This style clearly does not encourage others to build relationships with them. Consider how you feel when someone questions and directs you repeatedly; you probably do not choose to be with them much. And it is critical that we help our children be attractive partners to others.

This is not to discourage you from all questions and commands. They are certainly needed at times, but if they predominate your child is unlikely to have the extended conversations he needs. Take care to prevent a directive style from defining your relationship for fear that it will make your child a passive partner who rarely initiates and stays in conversations.

Consider how much of your child's life consists of being questioned or directed. Make a few circles on a paper. In one circle darken the amount you think represents the portion of your child's life spent in questions and directions. We have found that conversations with late-talking children are often controlling about as much as 80 percent of the time. That is, easy, undemanding exchanges comprise only about 20 percent of the child's interactions.

Using the same approach, look at a child a few years older with the kind of rich social life you hope for your child. Draw the circle again; how much of it is darkened? We find that typically social children spend much less than half of their interactions in conversations dominated by questions or commands. Rather, these children are communicating for many social reasons just to have a relationship and not to get an answer or accomplish something.

As we said, there are times when questions and commands are necessary, as long as they do not dominate your relationship. When you do need to be directive, your questions should get answers and your commands should get cooperation. Because children often ignore questions, consider a few ways to get responses.

First, try to cut down your "rhetorical" talk where you talk at your child more than talking for a response. Many adults ask questions but do not wait for or expect answers. For example: "Why did you mess up my clean floor?" Or "Where did you get that? I bet Davy had it. Did you take it from him? Is he angry?" In each case the child realizes that no response is required. Many of our children learn to expect to be talked "at" and not to need to respond. Similarly adults often give many commands but then fail to enforce them. In both cases—rhetorical questions and unenforced commands—the child learns that he is not required to talk with others. Talking is optional. For children with language delays, talking must be seen as necessary, not optional. All the child has to do is to ignore the adult and the adult will keep talking, entertaining him and relieving him of the responsibility to communicate.

Some adults are in the habit of asking strings of questions without waiting for a response. "Where's your brother? He's with dad, right? They went to grandma's. Didn't you want to go? You can go next time." When life is full of questions that do not allow a response, children may stop talking. We recommend that you practice asking only genuine questions, ones you really want answered and that you will wait silently to be answered. We strongly discourage many questions because they make communicating more difficult for the child and they often do not respond to the child's interests or show the child how to talk.

Case example: conversational development

John was four and had a vocabulary of over 300 words. He talked mainly to himself in rote phrases and rarely in conversations. His parents saw him as intelligent since he read at the first grade level, solved many problems creatively, and mastered computer games. They were concerned that he spent his time mainly in isolated and obsessive activities, resisting intrusions violently. When he began an activity he got lost in it with little concern about finishing. John had many cognitive skills and considerable language but little social communication or interest in people. He had limited social–emotional skills such as self-regulation and empathy.

He used his own language which no one understood. Unless he was in control of the situation he showed considerable anxiety that prevented interaction with others. Video records of John from 6 to 12 months revealed he had been interactive, playful, and beginning to talk. By age two he was resisting others' contacts vigorously, insisting on playing alone.

During the first month, we observed John for several hours, to assess his cognitive, motivational, communicative, and social–emotional development, since each varied across situations markedly. We identified the situations in which he would interact, then recreated them to begin the program. The first goal was to help John interact back and forth in ways not totally on his terms. We discussed with the family how to enter his world without threatening him and to learn to read when he was open to social contacts.

John's mother, Jodi, recalls an important early breakthrough when she began visualizing John and herself on a development staircase and that the closer she was to his step the more he would learn. She came to realize that she was often acting as if she was on the tenth step and John was on the second step of the staircase. She admitted that she wanted him to have adult conversations, socialize typically, and enjoy others. She came to realize that her expectations were far above what he was ready to do.

The program began by teaching Jodi to play in John's world and to accept anything safe that he did. His first pivotal goal was to tolerate joint activities with others. We explained that, regardless of how much language and knowledge John had by himself, he would develop only to the degree that he interacted with others. We discussed several topics over two months to understand how critical social interaction is to developing cognition and communication. We practiced several strategies such as balancing to build a reciprocal habit, making the interactions stress-free and enjoyable and matching their behavior to John's interests and abilities.

Joining into John's play took considerable patience on the family's part. They began by playing parallel to his play without intruding on his activity. He resisted at first but began to enjoy and attend to them when they imitated him with no demands. Jodi realized that she had believed she needed to teach him the "right" way of doing and saying things, which resulted in rage and resistance. Now she saw that when she simply joined in his play side-by-side, he began attending to her more and even imitating the ways she was playing at times. He now occasionally smiled and began showing her things he was doing, which was a first. She was learning to fine-tune herself to his interests, his emotional state, and to his current abilities. The more she acted like John, the more he attended to her and invited her into his activities. It appeared that he was more open to her once he was convinced that she was not going to dominate his play with directions to do things that did not interest him or that he might fail. Learning to be safe in social interactions was a first major phase of the program. The family was pleased when he began enjoying their company more, if even only occasionally, and when he began coming to them more to interact and to act and talk in ways they were doing.

In general Jodi was becoming a very responsive partner to John, and she found that when she did less in an interaction with him he did more. It was clear that there was some real basis for an emotional attachment between them when she accepted what he did and responded in ways that helped him succeed. John's mother no longer worried about whether he was talking or playing in the ways she thought were "appropriate." Her concern now was for him to accept her into his activities and experience success interacting with others.

The next phase of the program was to develop the pivotal goal of intentional communication. The family was very concerned that John rarely talked to others. While he did have some language, he rarely used it with others and it was generally hard to understand. When the family focused on helping him make sounds clearer, he was frustrated and avoided them. We discussed how any behavior can communicate and demonstrated that responding to any of his behaviors without correction would help him communicate more. The family found that when they responded to all of John's sounds and words without judging them, he began talking more to them and less to himself. His self-talk and insistence on his own topics still predominated, but his mother was enthusiastic that he was beginning to "talk to me at last."

John interacted more when they had a schedule of predictable routines on a one-to-one basis. Previously, most of his time had been in groups with considerable distraction. We discovered that John found many kinds of stimulation aversive and he retreated. The home program then focused on five daily routines that he would allow his parents into and that resulted in little agitation. Avoiding agitating situations became a major issue because, once John became anxious, he violently resisted social contact for up to several hours. Jodi was learning when John was ready to learn and when he was not. The daily routines were computer games, photograph books of the family, car rides, bath-time, and quiet bedtime.

In the daily routines, Jodi acted and communicated in ways John did and then occasionally translated his unclear speech into single words that were appropriate to the situation. Gradually, John began to respond more to her and to direct his words to her occasionally. The progress was slow but it was occurring. We needed to reassure the family that John's habits of not interacting were longstanding and that he would learn that interacting was safe and rewarding only slowly. John's family learned to ignore his undesirable behavior and focus on responding to the appropriate social contacts and language that were increasing. Jodi learned that, while her prior interactions had been mainly verbal, now she found that when she reduced her talk greatly John began talking more. We also noted that his speech became clearer when he directed it more to others than to himself and when we reduced our language to his level.

Developmental guide: your child's conversational life

Based on years of developing conversations with children, we have found a series of skills that help children become effective and enjoyable conversation partners. Many children with delays have language but do not effectively use it in conversations. Conversation, not language alone, is the key to successful relationships, learning, and success in society. The skills below allow a child to build a conversational life.

Four general attitudes seem essential to become a conversationalist:

1. Interest in sharing knowledge.

2. Interest in what others have to say.

3. Understanding that conversations have many purposes.

4. Confidence and enjoyment in interactions.

With these four attitudes, your child will become a successful conversationalist to the degree they develop the following skills.

Enjoys conversing with others

1. Seeks out others for conversation

2. Makes conversations playful times

3. Converses during literacy activities

4. Converses easily as part of physical play

5. Has pretend conversations

6. Makes games of conversations

7. Wants others to know what he knows

8. Enjoys the attention he gets in conversations

Stays on a mutual topic

1. Takes turns with others

2. Responds to others' meanings and intentions

3. Stays on one topic for several exchanges

4. Allows partner to lead the topic

5. Shows interest in what partner has to say

6. Understands when partner wants to change the topic

Converses for many reasons

1. Converses to get information
2. Converses to enjoy being with others
3. Converses to tell stories
4. Converses to get to know others
5. Converses to argue or compete
6. Converses to manipulate others
7. Converses to solve problems
8. Converses to share ideas
9. Converses during playtime

Possible problems

1. Insists on only his own topic
2. Interrupts others
3. Talks at rather than with others
4. Repeats his ideas excessively
5. Shifts topics rapidly
6. Ignores what others say to him
7. Initiates but does not respond
8. Responds but does not initiate
9. Dominates turns by constantly talking

Developmental guide: five strategies to help your child have conversations

The following are ways to help your child have conversations.

- Conversations mean exchanging words back and forth on a shared topic
- Start with strategies that come most easily for you
- Try one or two as you play with your child, then watch how he responds
- Keep doing the ones that keep your child talking with you
- If certain ones seem uncomfortable, do not push yourself. There are many different ways to be effective
- Try new strategies when little is happening with your child
- Determine success by what results in longer conversations on different topics
- Be patient and feel energized by every new communication. However small it seems, it is important for your child

Be balanced

1. Take turns with your child in conversations
2. Take one turn then wait for your child to take one
3. Avoid dominating the conversation
4. Wait for a turn silently with a clear expectation on your face
5. Make the conversation part of a turn-taking play activity
6. Keep the child for "one more turn" when he stops participating
7. Keep your child on one topic for several turns
8. Try to initiate and respond about equally between the two of you
9. Allow silence when your child does not immediately respond
10. Think of conversation more like a game of ping-pong than darts

Be matched

1. Respond to the personal meaning of what your child says
2. Encourage your child to respond to what you say
3. Talk in ways your child can talk
4. Talk about your child's interests half the time

5. Show your child how to talk about your interests some of the time

6. Discourage your child from talking only about himself

7. Talk about what your child is doing

8. Join into his activity and talk about what you are doing together

Be responsive

1. Respond verbally to what your child is doing

2. Respond verbally to what your child is saying

3. Respond once, then wait for your child to say more

4. Respond by showing your child a little more to say

5. Respond by staying on the topic

6. Respond more to positive than negative talking

7. Respond without judgment or criticism

8. Respond with a correction without judgment

9. Respond without demanding the impossible from your child

10. Respond in the ways that gets the most response from your child

Share control

1. Talk to behaviors you want more of

2. Do not talk to behaviors you want less of

3. Regularly ask yourself: Do I want this behavior to continue?

4. Look away when your child is doing something you want to decrease

5. Do not talk to your child when taking him to time-out

6. Remind yourself that your attention is like a fertilizer to your child

7. Teach your child's partners to attend to the positive and ignore the negative

Be emotionally playful

1. Make conversations more playful than task-oriented

2. Have conversations more for companionship than information

3. Respond to your child's emotions

4. Show affection and warmth

5.   Be animated

6.   Be more interesting than your child's distractions

7.   Laugh authentically

8.   Accept your child's ideas without criticism

9.   Talk about your and the child's feelings

10. Make conversations out of your child's play and pretend

Parents' experiences using Communicating Partners to help their child have conversations

Nick started to have conversations with children much younger than his age

"Nick had a great deal of language by ten but he rarely talked with people other than at home or answering questions in school. We tried many times to enter him in age-matched group activities but he isolated himself. Then at age ten he said he'd like to volunteer with five- and six-year-olds in the developmental delay class. Once he did this, he began having conversations with the children and told his parents how much he enjoyed helping the children. The children looked up to him and did not talk or move as fast as his age-matched peers. That is how Nick learned to have conversations…he did it with children who were at his developmental speed conversationally and who made him feel useful." (Anne)

A happy child is much more important than an "A" student

"The more I made learning hard work for Nick the more antagonistic we became. My husband Joe told us to 'stop the war.' It was a struggle and Nick withdrew more. I thought he had to learn so much for school that I did not realize he would learn to talk best when we played enjoyably together. Then I joined his world and he finally let me in. I realized that a happy child is much more important than an 'A' student." (Anne)

Aiden's first phone call

"Aiden began to talk well into his fourth year. Now he is six and we have been working hard at home at having conversations about anything he wants. Aiden got his first 'friend' phone call yesterday. So cute! A girl from his kindergarten just called to chat. It's kind of hysterical how these six-year-olds want to talk on the phone; I guess it makes them feel grown-up.

Anyway they talked for about five minutes. He told her what he did that day, responded to what she said (I think she invited him to a nonexistent party), and he invited her to a nonexistent sleepover. Then he told her he had to go and eat supper and that he'd see her tomorrow and hung up. He had a grin from ear to ear. I think the telephone is a good way to encourage conversation since it forces a back-and-forth exchange that face-to-face contacts don't." (Valle)

Conversations work better when the child has the lead

"I have really been tuning in lately to conversations with Aiden and I realize that we are now pretty successful at it. When I used to mainly ask him questions and make him say things, he clammed up. The times I was discouraged were the conversations that I tried to dictate, but when I allow him to lead the way, there are much better results. I overheard him talking to his dad [Phil] this morning when they were snuggling in his room.

Aiden:	Daddy, Casey (our dog) took my tape.
Dad:	Your tape? (Phil was confused. He hadn't awakened yet.)
Aiden:	Yeah, he took my tape.
Dad:	Okay, let's go get it.
Aiden:	Casey is downstairs.
Dad:	Okay, let's get up.
Aiden:	Wake up, sleepy head.

So off they went downstairs and took the tape, Aiden's music, out of the dog's mouth." (Valle)

11

Civil Behavior

The Fifth Stage in Learning to Communicate

Case example: John and Jodi and the elephants

John was six years old. He began to talk regularly to people at age five. His mother, Jodi, was so pleased that John was talking that she responded to anything he said. She had found early on that she needed to respond to any sounds or words John said even if to himself, so that he would learn to use words to communicate. This story is an example of the natural dilemma parents face when their child finally talks after years of fear and confusion. Jodi related the following dialogue during a visit to the zoo:

John: I want to see elephants.

Jodi: Okay, we're on our way.

John: Now. I want them now!

Jodi: That's where we're going, honey.

John: (screaming) I want the elephants, now!

Jodi: Honey, I told you that is where we are going, just be patient.

John: No, I want them now. (Starts screaming and lying down kicking)

Jodi: We won't get there any faster if you get mad.

John: (gets up and hits Jodi) No, I want it now!

Jodi: You don't want to hit momma.

John: Elephants, elephants, where are they? (screaming)

Jodi: Please stop. I've got a headache.

John: I want the elephants!

Jodi: We're almost there.

John: (drops to the ground crying)

Jodi: Stop crying or we'll go home.

John: (keeps screaming and kicking)

Jodi: (picks up John and carries him to the elephants) There they are!

John: No, I want to see the monkeys.

If this story is painful to read, consider how Jodi felt. When I asked why she kept responding to his negative talk and abuse, she said she thought she should always respond to him so he would keep talking. She did not want to discourage him since they waited so long for him to talk at all. She also believed that she needed to explain that, indeed, he was going to get what he wanted. Then she began talking to him to threaten him. Finally, she gave in entirely and took him to the elephants, at which time he was in such a negative state that he demanded something else. Imagine how you would feel after such a tug of war!

Jodi also said that everything was becoming a fight: getting dressed, eating, brushing teeth, and shopping. She had to admit that she and her family all felt obliged to respond to anything John said, however offensive or inappropriate. While the negativity tested their patience and made life difficult, they still felt "at least he's talking" and they had a palpable fear that ignoring him would drive him back to his nonverbal world.

I told Jodi that many parents had considerable success by ignoring their child's negative behaviors. She responded by saying, "I can't ignore it—he just keeps it up." But with a little discussion she had to admit that she had not really tried to ignore the boy very much. I realized that after worrying so long about John ever talking, she could not emotionally allow herself to ignore him. She viscerally feared that ignoring him would hurt him and perhaps even make him not talk again.

John and Jodi began working with me again. We had worked together for about a year in which Jodi learned to enter John's nonverbal world. She was excellent in helping him communicate first in his world of actions, then more and more in her world of words. I knew well that they had a strong and mutually responsive relationship that John enjoyed and thrived on. Consequently, my task was to convince Jodi that ignoring his negative behavior would not drive him away from her.

In order to help him talk, Jodi had had to respond to all kinds of talking just to get him convinced it was worthwhile. But now, since he clearly wanted to communicate, I was certain that ignoring certain kinds of talking was necessary to show him the kind of talk that would be accepted in society. I demonstrated how to respond to him when he was positive and ignore him when he was negative. I responded playfully to anything John said positively, but immediately looked away silently whenever he whined or acted rudely or abusively. Jodi saw that John continued to talk to me. She saw that ignoring him did not drive him away from talking but in fact resulted in him talking more to me in positive ways. I showed her that when I attended to his positive talk he did more of it, and when I ignored his negative talk he did less of it. In fact, he kept coming back to me to play and talk in increasingly appropriate and playful ways. I did have to tolerate episodes of resistance, but I took the time and it paid off.

However, I realized that carrying this out on a daily basis was going to be difficult for Jodi. I expected that ignoring might not work unless she was convinced how important it was for his inclusion into society. I reminded her how successful she had been helping a five-year-old nonverbal boy talk and convinced her that she could now be just as successful in teaching him how to behave more civilly.

We discussed two beliefs that Jodi had about John. The first was that ignoring him would hurt him and make him not talk again. The second belief was that she could successfully reason with him and talk him out of his negative behavior. Then, I suggested that she make a couple of images in her mind whenever John was nasty, negative, or inappropriate. The first image was that every word that she said was a 20-dollar bill and that the more she talked to his negative behavior the richer and nastier he became. I wanted her to realize that her responding to negative behavior was actually harmful to John as well as distasteful to others. She needed to learn that she, indeed, could actually teach him to behave worse by attending to the negative behavior. The second image I encouraged her to see when John was negative was to pretend that John was a brittle diabetic when he was nasty and that every word was a piece of candy. Then she could see that talking to him when he was negative was like giving candy to make a child sicker. We have found that these two images are very effective since they are clear analogs to what happens to a child when we attend to negative behavior. He becomes more negative and he becomes sicker, in a sense becoming less able to have positive relationships.

After a few weeks of practice, Jodi called to say that she and her husband, Andy, tried the suggestions. The first few days were rough. John went into several rages, which passed when they ignored them. But then he got the idea that certain behaviors would lose just the attention he craved. After persisting for a while, Jodi called to say that John was much less negative and that his most common phrase now was, "Don't ignore me, talk to me." Jodi and her family came to realize that John was going to continue talking and he would do so much more appropriately when people did not attend to his negative or disruptive words or other behavior.

Communicating with a child often involves a clash between two worlds: the child's idiosyncratic world of sensations, action, and perceptions and his partner's world of thought, language, and conventional expectations. This clash can result in conflicts and a variety of perceived "behavior problems." In fact if we consider a behavior problem as simply behaviors that are undesirable, many might view autism or a related disorder as a "behavior problem." We definitely do not view it as a behavior problem since it is clearly more a neurologically influenced condition than the environmentally induced behaviors often considered "behavior problems." However, the fact that much behavior is neurologically driven does not mean that it cannot be changed by environmental and interpersonal measures. The now well-documented "plasticity" of the child's brain has now been shown to be quite readily influenced by experiences.

While we need to understand and address the many socially undesired behaviors of our children, we must state emphatically that it will not be enough to eliminate these behaviors. We know many children with ASD and other delays who no longer exhibit "autistic" behaviors and are quite cooperative and compliant. Their families feel relieved and successful after long struggles with the child's difficult habits. However, the elimination of undesired behaviors should not be seen as a satisfactory goal for our children. We are more optimistic about ASD children than to accept only a "well-behaved" child who is not a bother to others. Do not accept the lack of negative behaviors as success for your child. We know many children with few "negative" behaviors but also with little clue about how to have genuine relationships. We know many ASD children who can become positive communicative partners with authentic relationships. We are not satisfied with a child who is well behaved and shows few "autistic" behaviors. We can expect much more from most of our children.

Why are we concerned about civil behavior?

A major concern for our children is the strong negative effects their unusual behavior can have on relationships. Given that our children experience a very different "world" to that of most other people, their behaviors may appear strange, undesirable, and even offensive. It is not surprising that these behaviors become "problems" that drive others away.

So, what does a parent do? One option is just to explain the behaviors away as "autistic" and learn to live with them. Another option is to try to eliminate them as enemies of development. On the contrary, we have found that much can be done without either accepting or eliminating the behaviors.

The answers are neither simple nor the same across children but often lie in places that we least expect them. When you begin to understand reasons for the behaviors and adapt your environment to your child, he can get on more of an even keel, even with the neurological differences, sensitivities, and developmental differences that may trigger the undesired behaviors. This is not to say that autism or a related disorder is primarily a "behavior problem" in the sense of being manipulative or due to inappropriate training. However, many of the behaviors called "autistic" need not be permanent and can be altered in sensitive, responsive relationships. The first step to improve your child's civil behavior is to be optimistic that the child can change and that the behaviors are not permanent. Martin Seligman and colleagues have found in years of studying optimistic and pessimistic people that, when parents are optimistic about their children, they interact more and promote more positive behavior in their children instead of attending to negative behaviors (Seligman 2002). We know many parents who have helped children behave more civilly when they realize that behavior problems are not a permanent part of their child's condition. The next step is to come to understand the reasons their children behave as they do. This chapter is intended to help you develop an empathy for your child by understanding why he does what he does and to see how you can help him behave more civilly.

The "two worlds" problem

Often when our children are not reacting appropriately or behaving correctly in our world, they are actually reacting to a different world to the one we experience. Throughout this book, we frequently return to a core notion: autistic children live in a world of action and sensation and we adults live primarily in a world of thought and language. Consequently when children and adults interact across the two worlds, expecting the other to be in their world, there are bound to be conflicts, disappointments, and "behavior problems."

Hundreds of cases have shown us that when adults enter and understand the autistic child's world, they can often prevent and moderate the undesired behaviors. They learn the reasons for the unusual behaviors and they learn to distinguish between ones to be addressed and ones that may disappear without attention. One major source of concern is the different sensory responses autistic children have to typical life situations that we have adapted to.

Many children feel so much stress in their body that they just cannot interact or communicate with us until the stress lessens. Unfortunately for parents, stimulation that stresses them is not the same stress that unhinges their children. Parents need to understand that their children's nervous system just cannot stand many ordinary events, such as the onset of a vacuum cleaner or a friendly touch on the head. It is critical that an understanding and preventative approach be taken with each individual. Punishing or trying to suppress a behavior that is the nervous system's natural response to stimulation that physiologically disturbs the child will be no more effective than punishing a child for rubbing his head in response to a headache.

Common reasons children behave in undesirable ways

In 30 years I have seen a wide range of behaviors that are considered undesirable in children with autism and related disorders. In fact, in more than 80 percent of cases parents and professionals have listed "behavior problems" as a major concern. By "behavior problems" they usually refer to behaviors such as: unusual physical movements like shaking, spinning, rocking; verbal behaviors like swearing, screaming, bizarre language; violent or aggressive behaviors such as hitting, spitting, breaking things; cooperation problems such as resisting, disobeying, and ignoring; civil problems such as rude, insensitive, or embarrassing behavior; agitated or over-active behaviors such as impulsive and unpredictable movements; isolating behaviors such as ignoring, escaping, and extensive alone time; and others that are often specific to each child and to the tolerance levels of the persons reporting the concern.

Note that many of these behaviors occur in typically developing children and others are actually the defining features of autism. So which are "behavior problems" and which are "autistic behaviors"? We believe there is no clear answer since typical children do many of what are considered "autistic" behaviors. In fact "autistic" behaviors in a five-year-old are often typical behaviors in younger children under stress or even in their natural explorations. Consequently, the issue is less what the behavior is ("autistic" or "normal") than whether it is disturbing others, interfering with learning, or damaging. It is important to realize that even if the behaviors are agreed to be part of "autism" (or any related condition), I strongly disagree with those who see them as unchangeable. In this chapter we will use "undesired" as a comprehensive term for any behaviors that you may be concerned about and want to alter in your child. This is not to say that we will be agreeing with you that all the "undesired" behaviors are actually developmentally undesirable or ones the child should never do. As you will see, we have found that many of the "autistic" behaviors that concern us are natural reactions to environments that do not fit the child. Some of them are also learned behaviors. And some are temporary manifestations of the child's developing nervous system. The point is that there are often reasons for the undesired behaviors that can be managed over time after developing empathy for the child's experiences.

There is always a reason for undesired behavior.

When children behave in undesired ways, their relationships and development can be seriously thwarted. This is especially true of a child with autism. In fact much of what we define as "autistic" might be considered undesired behavior. Just because it is undesired does not mean it is "wrong," even developmentally "incorrect" or useless to the child. It is much more productive to view all of a child's behaviors as "reasonable," perhaps not desirable, but "reasonable" in the sense that they are reactions of the child's nervous system and mind to a challenging environment. Once you understand your child's experiences you will see that his unusual behaviors actually "make sense" in light of the circumstances. That is not to say we will accept them and do nothing. No, in fact we have found that much can be done to reduce undesired behaviors and replace them with positive ones.

Enter into a "no fault" relationship with your child

You can help your child develop when you enter a "no fault" relationship with him. "No fault" means that there are always reasons for undesired behavior and that mindful parents can change many of these. By the way, "no fault" does not mean "no consequences" or "no responsibility." Children absolutely need to learn that their behaviors have consequences, both positive and negative ones. We reject the notion that autistic spectrum children cannot learn from consequences to their behaviors. They may need more time and environmental support than other children. However, it can be disastrous to take the attitude that "he's autistic and he can't stop himself" or "autistic children cannot learn to be responsible." Your child will not be able to stop some undesired behaviors at times and those behaviors may actually have positive functions for him. We also find that "perfect" behavior is not the goal, and so our children can develop well even while having habits such as rocking that may bother some people. The point is that parents can learn which behaviors to focus on and which to leave alone. When parents help their child interact and communicate, the undesired behavior often decreases markedly.

Reasons for undesired behavior

Often parents say to a misbehaving child: "There is no reason for that!" While it may be hard to see a reason, there always is one, perhaps not an acceptable one, but a reason nonetheless. When you realize there is a reason, you can then discover whether you can or should address it. Reasons for undesired behavior can be found in at least three places: in the child, in his relationships, and in his living and learning environments.

Reasons for undesired behaviors in the child

Autistic children have a more difficult time than other children just negotiating the stimulation, changes, and demands of their environment. The world they see is often designed by and for people who perceive it very differently. Authors who have lived with autism (Grandin 1995; Kaufman 1976; Williams 1994, 1996, 1998) describe how the conventional world is painfully out of synch with their nervous system. In fact, a boy we knew for many years, John, expressed it well after a few years out of school when he said, "My nervous system is ready for school now." We need to understand how our children experience the world and believe them when they show us that they need changes in the world.

While each of us operates from a unique "nervous system," autistic children do so in markedly different ways than most. It is important for parents to realize that their children are not really experiencing the same world as we are. Consequently, such children behave in "unusual" ways when they perceive the world differently and have a different belief system. The more that parents understand a child's perspective, the more they are able to address "undesired" behaviors. When undesired behaviors concern you, realize that your child is not responding to the same world with the same nervous system as you are. You will then not expect your child to respond in the ways you would. "Putting yourself into your child's shoes" is an expression parents learn. I prefer the notion of "putting yourself into your child's nervous system" since seeing the world from your child's perspective is often as different as seeing the world from the ground or from a moving roller-coaster. For many autistic children, the world is much like a moving roller-coaster that changes speeds but never stops. Parents have the daunting task of joining the child and becoming an engineer of that roller-coaster so that the child can develop within its constraints.

THE CHILD IS FAILING AT A TASK

One common "undesired behavior" is the child's emotional reaction to failing at a task. Actually, this is the child's reaction to "feeling" he is failing at a task. It is so easy for a child to come to believe he is doing something wrong or failing when he is simply doing what his nervous system allows or what he is developmentally ready to do.

Three basic assumptions of Communicating Partners relate to the issue of "failures":

1. Children do not make developmental mistakes; whatever they do is what they can do at the moment on the basis of their abilities, history, and environment.

2. One of the most harmful things we can teach a child is to feel that what he is doing is "wrong" and that he should be someone he is not.

3. Each child, regardless of his developmental delays, has some "signature strengths" that can be supported to help him build interactive relationships.

The goal of Communicating Partners is not to fix or repair problems but to build on the child's signature strengths.

THE CHILD IS BORED OR LOST FOR SOMETHING TO DO

It is absolutely natural for a child to be doing something. His life is action. We worry when a parent says, "She was such a good baby; I could get so much housework done and she never bothered me." This is a frequent report on autistic and other late-talking children and it is a serious concern. Children should not be quiet and easy. They need to make noise and move to grow and learn. Those movements are going to get in your way at times. So if your child is not doing something constructive, it is reasonable to expect that he will do things that will bother you.

THE CHILD DOES NOT HAVE ENOUGH "DOWN" TIME

While our children are often too isolated, many need time alone more than many other children. Not only do they need time alone, they often need more "waiting" time from others. We have found time and again that when we give children some quiet time they often move into our world more easily. We also find that our children are easily overstimulated and so they need quiet time for their nervous system to recover from stimulation since it affects them differently to us.

THE CHILD IS UNCOORDINATED

When children learn new things, they may naturally be disruptive in ways that look like "misbehaving." If a child is learning to walk and topples over your coffee cup, try not to react as if it were deliberate and keep breakable things from his reach. This is not to say that autistic children are less coordinated but they are often less attentive and more impulsive in ways that can look like coordination problems. A child learning to negotiate a world physically that they see differently to us may look like a "bull in a china shop" and that is why we usually keep china away from bulls.

THE CHILD IS INATTENTIVE OR DOING TOO MANY THINGS AT ONCE

As a child develops he will be paying attention to many things at once. Sometimes he just won't "see" the coffee cup on his way to something he wants. We often find that simplifying the environment and helping the child focus on one activity at a time helps avoid the distractions that can lead to undesired behavior.

THE CHILD INTENDS TO GET SOMEONE ANGRY

Some children do intentionally try to get others angry. For some, it is actually enjoyable, giving them a sense of control. However, in my experience, this is a very uncommon reason. When children try to get others angry, they are often seeking the attention the anger got them in the past. Unfortunately for children who feel emotionally deprived, any attention may be reinforcing. It is almost as if they are saying, "Love me or hate me, but don't ignore me." It is sad to see abused children deliberately antagonize others into punishing them since negative attention is the meaning of emotional attachment to them. It sounds bizarre that being abused would be more desirable than being alone, but it is often true.

THE CHILD HAS NOT LEARNED TO "SELF-REGULATE"

For autistic children, their sensations and emotions can be so intense that it is very difficult for them to resist acting out. As a child's sensitivities mature, he often becomes less disruptive. For some children, it is possible to address their compulsive behaviors both physically and cognitively. By physically restraining or signaling a child to stop, some children learn to regulate their behavior. We find this physical approach is much more effective if it is not accompanied by talking, which can actually reinforce the child. The cognitive approach can work with verbal children who can generalize "moral" instructions from one time to another.

THE CHILD IS AFRAID

A normal response to being in a strange land is fear. Our children often fear events that seem "normal" to others. We must understand that much of the world that we see as "normal" is strange and unsettling to our children. We should not be surprised when a child responds with aggression to being afraid. It takes careful observation to learn what triggers fear in your child. Do not assume he will be afraid of the things that frighten you. Some of your greatest fears, like snakes, may not affect him at all. His history of failures and his perceptions of the world are very different to yours. He has sensitivities that you do not experience. Abrupt changes or unexpected events can trigger considerable emotion in an unsuspecting child. Transitions can also be very upsetting and the unknown is full of potential fear for our children.

THE CHILD IS IN PAIN

Closely related to fear, as a trigger to undesirable behavior, is the general range of experiences children feel as pain. Children with autism often have sensory thresholds very different to ours. Certain kinds of sounds might disturb them while other sounds might not. Certain sights can trigger pain. Our children often tolerate internal pain without letting others know. The point is that some of the neurological experiences that accompany autism and related disorders are often very little known to others.

> Mario often tried to repress his nervousness and then just exploded by striking out or abusing himself. It actually looked like his agitation was painful to him. He had been told to "calm down" so it was apparent that he felt he should not feel what he was feeling. The

more he tried not to move in an agitated way the more agitated he became. His mother was very sensitive and simply stayed with him quietly when he was nervous, not trying to change him but joining with him so he was not alone or feeling wrong. His mother did not take his behavior personally but tried to discover how to change the situation so that it was not so painful for him.

THE CHILD HAS OBSESSIONS THAT ARE DIFFICULT TO REGULATE

One of the hallmarks of autism is behavior that seems not to have any practical function. The child may repeat actions, sounds, or words over and over. He may have ritualistic ways of doing things. He may become obsessed with connecting with things in peculiar ways. He may have to have things arranged in consistent ways. He may be very resistant to changes in the environment, such as the location of a bed or plates on a table.

Sean in Pittsburgh met me in a room where he was running and tapping nonstop. I wanted to show his parents how to keep him interacting. They had been told that before they interacted with him he needed to stop his repetitive behaviors. When they tried to stop them, he became agitated and even more isolated. I decided that he and I were going to interact by throwing a pillow back and forth. I kept him physically with me by holding his legs. I physically prompted him to exchange the pillow as he waved his hands, rocked, and made repetitive sounds. I focused on the interaction and allowed him to do anything he wanted as long as he interacted in the one way with me. After about eight prompted turns back and forth, Sean began throwing the pillow voluntarily and in an easy turn-taking volley. I gave him a break as I explained what happened to his parents. We were all surprised and pleased when Sean, after a short self-stimulating break, came back to me and resumed the pillow game. He was still showing his agitated behaviors, but less than before. He was even staying now without me holding him. It became clear that he did want to interact with people but he had to do it while also moving in his own ways. Again we stopped as I talked to his parents, who were surprised to see him stay interacting. He had usually put up a fight when he was stopped before, but now he learned he had to stay briefly but could still do his "autistic" behaviors, he showed that he actually enjoyed interacting with me. I had thought he was finished with me when all of a sudden he sat on my lap. His parents said they never saw him do that with a stranger. I allowed him to be himself and he stayed with me.

Reasons for undesired behaviors in relationships

One of our most positive findings has been the success parents have on reducing negative and increasing positive behavior in children. They do this by making subtle but powerful changes in their relationship with the child. We have repeatedly found that once a parent and child have a *mutually responsive orientation* to each other, the child replaces many of the prior negative behaviors with positive ones. Many parents have come to us believing that undesired behaviors, such as resistance, acting out, and bizarre actions, were a necessary part of their child's condition. They often felt powerless and defeated. They usually believed that only professionals could help.

Once parents learned that becoming responsive play partners was more effective than being directive, they came to enjoy their child more and the child behaved more positively. Teaching parents to see the consequences of their interactive styles and attitudes on their child is a major task in our work. Parents become more effective when they see the many choices they have in ways to interact with the child.

This section discusses reasons for undesired behavior due to the kinds of relationships children have. In no way are we implying that parents are responsible for a child's "autistic" behaviors. A child's behaviors have a profound impact on parents. The changes we see in relationships are natural effects of parents being subjected to unusual and frightening behaviors they do not understand. As long as parents view their child from their adult perspective of thought and language, they will continue to be emotionally affected and will maintain conflicts with the child. Once parents enter their child's world of sensation and action, they will appreciate how the child behaves and the ways to help him behave differently.

THE BEHAVIORS GET YOUR ATTENTION

Many parents do not realize how important any personal attention is to their children. Especially when children are just beginning to connect with people, they will do a great deal to get any kind of attention. It is very difficult for parents not to attend to behaviors that are irritating, abusive, or inappropriate. But we have also found in hundreds of families that when parents do ignore "misbehavior" it decreases. This is not to say that ignoring is easy. It is usually very difficult and takes real effort. It also takes an understanding that attention will mainly increase just the behaviors you want to decrease. However, ignoring pays off incredibly by decreasing the child's behaviors and relieving partners of conflicts that perpetuate themselves.

THE CHILD'S PARTNER DOES NOT UNDERSTAND HIM

Your child may misbehave when he feels misunderstood. It is lonely and frightening for many children to lose connection with you when you misunderstand or misinterpret them. Many parents have helped their children behave civilly by simply entering the child's play world and understanding their experiences. Many adults think they need to understand the child in terms of thoughts and language while the child is often experiencing the world in terms of sensations and actions. Many parents have been surprised to see how better behaved their child becomes when they do not try to "understand" the child in ideas but in actions. The point is that you will be able to interact more effectively with your child when you understand his actions by acting just like him. Understand that working with your child is not a thinking project, rather it is a sensory project to learn how the child is feeling.

THEIR PARTNER JUDGES THEM AS DOING SOMETHING "WRONG"

Autistic children will do many things that others consider "wrong" or "bothersome" when they are simply natural reactions of their nervous system to the current stimulation. When a child is criticized or chastised for something he cannot control, he will often react with resistant or otherwise undesirable emotional behavior.

> John's father, Andy, was irritated by the boy's constant tapping on furniture around the house. His mother knew that John tapped when he was anxious and that he was doing it much less than before. Consequently, she did not try to stop him since it calmed him. His father continually told him to stop and saw the behavior as disobedient. A daily tug-of-war between father and son developed and John had rages when his father scolded him. John's mother helped her husband realize that the criticism did not stop the tapping, but it seemed to result in rages. We discussed with the father how he would feel if every time he smoked a cigarette, someone

would take it from him. John's father understood that smoking relaxed him. He came to understand that John's tapping had calming effects on the boy as smoking had on him. He even came to realize that for John his tapping was "safe smoking."

THEY DO NOT HAVE ENOUGH ENJOYABLE AND MATCHED PLAYTIMES WITH YOU

Our children often "misbehave" when they have not recently had enjoyable personal contact with people. Even the most autistic children we know actually do want to interact with you but they need to do it in unconventional ways. Often just a little frequent access to you in a playful way where he is not controlled can offset a child's many "behavior problems." It is understandable that parents, anxious to help their children, will often engage in so many task-oriented interactions that the child views social life as hard work and failure. Such children behave in undesired ways just as a relief from so many expectations for him to do the impossible. Contrary to some beliefs, our children can feel disregarded and disrespected. They are not immune to understanding that others do not really care about their interests since their interests may not be what parents are hoping for the child. We often see anger and misbehavior when a child feels disregarded.

THE CHILD IS RESPONDING TO CRITICISM OR JUDGMENT

As your child develops it is natural for him to do things that are not mature or acceptable; what some call "mistakes" are natural steps in development. When children are criticized for doing things that come naturally to them, they are likely to rebel and resist because internally they are simply following their developmental flow. They are usually not intending to do "wrong," they are simply doing what they can do at the moment. Such a critical pattern can harm a child if the person does not immediately show the child how to do the behavior more acceptably. Criticism can in itself, over time, convince the child that he is incompetent and drive him away from just the regular interactions he needs to grow.

THEY EXCEED THE EMOTIONAL LIMITS OF THEIR PARENTS' BOUNDARIES

It is too obvious to note that interacting with autistic children can challenge the emotional limits of even the most tranquil person. Unless that person expects the unexpected from a child, our children often do things that downright surprise and offend even a kind-hearted person. Many children we know learn how to test their parents' limits when they see them being vulnerable. Parents can avoid unnecessary conflicts by coming to know when they are most vulnerable to the child's challenges and try to limit their interactions at those times. This will often not be possible but with practice parents can teach themselves to be mindful of times they are particularly tired or distracted and attempt to limit their interactions with the child to a minimum. For example, when you are late for work and your child still does not have his shoes on, you see that he is testing you with whining and dawdling. Rather than requiring him to do the job himself, it is wise to put the shoes on him quickly without discussion and get out the door in time. He will learn that he cannot buy time and your attention by such behavior. Parents often find it emotionally difficult to "get the job done" briskly without conversation with a child who may not talk much. Parents need to teach children that there are times to talk and times to move. Such discipline will teach the child an important life lesson.

THEY ARE RESPONDING TO DEVELOPMENTALLY UNREASONABLE DEMANDS

Children, especially ones with a history of frequent failures, may behave unacceptably when others make demands on them that they are unable to do. In the hope for a child to "act his age" many parents try to get the child to do things he is unable to do. A developmentally unreasonable demand is one that attempts to get the child to do something that may be accepted for his chronological age but he is simply at a much lower level developmental age. Often we see children begin to talk at four or five. They may say a few words but actually be performing more like a two-year-old. We have observed many persons look at the child and talk to him as if he was at a four- or five-year level. They talk far over his head and the child is not able to converse at all. Parents are often frustrated when a child does not talk to them. The problem is that, as soon as the child talks, others see him as a full "talker" when he is only beginning to talk.

When you expect more than your child can do frequently, he may begin to react in destructive emotional ways since he is frustrated. He might resist interacting with you and become angry at his failure to communicate. We work hard to encourage parents to learn where their child is developmentally and then to expect and prompt him to perform at that level and a little above. For example, when you see a six-year-old talk in single words, respond to him in single words and occasionally showing him a few new words. Try to avoid talking to what you would expect of his chronological age. If your six-year-old is talking at a two-year level, respect and accept that fact and proceed to interact with him as if he were developmentally two years old. He will have more successes and probably show less undesired behavior.

Environmental reasons for undesired behavior

One common view of children with autism is that they need structure in their learning situations. Many feel that they need predictable routines and consistent contingencies. Often this belief is translated into directive teaching situations where the child is programmed to carry out activities decided upon that "typical" children at the child's age would do. This kind of structure may benefit children who already have the social and communicative skills to use in daily life the knowledge they get in the structured education. But this may well be wasted time for children who are not yet social and communicative.

We have found that the kind of structure children need first to become natural social learners and to have relationships is *mutually responsive social structure*. Children need to know how to interact with others. The rules they need to learn include more than compliance and following directions. The structure they need involves learning the rules of relationships such as reciprocity, turn-taking, spontaneous social modeling, imitation, and other skills that address the question: What does it take to function in a "socially disciplined environment?"

The notion of discipline usually refers to ways to get children to behave to meet others' wishes. We have found that children will learn to communicate best in socially disciplined environments, where social discipline means that the child and his life partners follow social rules that insure that both partners are actively participating and are responding sensitively to the other. Consequently it is not only the child who needs to learn this kind of social discipline; his life partners need to learn this rule as well. The basic components of an interactive environment that appear to predict positive cognitive and social development in children are those interactive skills that both the child and his life partners share, including the following major responsive strategies: balancing, matching, responding, sharing control, and expressing positive affect.

When we observe frequent undesired behaviors, we often find that children are in an environment that is not very disciplined in social terms. Their relationships may not be predictable and they are not having interactions that are responsive to their interests and developmental needs. An undisciplined environment is also one in which the child is not encouraged and required to be responsive to others. He is allowed to stay in his own self-absorbed world and does not learn that giving back to others is a basic responsibility of any human being, or he is allowed to dominate interactions without much regard for others' rights and concerns. Many believe that children with autism and other delays are incapable of truly responsive relationships. Consequently, they are allowed to live a life that shows many of the features of learned helplessness that Seligman and others have noted in socially ineffective children. When children are not required to participate socially, they learn many antisocial patterns that further limit their development.

Children are frequently in environments in which they are expected to be social or act according to society's rules of give and take, reciprocity, concern for others, responsiveness, sharing control, and empathy. Consequently, when our children violate those rules that are new to them, they are often seen as misbehaving. Our children have not learned these rules and then they are accused of "misbehaving" when in fact they have simply not been taught how to relate. We categorically reject the common notion that autistic children are not able to have relationships. Even the most isolated and asocial children can learn to take turns, respond meaningfully, and succeed in the common skills for relationships. Their environments often neither expect nor prepare them for these skills. In fact, many natural environments actually work against our children learning the social rules by structuring their lives in such directive ways that they see relationships as one-way events rather than reciprocal events.

Helping your child to communicate for relationships, then, is actually a matter of designing and supporting environments that make interacting successful and enjoyable for the child. Many parents have learned to help their child into a social world by evaluating their child's learning environments in terms of how they facilitate a successful and responsive life for the child.

Use the MRE survey box to understand how your child's natural environments might be supporting or interfering with him learning to communicate. Many parents report marked changes in their child's social and communicative behavior when they make even small changes in his environment. Many times the changes have been simple to accomplish while others required new efforts and understanding.

The MRE survey: your child's mutually responsive environment

How much are your child's living environments supporting or limiting his social and communicative environment? Use the survey to understand how your child's environments may influence his development either positively or negatively. You can then make the easy changes so that your child spends more time in supportive environments and less in unsupportive ones. Some changes will be much easier than others, but many parents have found that just increasing the positive environments a little can open a child to a more social life.

Potentially supportive features

1. The child is free to interact with others
2. People interact with the child in a turn-taking way
3. People respond to the child's interests
4. People act in ways the child can try to do
5. One-to-one interactions are available
6. People wait for the child to respond
7. There is a sense of give and take in the interactions
8. The child clearly enjoys himself
9. The other people clearly enjoy the child
10. There is the possibility of quiet time
11. The child is given enough time on an activity
12. People respond to the child's spontaneous play
13. People play in the child's chosen activity

Potentially limiting features

1. People expect the child to do impossible things
2. The level of stimulation is overwhelming
3. Little participation is expected of the child
4. The child has little control over the interactions
5. The child is corrected or criticized
6. The child plays mainly alone or parallel with others
7. The interactions focus on accomplishing a task
8. People talk to the child when he "misbehaves"

The following conditions are ones that parents are able to change in their environments so their child behaves more positively and civilly.

AUTISTIC CHILDREN HAVE MANY "ENVIRONMENTAL ALLERGIES"

When a child has food allergies we see the symptoms on his skin, in his breathing, or in his behavior, and we respond by changing his food and environment to reduce the symptoms. Similarly, we can help autistic children behave more appropriately when we see his behaviors as the result of other "allergies" to the environment, such as too much sound, sight, movement, or changes. Many of our children show clear neurological reactions to stimuli that most people have adapted to. When we understand that many normal sensory stimuli can disrupt our children and result in upsetting behavior, we can then begin to manage the environment to allow them to function, just as we do when they have other physical allergies, such as to foods or pollen. Many persons with "autistic" histories describe how difficult it is to put up with stimuli that others have no problems with (Grandin 1995; Williams 1994, 1996, 1998). They report neurological effects of many sights, sounds, and touches that can be managed by observant parents.

THE NORMAL ENVIRONMENT IS FAR TOO STIMULATING FOR THE CHILD

One consistent feature of our children is that their nervous systems react disruptively to natural stimuli that other people can adapt to and function within. When parents learn that "normal" events can trigger difficult behavior, they can come to redesign the environment to avoid unnecessary attacks on the child's nervous system.

> The author Don DeLillo, in his contemporary novel *White Noise*, describes a household in which there is a constant barrage of sights, sounds, and movements that make it difficult for anyone to concentrate on much of anything. One character in the book is a four-year-old son who shows many autistic features, especially when taken out of daily routines. He actually falls apart when he is not alone or when he cannot connect quietly with someone. His father takes him to a therapy lesson where he screams and becomes self-destructive. The mother believed that a lot of therapy was necessary.

The father decided instead to take a drive with the boy in a parking lot and let him quiet down. They drove around in circles slowly with the boy on his lap moving the steering wheel. In the quiet situation where the child could have control over something and without the "white noise" of the world, the boy calmed and enjoyably interacted with his father. He began to talk softly back and forth in a way that he rarely did in the chaos of the home. The boy's father came to understand how much his son needed him in quiet, nondemanding interactions. The themes of DeLillo's novel suggest that we often live among such "white noise" of random distractions that it is difficult for even nondelayed individuals to have intimate personal relationships.

This story is even more striking when applied to autistic children, for whom "normal" stimuli can disrupt their sensitivities to the point that they retreat into "autistic" behaviors that may actually calm them and relieve their anxiety. When a child is "misbehaving," we should evaluate his environment in terms of the demands it puts on a sensitive nervous system. In this case the father could help the boy develop by insuring that he had several quiet one-to-one interactions every day in which he could attend to others and communicate without competing with an impossible environment.

In our experience, overstimulation is one of the major reasons children become upset and misbehave. Often adults are not aware of how actually abusive some sights, sounds, and touches are to children. I know many children who literally suffer from too much stimulation. They may cover their ears, close their eyes, and recoil from friendly touches. Many will actually strike out and scream as if they are being attacked. Many parents have learned that, indeed, these children actually feel attacked when exposed to a crowd, too many choices, new sights and sounds, or abrupt changes in the environment. When seen from the child's perspective, it is not surprising that a child may look like they are misbehaving when they are actually protecting themselves from painful experiences. Try to appreciate that you might do the same if you felt as they do.

THEY HAVE LEARNED FEW OR NO BOUNDARIES

When the child is finally out of his isolated world and interacting, you will need to address the major problem of "boundaries." Your child may not understand when, where, and how much he should be doing his new social behaviors. He may ask 40 questions in a row nonstop. He may hug strangers. He may say inappropriate things to strangers. He may interrupt others. The problem of boundaries involves many issues.

The fact that appropriate boundaries will be constantly changing as the child develops makes it very difficult for parents. At first we want a child to say "anything" and then only appropriate and civil things. Early on you may want an isolated autistic child to touch you in any way and then you will establish boundaries for where, when, and how much to touch. What is developmentally appropriate at one age will be unacceptable at other ages. But we must realize that the age to consider is the child's "personal developmental" age, not the chronological age. Consequently, while we may not want a child who is seven years chronologically to touch and talk and play with you as a two-year-old does, many parents would be very pleased if their seven-year-old autistic child did so if he had generally been isolated and noncommunicative. Jodi realizes that John, now 12, sometimes still needs the physical affection that we might expect of a three-year-old. She recalls when he was younger that he would not tolerate the touches that he wants today. Jodi feels that he is still emotionally a three-year-old and she accommodates him, but only alone, and she makes it clear that it is not acceptable in public.

Teaching a child physical and social boundaries is a major part of socializing him. Showing your child what to do will usually be more effective than telling him about it, since talking to him when he is inappropriate can serve to encourage the undesired behavior.

THE ENVIRONMENT SETS UP FAILURES FOR THE CHILD

One common recommendation we make to parents is to make sure that the child's environments and tasks are "possible" for him. Many parents have become very sensitive at assessing a task or situation in terms of how possible it will be for their child to negotiate it socially. When a child fails at a task, he may behave in undesirable ways. He might cry, scream, strike out, or otherwise express emotions destructively. Teaching a child to proceed calmly through a frustrating task is a major challenge in helping a child develop in civil ways. For many of us adults, it remains a task that we face many times a day. Consequently, it is very important to design a child's natural environment so that he sees social situations as "successes" not "failures."

When your child fails at a task, you can help by asking the following questions. First, is the task developmentally appropriate or is it requiring the child to do something he is not ready to do? Often when we press a nonverbal child to say words they are ready to say, the child resists and frets. This is important because consistent demand to do the impossible can seriously hurt our relationship and drive the child away from interacting with just those people he needs for learning. We see many children isolate themselves from people who expect them to do more than they can do at the moment. This can be disastrous for the child's development if he interacts increasingly less with the people he needs.

Second, are you expecting your child to know what to do or do you show him how to do it? Children often do not understand what you want them to do until you carefully show them the steps it takes to do what you want. Do not assume that just because your child understands the words, he will understand what you want him to do with those words. You may also need to show him what to do if he has not followed the same instruction in a similar situation.

The power of your communication on your child's civil behavior

Parents are often unaware of the powerful influence their communication has on their child's behavior. We have observed two major findings with hundreds of parents and children: first, parents immediately talk and attend to a child when he does something undesirable; and second, when children are acting positively, often parents do not respond to them. In extensive video analyses, we found that the more a parent attends to undesirable behavior, the more the child continues doing it. Conversely, the more a parent ignores undesirable behavior, the less the child does it. We also find that the more a parent attends to spontaneous positive behaviors of a child, the more the child does them. This may seem a very simplified analysis and we realize that this is only part of the answer. However, our findings have been so consistent that we make two major recommendations to most parents: first, pay more attention to your child's positive behavior; and second, pay less attention to his undesired behavior. Once parents realize that their child will do more of the behaviors that others attend to and less that others ignore, they then have a rather simple decision to make whenever faced with abusive or undesired behavior: talk more to positive behaviors and less to negative ones. In other words, talk to the behaviors you want more of and ignore the behaviors you want less of.

While it takes parents considerable practice to ignore negative behaviors, many have found the habit very effective in reducing negative behaviors. However, ridding the child of negative behavior is not enough. We must not be satisfied only with decreased negative behavior. Surprisingly, it appears to take even more effort to attend habitually to positive behaviors than to ignore the negative ones. Parents are often so drained from their child's undesired behaviors that they often leave their child alone when he is playing constructively and positively. We are very concerned that when children act in "autistic" ways, they focus on the negative times and think of autism as a "disorder" to get rid of. We strongly encourage parents to turn their habits around and spend much more time with the child when he is positive, not to get something done or to teach something, but to convince the child that people will attend to him more when he is relaxed and productive.

Clearly, managing undesirable behavior is much more complicated than just ignoring it and attending to positive behavior. We are certainly not inferring that this is a simple solution. However, we have known many parent–child relationships that get stuck and distant when they focus on the child's undesired behaviors. It often takes parents considerable time to even believe that they can have positive times with some children with whom they constantly compete and struggle.

We have found that a mutually responsive relationship results in a steady increase in positive behaviors and a decrease in undesired behaviors in many of our children. The five responsive strategies can help a child become emotionally civil and cooperative as well as helping him be more social and communicative. When you are responsive to your child in these ways, we find children more optimistic about interacting with others. These five strategies are at the heart of the Communicating Partners program and have been presented in earlier chapters of this book where we describe how to help children play, interact, communicate, talk, and have conversations.

The key to the five strategies is that you will become much more child-oriented and less task-oriented. As you practice each strategy, you are showing your child how to behave with others in a more positive and civil way. Consequently, we hope that you look at these strategies both as something for you to learn but also as very important skills for your child to build relationships.

Much of the literature on autism and related areas revolves around negative problems. In reviewing many cases over the years, we have taken the perspective of contemporary "positive psychology" to identify the times that the children we know show the most positive behavior. So much of what we think we know comes from evaluations of children's behavior in situations that pressured them to perform according to others' wishes rather than their interests. Consequently, we seem only to have a "negative psychology" about autistic disorders; that is, a view of the destructive developmental and emotional behaviors.

However, we have taken a positive view by asking in what kind of relationships our children behave most positively. Clearly, our children are not behaving "autistic" all the time. We have found it very instructive to analyze the differences between the times a child is acting "autistic" and in antisocial ways. In over 30 years of research and clinical work, we found that when parents use five general strategies as they interacted with children, negative behaviors decreased and a more healthy social and communicative life became possible. We do not see any one strategy as a sure-fire way to improve behavior, but together they lead to more communicative relationships. Not only are these strategies for you to use, they are also powerful interactive ways for your child to develop. Rather than the traditional focus on getting rid of negative behaviors, we have found it much more successful to focus on building the child's signature strengths, skills, and values. Using the analogy of a gardener to a parent, it is not enough to get rid of the weeds, you also need to grow strong plants that will multiply and overcome the weeds.

What follows is an account of ways in which you and your child can interact to increase his positive and decrease his negative behavior.

Be balanced

One strategy to help your child be more cooperative and socially appropriate is "balancing"; that is, insuring that the child interacts fairly by taking turns with others and making sure that neither person plays a dominant or passive role. We have been amazed at the power of turn-taking in teaching a child the basic social discipline of treating others in a give-and-take manner.

To begin this, parents learn to play and communicate habitually in a turn-taking way with their child. Perhaps the hardest skill to learn is waiting silently and letting the child have his turn, interacting with any behaviors he can do. The goal for the child is to convince him that interacting can become an enjoyable "flow experience" (Csikszentmihalyi 1990) in which people interact not to accomplish anything but for the personal involvement in interacting. The child learns that communicating is not a one-way street but that it will go better if he learns to talk and then wait and listen.

One of the most disturbing behaviors of some autistic children is their constant talking. People will generally avoid a child who insists on talking and ignores what others say. Parents are often dismayed after spending years teaching their child to talk only to see that no one enjoys talking with him. The value of turn-taking is that it tells the child to act as if there were two persons in the relationships. We are concerned that with all the energy spent teaching children language there is very little effort made teaching them how to communicate in social acceptable ways.

Children learn and behave more positively when they are allowed the time and freedom to explore and participate in interactions. I still find it easy to take a child's turn if he does not respond immediately. We have found, in fact, that one way to help a child behave more positively is to play silently with him with no demands and to mainly respond when he talks. This is a powerful way to show your child that he can succeed with you and that you will give him the time.

However, your child also needs to learn to allow others to participate. When neither person is dominating the interaction, children behave more appropriately. We have found that a fundamental thing children need to learn is to participate fairly by allowing others to take their turn and by sharing in the choice of direction of the joint activity.

Be matched

We have found at least two major reasons for undesired behavior in our children: over-stimulation and impossible challenges. Autism and many developmental disabilities involve sensitivities that other children seem never to have or adapt to more easily in time. For autistic children certain kinds of stimulation—visual, tactile, auditory, linguistic, and emotional—that occur naturally in daily life are incompatible with the current demands and limits of their nervous system. This reminds us of our young autistic friend, John, who announced after a hiatus from group schooling, "I want to go back to school. My nervous system is ready now." In our honest determination to "normalize our children" we often forget that their nervous systems can tolerate daily life in different ways to typical children. Several autistic children who became verbal have told us that their nervous systems just could not tolerate many sights, sounds, and touches that were totally acceptable to their peers. Donna Williams describes many instances of sensory overload that prevented her from even thinking clearly, let alone communicating effectively (Williams 1994, 1996, 1998). In fact she even refers to the world at times as a "stimulus hell" which often takes her away from her life alone—a life which she often experiences as a "stimulus heaven."

Related to the over-stimulation problem is the problem of facing children with impossible tasks. One solution for over-stimulation and impossible tasks is the general strategy of matching. Matching simply means that we try to insure that our child is faced with stimuli and tasks that he is able to tolerate and to do. On a personal level, matching means that you will act and communicate in ways the child can try to do. This will mean that you will act like him at times and then show him a feasible next step at other times. Matching your child increases the likelihood that he will interact with you more spontaneously and not only in directive teaching situations.

The second reason matching is so important is that children often act undesirably when faced with a partner or a task that is too difficult for them. When your child is becoming social it is other persons who are the critical tasks for the child to negotiate. When adults act and communicate in ways that are impossible for the child to try to do, that person will become an impossible task for the child's social and emotional development. When you realize that every interaction is a developmental task for your child, you will understand that the more your behavior matches your child's ability and interest, the more he will develop with you. Even autistic children do want to develop and succeed in life, and when that is thwarted, they are likely to behave undesirably, just as we adults occasionally do when frustrated. The more we match our spontaneous behavior and demands to what the child can do and to his interests, the more successes he will have and the better our relationships with him will be in the long run.

Be responsive

Respond more to positive than negative behavior. Barbara Mitchell, a mother involved in Communicating Partners with her son Mark for 13 years, now communicates with many parents of autistic spectrum children. Recently, she sent me a message about improving children's behavior: "I think the most important key to improving behavior is for adults to focus on more emotionally positive, matched, and balanced interactions that follow the child's lead and interests. More positive interactions DO help improve behavior. I really believe that." Barbara is also the mother of seven remarkably civil and enjoyable children, especially Mark.

The more we interact in positive emotional ways, visibly enjoying each other, the fewer children misbehave. While it may seem too simple a solution, we repeatedly find it effective. But, it is not at all simple. Interacting positively with an autistic child means finding positive behaviors your child does have and not focusing, as we all easily do, on his negative or undesired behaviors. In our anxiety and concern about "fighting" autism, we often attend far too much to "autistic" behaviors and far too little to the many positive behaviors that can replace the undesired ones.

As in the story of John and Jodi earlier, you can see how John kept up his annoying behavior when his mother responded to it. She then learned that when she ignored his negative behavior and spent more positive, playful time with him, his undesired behavior decreased markedly.

Many researchers in early socio-emotional development (Koschanska 1997; Maccoby 1999) have found repeatedly that mutually responsive interaction between parent and child predicts much more civil behavior of children at later years. When young children and their mothers were mutually responsive to each other in positive ways, the children developed more of a "conscience" by abiding by the social rules and concerns of the mother. They found that it is not enough for parents to respond to children, but that the children need to respond back. Thus, when we teach parents the importance of responding, we emphasize that it is mutual back-and-forth responding by both persons that is critical.

Parents need to learn that whenever they respond to their child, that response may well reinforce or increase whatever the child was doing at the moment. Parents need to understand how important their casual responses are to their child. I spend considerable effort with parents trying to show them that their everyday casual communication is much more influential on their children than the times they are deliberately teaching the child.

We encourage parents to think of their attention as if it were a powerful fertilizer to their child's behavior and, as with flowers, the more one fertilizes them the more they grow. Many parents learn to support positive behaviors by treating their child's behavior in two ways: some behaviors are flowers you want to grow and some are weeds you want to eliminate. Then, when a child does something, parents can ask themselves: Do I want more or less of this behavior? Then, if they want more, they should respond to it, and if they want less, they should not respond to it.

In our experience, few parents value how important their daily interactions are to their child's civil and behavior development and to the kind of ethical and considerate person the child can become. However, when these parents see that their child increases positive behaviors and decreases negative ones, when they attend more to the positive than the negative, they are more successful in helping their children behave.

Contrary to some popular opinion, ignoring a child's negative behaviors will not damage the child if parents are also frequently playing with him during positive times. Many parents feel they will hurt the child by ignoring him, especially if the child is delayed in developing. We have found just the opposite. Rather than hurting the child, ignoring negative behaviors actually helps the child learn right from wrong and develop stronger moral character. Responding to negative behavior actually teaches that negative behavior will work. This can be disastrous for a child with delays because he already has trouble in relationships. Once parents deeply understand the power of their responses, they come to realize they have an ethical responsibility not to encourage negative behaviors by attending to them in any way.

Share control

Children appear to behave more positively when they have control over their immediate environment. The undesired behaviors often arise when that control is thwarted. Unfortunately, interacting in the world constantly involves giving up some control to your partner, at least by waiting for him to take his turn in a conversation. Again, this may seem like saying the obvious, but for autistic children relinquishing and sharing control with others is a fundamentally difficult task and a frequent source of reported behavior problems.

Learning to give and take in social relationships requires that parents carefully help their child to self-regulate their behavior socially by learning that it takes two to have an interaction. Sharing control also requires that you will have to limit your habit of questioning and directing the child. Even when the child seems unable to engage with you, we recommend that you give him time to do what he can do and accept that.

> Kenny was six. He had considerable language but used it rarely to communicate with others. We observed him with his mother for about 20 minutes. She was watching him play with his cars and trucks. Of the total verbal interaction, she dominated over 90 percent of the talking. She asked Kenny an average of 20 questions per minute, which took him from his toys. He began to interact but then avoided her and resisted when she brought him back. He frequently refused to comply with her controls. She never joined in his activities

or gave him any sense that he could have effects on her. Clearly the agenda for the interaction verbally was hers; he had little chance to talk about his ideas and when he did she did not respond to them but usually posed another question. She considered him resistant and reported that this habit was a real behavior problem in school. He was getting the reputation of an "oppositional" child.

As we played with Kenny, we let him take the lead and at least half the time we responded to his actions and words with ones that followed his lead. Rather than asking questions, we made comments instead that built on what he was doing. We showed him how to talk about his play rather than testing him with questions. For example, when he pushed his fire truck, rather than saying "Is that your fire truck?" as his mother had, we pushed the truck back to him and said "Fire truck's going fast" or "Let's go help the fire." We found that he stayed talking in a back-and-forth manner when we reduced our control with questions and simply gave him ways to continue the conversation. After a few months of practice Kenny's mother was surprised to see that when she stopped her questions and let him have at least half the control in interactions, he began talking more and resisting her much less. His oppositional behavior decreased in situations where he was allowed to have some but not all control—in interactions, both in terms of the activity and the content of the talking.

Be emotionally playful

We have seen time and again with our children that the more playful and enjoyable the interaction is, the better the child behaves, cooperates, and stays learning with others. While this may seem obvious, it is often difficult to find ways to have enjoyable stress-free interactions with autistic children. Parents have found that to be more enjoyable to your child, you first need to understand that the more fun you have with him, the more he will interact and communicate. Often parents are so drained by the task of "curing" or teaching or managing their child that they take little time simply to enjoy the child in any ways they can. Imagine having an acquaintance that interacted with you only to change you or get you to do things their way! If you absolutely had to interact with him, you might do so but it is unlikely the two of you would become friends. No matter how much your child can learn, we have a strong belief that the best way to be a learner is to have positive relationships with others—in other words, friends.

Consequently, the fifth strategy to help a child become socially behaved and civil is for you to become emotionally enjoyable with him. We find repeatedly that the more playful and childlike you are, the longer the child will stay and learn. Our children must learn that people can be enjoyable. And to be enjoyable, people have to respond sensitively to the child as he may not be as they want him to be. Many of our children avoid people when they experience failures, demands, or criticisms, thus losing all chances to learn socially.

A fundamental goal for many developing children is simply to initiate and interact more frequently with people. In order for children to learn and develop they need to see people as enjoyable and reinforcing to be with and not just as tools to satisfy their needs.

Case example: Molly

Molly was a three-year-old girl whose family members were concerned that she was emotionally erratic and extremely uncooperative. Testing was difficult with Molly but a psychologist estimated her development from parent interviews and observations, as follows: cognition, 12 months; communication, 14 months; social–emotional functioning, 4 months; self-regulation, 4 months; motor functioning, 30 months; adaptive functioning, 12 months.

Molly presented the following profile.

Cognition

Molly rarely stayed in social play or modeled others' behavior. She did show she could learn from others, but only rarely and at a later time. She initiated activities occasionally but only briefly. She did have a few favorite games by herself that showed she was cognitively capable of creating and experimenting. In her rare calm moments, she pursued a few problem-solving events, but she usually gave up in a tantrum when frustrated.

Communication

Rarely did Molly attend to others or join in activities with them. She was a loner, except when she wanted something. She made many speech sounds and some word attempts, but more as self-stimulation than communication. She intentionally communicated occasionally to get her needs met and resist social contact. She showed little or no interest in conversations.

Social–emotional functioning

Molly occasionally showed attachment to her mother, but mainly on her own terms and not in response to others. She appeared not to trust many people. She showed little or no empathy and no concern when she clearly bothered others with her resistance and violence. Molly was almost never cooperative and she showed little self-regulation in that her acting out often lasted up to an hour.

Motivation

Molly seemed to be interested only in her own chosen activities and in doing them alone. She rarely persisted in an activity. She enjoyed playing alone with dolls and picture books, as she smiled and sang to herself at times. While it was difficult to determine how competent she felt, she insisted on controlling her environment, which suggested a low level of confidence.

While Molly had marked delays in cognitive, communicative, and adaptive functioning, her family was mainly concerned with her social–emotional functioning, specifically her resistance to people. They were discouraged with the struggle that taking care of her had become. Often they were too fatigued to spend positive learning times with her. Consequently, the program focused initially on social–emotional functioning to increase positive learning between Molly and her family. We discussed several topics to help the family understand Molly's behavior problems as a function of her other delays. We explored the reasons for her behavior while we helped her develop a trusting attachment with them. We discussed why we were postponing direct teaching of communication and cognitive skills. We explained that when she became social and emotionally available, she would be ready for the other goals. The first pivotal goals included trusting others, joint attention and activity, and cooperation.

To build a trusting attachment with Molly, we discussed several topics related to the importance of calm and trusting relations for learning. We also practiced playing in Molly's world, illustrating the messages in the topics.

To address her cognitive development, we focused on teaching social play, which is critical to both social–emotional function and cognition. Molly's parents said life was generally a struggle and that when the girl was calm they left her alone, not wanting to disturb her and raise more problems. Consequently, they played very little with her in positive ways. After discussing at length the importance of enjoyable, trusting play times, we demonstrated ways to play in Molly's world in a parallel way. We showed them how to be available and not intrusive. We practiced several strategies over three months. We showed the family how to play frequently together and to do it in a parallel way, mirroring her behavior but not demanding anything in particular. Our intention here was to have Molly allow others into her world without resistance and rage. The family then learned that when they imitated her actions and communications, she attended to them more.

The parents also learned to observe Molly silently to determine her interests and to discover the situations that helped her to respond. Previously they believed that their responsibility was to teach her many skills for school. We spent considerable time helping them shift from the role of directive teachers to play partners who were animated and interesting and who acted in ways that Molly could try to do. We took care to spend a full session on only one topic and no more than two strategies at a time. While many of the strategies may sound like common sense, they are often difficult to do since they involve changing the parents' expectations of both themselves and the child. In this case, they thought they should be teaching her to get ready for school and we were trying to help them become emotionally attached play partners.

After nine months of careful and persistent play in Molly's world, her parents reported that she was initiating and occasionally staying in back-and-forth play with much less resistance. While she still insisted on the play going her way, she was spontaneously joining them in daily activities, at times on their terms. The progress was not rapid. The family learned to ignore many of her tantrums and at the end of the year her outbursts took less than 10 percent of the time they did at the outset of our work together.

Molly was now imitating others and was occasionally using her words to communicate. Previously, she had only talked to herself and never in response to others. Molly's mother had also changed in marked ways. She no longer thought that her job was to be Molly's teacher but rather to help her enjoy being with people. She came to respond much more to the positive things Molly did than to the problems, which had been her habit. While she learned to be animated and playful, she also learned to discipline Molly and gently but firmly insist on cooperation. She did this by going past the girl's resistance without discussion and continuing interactions even when Molly was not cooperative. Before the program, her mother was afraid she would further delay the child if she insisted on cooperation; now she had learned just the opposite. The most beneficial change seemed to be that Molly had become more interested in pleasing others and in doing things with them. After this nine-month period, I certainly found Molly much more enjoyable to be with and her teacher, who was part of the program, reported that Molly was beginning to enjoy learning with other children whom she had previously ignored or dominated.

Developmental guide: your child's civil behavior

What your child needs to do to become a self-respecting and acceptable social partner

Cooperation

1. Follows directions that are developmentally appropriate
2. Cooperates willingly without being coerced
3. Cooperates in activities that fit his development
4. Complies willingly but not in a rote or passive manner
5. Responds to others' wishes and behaviors as well as his own
6. Shows more voluntary cooperation than mindless compliance
7. Maintains his own interests and motivations as he cooperates
8. Maintains his own integrity while cooperating

Trust and confidence

1. Approaches people without fear
2. Responds to people without fear or resistance
3. Interacts without needing to have full control
4. Shows comfort and relaxation with people
5. Avoids people who show little acceptance

Civil behavior

1. Treats others with respect
2. Treats self with respect
3. Treats others with kindness
4. Learns from consequences to his behavior
5. Regulates his emotions reasonably

Self-regulation

1. Controls his impulses and emotions reasonably
2. Expresses emotions effectively and without excess
3. Checks himself when beginning to act out or lose control
4. Tolerates frustration without losing control

5. Calms himself when anxious or disrupted

6. Tolerates transitions without great difficulty

7. Recovers easily when upset

Emotionally appropriate behavior

1. Asserts self without aggression

2. Shows humor

3. Shows negative emotion appropriately

4. Shows postive emotion appropriately

5. Accepts affection

6. Shows affection in socially acceptable ways

7. Recovers easily when upset

8. Tolerates transitions easily

Emotional attachment

1. Develops attachments with responsive people

2. Avoids attachments with people who are not responsive or accepting

3. Attachments are flexible and not obsessive

4. Seeks comfort in times of distress or anxiety

5. Shows similar emotional patterns as his life partners

Empathy

1. Shows concern for others

2. Is affected by others' emotions

3. Listens to others

4. Actively tries to please others

5. Actively helps or supports others

6. Takes others' perspective/point of view

Possible problems

1. Disregards others' feelings or ideas

2. Talks in rude or insensitive ways

3. Interrupts others

4. Talks loudly or otherwise inappropriately

5. Dominates conversations

6. Abuses others verbally

7. Abuses others physically

8. Shows little emotion

9. Shows excessive emotion

10. Fails to learn from consequences

11. Ignores others or acts as if they do not exist

12. Fears contact with people

13. Makes attachments to people who are abusive or not accepting

14. Shows little sustained attachment to people

Developmental guide: five strategies to improve your child's civil and appropriate behavior

The following are ways to help your child improve his civil and appropriate behavior

- The goal is for your child to communicate in civil and socially acceptable ways.
- Start with the strategies below that come most easily for you
- Try one or two as you play with your child, then watch how he responds
- Keep doing the ones that work with your child
- If certain ones seem uncomfortable, do not push yourself. There are many different ways to be effective
- Try new strategies when little is happening with your child
- Determine success by what results in less negative and more positive behaviors
- The goal is for your child to treat others with respect and appreciation
- Be patient and feel energized by each new positive behavior. However small it seems, it is important for your child

Balance

1. Avoid doing much more than your child in an interaction
2. Wait for your child to take a turn
3. Wait silently and with clear expectation for him to respond
4. Gently insist on taking your turn
5. Be sure neither of you dominates the interaction
6. Explain the "50/50" rule: when interacting, try hard to do no more than half of the talking
7. Think of communicating as more a "give and take" than just giving information or directions
8. Be sure your "turn" responds to what the child just said or did
9. When the child dominates the interaction, silently terminate it briefly; do not support excessive behavior that will limit your child in society

Match

1. The more you act like your child the more he will cooperate
2. The more you talk in ways your child can try, the more he will respond
3. Evaluate your child's environments for over-stimulation
4. Understand and reduce environments that disrupt your child
5. Understand and increase environments in which your child behaves well
6. Define "good behavior" as positive interactions, not only as "not doing anything wrong"
7. Change your child's environments so he interacts more positively
8. Be sure to give your child tasks he can succeed with
9. Try doing only one thing at a time when playing with your child

Respond

1. Talk to behaviors you want more of
2. Do not talk to behaviors you want less of
3. Regularly ask yourself: Do I want this behavior to continue?
4. Look away when your child is doing something you want to decrease
5. Do not talk to your child when taking him to time-out
6. Remind yourself that your attention is like a fertilizer to your child
7. Teach your child's partners to attend to the positive and ignore the negative

Share control

1. Allow your child to control your interactions at least half the time
2. Follow his ideas and actions at least half the time
3. Be more responsive than directive; that is, respond supportively more than controlling in a directive way
4. Limit your questions to necessary ones and less than 20 percent of your talk with him
5. Make sure that he allows you to have some control
6. Comment on what your child does or says, then wait for a response

7. Make your interactions more a playful flow than a task

8. Avoid pressing your child for specific answers more than 20 percent of the time

9. Teach the child by example that he can have successes in conversation

Be emotionally playful

1. Genuinely enter into your child's activities of interest

2. Play with your child when he is acting positive

3. Comfort your child when he is genuinely fearful

4. Make sure to discipline quietly and quickly

5. Learn to read your child's emotions

6. Show him that you genuinely enjoy him

7. Learn to "read" when he is available

8. Build on his "available" times by joining him in them

9. Respond to the positive things your child does

10. Ignore the undesired things your child does

11. Avoid judging your child's behavior

12. Invite your child into activities you enjoy

13. Understand your child's fears and limitations

14. Reduce stress in your interactions

15. Be more concerned with the interaction continuing than "right" answers

16. Tolerate your child's play even when you do not understand it

17. Be animated and more interesting than your child's distractions

18. Comfort your child when he is distressed

19. Show your child clear boundaries to abusive behavior

Parents' experiences using Communicating Partners to influence their child's civil behavior

Does zero tolerance work?

"If you have 'zero tolerance' for your child's behaviors, he may come to have 'zero tolerance' for you. I worked hard for several months to get Sean to keep his hands from flying, his feet from tapping, and his body from gyrating. It had become a full-time job and he was staying away from me more and more. I had been taught to have 'zero tolerance' for his self-stimulating behaviors because the belief was that he could not learn while he was doing it. Then I learned that was simply not true. Sean could learn many things while he still did these things that actually seemed to calm him. What I found worked best was to pay more attention to the positive things he did and ignore the less productive ones. And, voila! He did less and less of the ones that disturbed so many people. I came to know that if he was going to communicate he had to be with people more. And if people were going to have 'zero tolerance' for certain behaviors by suppressing them, he was going to have 'zero tolerance' for being with them. And then all social learning is lost." (Amy)

I thought Mario had unreasonable fears

"Mario is 12 and has been afraid much of the time since he was two. When this happens he has done all kinds of undesirable behaviors. I have tried many ways to explain to him that his fears of specific things (open doors, dad leaving, changes in routines) were not real and that he would not be hurt. Then I realized I was wrong. Those fears were real and they were hurting him in many ways. He lived in a world that was so strange to him. Then I realized that when I am in a strange place, I often feel afraid and stand back at first. Then I realized that most of the time Mario was in very strange places. He lived in his head but he was constantly confronted by our 'real' world that simply was not yet 'real' for him.

When things got too strange for him, I learned to stop all the demands and just get into Mario's world. The more I did this by being silent, responding to him, and acting in ways he could tolerate, the more I got to understand him and see that he had real reasons for his fears that I could control. Just by quietly being in his world, I was able to redesign the outside world so he could function again. Now he reminds me of times he was afraid of things and felt compelled to do things that he remembers as just memories now without shame or guilt." (Elaine)

Mario had a wonderful personality and I didn't want to lose it

"However much Mario drove us crazy with his moving and talking to himself and touching everything in sight, I didn't want him to be a different person. We enjoyed his personality, and much of the bothersome behavior seemed to allow him to be himself. The way we finally got him to be with us was to join him in what he did, however silly it may have seemed. When we did not join him, we lost him and became of no use to him at all. This took some years, but now at 11 he has great self-esteem and is having conversations that really consider what the other person wants to talk about. That was a big change but only after we kept him longer in interactions on what he wanted.

I saw his personality and I did not and still do not want to mess up a good thing. Mario has some peers who behave much better but do not enjoy people the way Mario does. I'd rather for now that he is a charmer than an obedient but unhappy child. Most people always enjoyed his personality and I did not want him to lose that personality." (Dave)

My nervous system is ready for that now

"We had to learn from John what environments he could function in and which were just too much for him. Eventually when he was about nine, he came to verbalize something that helped us all a lot. He would say 'my nervous system cannot take that now,' for example when we planned to go shopping, or 'my nervous system is ready for that now' as when he announced he was ready to go back to a crowded school." (Jodi)

Avoid making the world impossible for your child

"As his grandmother, I always knew that Jeremy was intelligent. So when he was still not talking at three, we started teaching him all kinds of things for school. The more we taught, the more he stayed away from us, even running when he saw us approaching with a 'teaching tool.' Then you showed us that we were busy teaching him things that were impossible and that he did not care about. Then once we began responding to anything he did and entered his play, he begun interacting much more. We used to think he did not want to be with people and then we discovered that he just did not want to be with 'impossible' people. Our first big step was to make him feel successful doing anything he could, but now doing it with people, that is what was new. We now know that it is more important that he becomes socially aware than that he knows facts that he will not use with other people." (Pat)

Who says autistic children cannot be empathetic?

Nick was isolated and afraid of most people until he was about ten. He was very sensitive and learned to talk about feelings with his parents a great deal. When he was 12 he was in a foot race with an obese boy who never succeeded in sports. Nick's mother, Ann, was rooting for Nick and then she saw him slow down to let the boy catch up with him and they tied in the race. When Ann asked him why he slowed down he said, "Well, Bill never wins anything and I know how he feels. Did you see how happy he was?" Who says autistic children cannot be empathetic?

Part 3

Following Your Child's Development from Isolation to Civil Conversation

12

The Adult–Child Relationship Map for Assessment and Planning

If you want to change something, the first thing you have to do is…to see it exactly the way it is.

Often a child is perceived and treated in terms of a test score, like an IQ, or his chronological age, or a diagnosis, like autism, Down syndrome, or attention disorder. People then assume from the label that the child can or cannot do certain things without actually observing him. It is easy to fall into the trap of expecting the child to act or not act in certain ways because of a label: for example, because his tested IQ is 70, or he is three and a half years old, or he is called "autistic." Then many problems occur. People respond to the child according to their expectations because of the score, age, or diagnosis rather than in terms of his behavior. They do not respond to what the child can do but to what we think he "is." Fundamentally they are not responding to who the child actually is. We frequently hear statements like these:

- "He cannot do that—he's autistic."

- "People with that IQ will never get married."

- "She will probably never talk since she's nonverbal and five years old."

These judgments are often made without observing the child in his most supportive relationships and in situations that are comfortable for him. Professionals frequently focus on what the child is not doing or what he is doing "inappropriately." They do not usually build upon the signature strengths that every child has. Traditional approaches often decide what a child needs by evaluating the child alone and not considering the natural influences his life partners and living environments have. Communicating Partners is based on the conviction that a child does not develop alone. He develops in great part as a function of the environments he lives in and the kind of relationships he has with people.

Evaluating the child alone can harm the child's development and discourage his natural teachers—parents—if it results in focusing on the child's perceived deficits and ignoring the child's natural successes that are the key to his development. It can also set the child up for discouraging failures when we expect behaviors for which he is not developmentally ready.

We also too easily judge as "wrong" many behaviors that are appropriate for the child's current development and useful for him. We need to understand that the best way to help a child change is to accept him and effectively respond to what he can do. Demanding that a child do the impossible discourages him from interacting, feeling competent, and developing as he can. Then he often does not even try to do what he can do.

The Adult–Child Relationship Map (ARM) helps you see a child for who he is, what he can do, and exactly where he is now developing. When we connect with a child precisely where he is, he will learn best with us. Unless we meet the child where he actually is, it will be like throwing a ball to a batter outside the range of his bat and then concluding that the batter was not able to hit the ball.

The ARM is the result of over 30 years of clinical research with more than 600 children with language delays. The children ranged from infancy through adolescence. Most were nonverbal or pre-conversational. The diagnoses included "late talking," autism, PDD and Asperger's syndrome, Down syndrome, motor disorders, seizures disorders, cerebral palsy, hearing impairment, and other conditions affecting communication.

The research was conducted at the Nisonger Center of the Ohio State University, the Family Child Learning Center in Ohio, Case Western Reserve University, the Communicating Partners Center, and the Logan County (Ohio) Program for Developmental Disabilities. The research focused on studying children in the contexts of family and classroom interactions.

The major research questions were:

- What do children need before they speak habitually?

- What strategies help children communicate both preverbally and verbally?

- What are common barriers to learning to communicate?

- What are the specific communication problems of late-talking children and ones with autism and Down syndrome?

- What interaction skills are necessary for social use of language?

- How does a child's play life influence communication development?

- What roles can parents play in helping children communicate at home?

- How can children learn to communicate in group settings?

- What are the most effective kinds of social interaction for fostering communication?

The ARM introduces you to the inner workings of a child so you can genuinely connect with him and not expect too little or too much. Many parents and professionals are not aware of the many little steps a child needs to make as he is becoming more social and communicative. Speech and language do not just "happen" like hair and height seem to grow; speech and language come from many subtle skills of the child, of which we are often unaware. Speech and language also come from the ways we interact and communicate with children. If we do not join in the child's world where he is, we are unlikely to help him develop.

The fundamental purpose of the ARM is to help you enter your child's world so that you both develop communicative relationships where each of you interacts reciprocally or "in synch" with each other. The ARM recognizes that your child will not learn to be social and communicative on his own; he will do so by living an interactive life with people who join his world of sensations and actions and gradually lead him into their world of thought and language.

When you use the ARM, you will get to know the child in terms of five of the lives that contribute to having full social and communicative relationships: interaction, nonverbal communication, social language, and civil-emotional behavior. When you accurately see where the child is in each of these five worlds, you will more easily connect with him and help him grow.

Each of the five separate scales includes a guide for strategies both adults and children need to learn to help the child become as fully communicative as he can. You can use the strategies sections to discover how you are now interacting with your child. You will also be able to identify a few strategies you can begin to change so your child stays interacting and communicating with you more. You will then have a map to guide you to use strategies that many parents and professionals have used effectively to help children communicate. You will learn how to make the five strategies a natural part of your relationship with your child: balance, match, responding, sharing control, and enjoyable play.

When you use the environment form of the ARM, you will learn how life situations may influence your child and how changes in his environment may help your child become more social and communicative. Many environments that typical children may adapt to easily will be disruptive for your child. The form alerts you to the kinds of changes that you can make to allow your child to become social and communicate more easily.

Use the ARM to identify the child's current strengths so that you can begin interacting in ways that give him successes. A primary assumption of Communicating Partners is that children develop to the degree they have effective interactions with life partners.

Each child deserves to learn and each child can learn. Each child will learn best when his life partners respond to what and how he is learning at the moment. The ARM is concerned that your child becomes a "spontaneous social learner," not just a compliant student, and that means that he learns whatever he can while interacting naturally with people. Many children with differences such as autism, attention disorders, Down syndrome, or other conditions learn on their own or when directed but do not socialize and communicate with people. Consequently, they miss out on the learning that other children do in frequent daily interactions.

The ARM is a practical tool to help your child become more social and communicative. By using the ARM, you will learn about your child in three ways:

1. You will identify what your child is doing now that can help him become more social and communicative.

2. You will learn specific strategies to help your child be more social and communicative.

3. You will discover how your child's living environments can be helping or hindering his social and communicative development.

What are the underlying assumptions of the ARM?

1. Children learn to communicate in their daily relationships with people more than in teaching lessons.

2. Late-talking children and ones with delays often interact much less than typical children.

3. Consequently, the first and most important task is to help the child become a social and communicative person.

4. Every child with delays has signature strengths that are the best source of his development.

5. Even when the child has cognitive delays, the most effective path to helping him is through increasing his social and communicative life.

6. Children have a great deal of work to do before they talk; preverbal skills are critical for sustained development.

7. The way a child's life partners interact and communicate with him is a powerful influence on how the child becomes social and communicative.

8. There is now research-based evidence to support certain adult strategies that help children be more social and communicative. The ARM provides a map of these strategies.

9. While parents and other adults are certainly not responsible for a child's delays, they can do much to help him build the relationships needed to progress.

10. Parents and any life partner can learn to help a child be more social and communicative.

What can the ARM do for you?

1. Help you to know your child more intimately.

2. Help you identify and focus on the current strengths that are the source of your child's progress.

3. Learn what children need to do to become social and communicative.

4. Learn how important your behavior is for your child's development.

5. Learn about common problems that can interfere with a child's development.

6.   Learn what you and others can do specifically to help your child be more social and communicative.

7.   Help you and professionals decide on developmentally effective treatment goals.

8.   Help insure that your child's treatment goals lead to success.

9.   Help you monitor your child's progress over time.

10. Help evaluate the success of treatment or education.

11. Show you how complex it is for your child to become social and communicative.

12. Alert you to respond to many child behaviors that you may not believe are important for your child's social and communicative development.

13. Provide you with a long-term map to guide your child's journey to a social and communicative life.

14. Help you know what to expect from your child, so that you are expecting what is possible for him.

15. Help you build confidence in interacting with your child in ways that help him.

16. Provide practical guides you can give to anyone interacting frequently with your child.

17. Inform you about how your child's daily environments may be helping or hindering his development.

18. Provide you and professionals with a way to teach others how to communicate effectively with your child.

19. Provide you with home-based information that you can use in working with professionals.

Who is the ARM for?

The ARM is for any person who is developing social and communicative skills, including typically developing children, late-talking children, children on the autistic spectrum, children with organically based conditions like Down syndrome and others, and children with emotional and behavioral concerns. It is also for any other person who has yet to develop habitual and positive conversational relationships.

Who can use the ARM?

Any person can use ARM who is involved in the social and communicative development of a child. The ARM has been developed and tested with hundreds of parents, therapists, and teachers. Someone who knows the child across many natural situations will most validly use the ARM. It is not to be used as a traditional test but for observation and interview. In addition to providing information on the child, it is also a teaching tool for educating people about the range of behaviors in the child and his partners that influences the child's social and communicative development. Consequently, it can be used by anyone teaching students or professionals about child development.

How was the ARM developed and tested?

The ARM is the result of over 30 years of research and clinical work with over 1000 families of children and adolescents learning to socialize and communicate. The children included typically developing children as well as ones with developmental concerns such as autism, attention disorder, Down syndrome, apraxia and other neurological speech conditions, emotional and behavioral issues, and a variety of late-talking children.

The child and adult components were selected in several ways:

1. They were the results of several studies of pivotal behaviors that children need to be more social and communicative.

2. They were the results of several studies about which adult strategies are successful in helping children socialize and communicate.

3. They result from comprehensive literature searches on early child development from social, cognitive, and behavioral perspectives.

4. They result from the analyses of over 100 parent-based treatment programs.

5. They result from several years using the model in schools and therapy programs.

Will the ARM tell me what my child should be doing at certain chronological ages?

No. The ARM is based on each child's individual development. Its purpose is to identify where the child is performing now and to direct you to his next developmental steps. The ARM operates more on the notion of "personal best" than "peer competition." That is, the ARM proposes that the most effective goals for a child are ones that derive from his current strengths and not from what children of the same chronological age can do.

For how young a child is the ARM useful?

The ARM addresses the earliest forms of social and communicative behavior. Consequently it is useful for children from birth to those with a full conversational life. Since the ARM is a guide for the behavior of parents and other adults, it is designed for any adult who wants to strengthen her communicative relationships. In fact the ARM has been used to educate teens and expectant parents as to what to expect and how to interact with future children.

For how old a child or adult is the ARM useful?

The ARM is not age-dependent. It is useful for any person who has yet to develop a full conversational life. The ARM has been developed with many older children identified with Asperger's syndrome, where conversational and civil behavior are of paramount concern.

How can the ARM be used in the home?

Parents can use the ARM as a developmental map to follow their child's progress and to identify where to focus their responsive strategies. Parents use the adult form to guide them in fine-tuning their interactions to the child's abilities and interests. They use the environmental form as a way to evaluate the child's learning environments and make changes to increase the likelihood of his learning to be social and communicative within them. The ARM can also be a record of the child's progress for comparison with his progress in professional settings. The ARM can provide information on the degree of success of treatment programs.

How can the ARM be used in a school setting?

The ARM has been used in schools in the following ways:

1. To monitor a child's progress.
2. To teach school staff effective ways to communicate with children.

3. To assist in program planning, such as individual education plans (IEPs).

4. To educate professionals into the preverbal stages of development.

5. To assist in designing learning environments that address the many interferences that can occur in educational settings.

6. To provide an evaluation of the effects of education programs.

What training is required to use the ARM?

The ARM can help anyone observe a child comprehensively without training. The Communicating Partners text goes into considerable detail about the rationale for, and use of, the developmental processes.

What do you do with the information from the ARM?

1. Identify your child's strengths, which are the first behaviors you can respond to.

2. Understand what your child needs to develop.

3. Follow your child's progress over time.

4. Identify your child's successes and use them as motivators for yourself.

5. Learn strategies you can use that others have successfully used with children.

6. Identify developmentally appropriate goals for treatment and education.

7. Learn what to expect of your child next.

8. Collaborate with teachers and professionals to insure your child's treatment fits his needs.

9. Allow you to be an "informed" parent who can advocate for your child's needs.

There are five separate developmental guides and related stratgey sheets to address the five critical stages of communication development. The Environment Form (see Chapter 13) identifies potential barriers to your child's communication and helps you make changes in your child's world that will help him communicate more. The Interactive Map is a practical tool to guide your daily interactions with your child by selecting child behaviors and adult strategies from the ARM.

Stage 1: your child's interactive life
What your child needs to do to become interactive

Social play
1. Notices the presence of others
2. Allows people in his presence
3. Initiates contact with people
4. Responds to others' contacts
5. Joins in others' activities
6. Seeks out or invites others for contact
7. Prefers being with people than alone
8. Plays parallel with people
9. Plays reciprocally or back and forth with people
10. Stays voluntarily in interactions
11. Actively keeps others interacting with him

Imitation and modeling
1. Tries to act in ways others do
2. Imitates others immediately
3. Imitates others at a later time
4. Imitates others' emotions
5. Learns by observing others
6. Imitates actions
7. Imitates sounds or words
8. Imitates from media (e.g. TV, video, computer)
9. Plays alone in ways he has seen others play
10. Invites others to imitate him

Reciprocal turn-taking
1. Plays in a give-and-take manner
2. Takes turns with actions
3. Takes turns with sounds

4.   Takes turns with words

5.   Waits for other to take a turn

6.   Stays in 2–4 turn exchanges

7.   Stays in extended turn-taking (more than 4 turns)

8.   Offers or signals others to take their turn

9.   Responds appropriately to partner's turns

10. Stays interacting longer when requested

Possible problems

1.   Ignores people

2.   Avoids or resists people

3.   Prefers being alone to being with people

4.   Rarely acts in ways others act

5.   Appears self-absorbed

6.   Rarely takes turns with others

7.   Dominates interactions with others

8.   Plays a passive, nonresponsive role in interactions

9.   Reacts emotionally when others interact with him

Five strategies to help your child be social

The following are ways you can help your child to interact more with people.

- Select first the ones that come most easily for you.
- Increase them and watch how your child responds.
- If certain ones seem uncomfortable, do not push yourself.
- There are many different ways to be effective.
- Try new strategies when little is happening with your child.
- Determine your success by observing your child interacting and enjoying people more.
- The goal is for your child to interact with you more frequently and for longer times in a gradual process.
- Be patient and feel energized by every new interaction.
- It may seem small for you but it can be a big step for your child.

Be balanced

1. Do about as much as your child in play together
2. Do one thing then wait for your child to respond
3. Take turns with actions
4. Take turns with sounds
5. Take turns with words
6. Allow silence so your child can respond
7. Act reciprocally; respond meaningfully to what your child does
8. Insist on taking your turn if your child dominates the time
9. Keep turn-taking exchanges going a little longer
10. Interact more like a ping-pong game than darts

Be matched

1. Act in ways your child can try to do
2. Communicate nonverbally in ways your child can do
3. Talk in ways your child can try to do
4. Communicate about your child's activity
5. Show your child a next developmental step
6. Expect behaviors your child can do
7. Avoid expecting the impossible

Be responsive

1. Accept your child's actions as meaningful to him
2. Psycically join into your child's activity
3. Respond to your child's actions
4. Respond to your child's sounds and other nonverbal communications
5. Understand what is meaningful for your child
6. Respond without judgement or criticism
7. Act like your child, then wait for a response

Share control

1. Make sure your child has clear effects on you
2. Change your behavior until you have effects on your child
3. Share the agenda or direction of the interaction
4. Make the interaction more playful than task-oriented
5. Follow the child's lead about half the time
6. Take the lead about half the time
7. Limit directions and commands to less than 20 percent of your behavior
8. Limit questions to less than 20 percent of your talk

Be emotionally playful

1. Find ways to enjoy your child
2. Make sure your child has successes
3. Make interactions relaxed and unstressful
4. Accept what the child is doing and join his activity
5. Interact in flexible not rigid ways
6. Be animated
7. Be more interesting than the child's distractions
8. Play in the way your child plays
9. Do more of whatever behavior gets your child's attention
10. Show your child you genuinely enjoy playing
11. Express affection
12. Laugh and smile authentically
13. Touch your child warmly
14. Comfort your child during distress

Stage 2: your child's nonverbal communication

What your child needs to become communicative

Nonvocal communication

1. Communicates with facial movements
2. Communicates with hand movements
3. Communicates with body language
4. Communicates with natural signs, pointing, or gestures
5. Communicates with learned signs
6. Communicates with pictures or symbols
7. Communicates with touches

Vocal communication

1. Makes sounds to himself
2. Responds to others with sounds
3. Initiates communication with sounds
4. Makes nonspeech sounds
5. Makes conventional speech sounds
6. Takes turns with sounds
7. Makes strings of sounds
8. Imitates others' sounds
9. Makes unusual sounds
10. Yells or screams
11. Changes his sounds to be more like others' sounds

Reasons your child communicates

1. To get his needs met
2. To show affection
3. To express emotions
4. To protest
5. To get attention
6. To accompany play

7. To imitate
8. To get information

Receptive communication

1. Understands others' emotions
2. Understands single words
3. Understands sentences
4. Understands nonverbal communications
5. Understands others' intentions
6. Follows directions

Possible problems

1. Rarely communicates in any ways
2. Communicates only with movements
3. Communicates only with sounds
4. Communicates more to self than others
5. Communicates mainly to get needs met
6. Rarely responds to others' communications

Five strategies to help your child become communicative

The following are ways to help your child become a communicator with any behaviors he can do.

- Communication here does not mean talking; it means exchanging messages with people
- Start with the strategies below that come most easily for you
- Try one or two as you play with your child, then watch how he responds
- Keep doing the ones that work with your child
- If certain ones seem uncomfortable, do not push yourself. There are many different ways to be effective
- Try new strategies when little is happening with your child
- Determine success by what results in more communicating
- The goal is for your child to communicate more frequently and in new ways
- Be patient and feel energized by every new communication. However small it seems, it is important for your child

Be balanced

1. Communicate once then wait silently
2. Take turns back and forth with actions
3. Take turns back and forth with sounds
4. Avoid dominating the interaction
5. Do not allow the child to dominate the interaction
6. Get into the habit of give and take with your child

Be matched

1. Act in ways your child can act
2. Communicate nonverbally as your child does
3. Talk in ways your child can talk
4. Show your child a next step
5. Match his action with a sound
6. Match his sounds with a word
7. Imitate his sounds playfully

Be responsive

1. Respond to your child "as if" he were communicating
2. Respond to your child's spontaneous movements and wait
3. Respond to your child's sounds and wait
4. Respond to your child's play and wait
5. Respond more to positive than negative behavior
6. Respond with a behavior your child can do

Be emotionally playful

1. Play with sounds back and forth
2. Be animated and noticeable
3. Do the unexpected
4. Do more of what your child finds funny
5. Be physically playful
6. Play pretend
7. Do pantomime games
8. Be affectionate

Share control

1. Initiate as much as respond to the child
2. Respond as much as initiate to the child
3. Take the lead half the time
4. Let child take the lead half the time
5. Avoid being dominant or passive

Stage 3: your child's language
What your child needs to become a habitual social talker

Form: how a child talks
1. Single words
2. Two- to four-word combinations
3. Sentences
4. Appropriate grammar
5. Strings sentences together
6. Dialog—back and forth
7. Monologue—one way

Content: what a child talks about
1. Objects
2. Activities and events
3. People
4. Emotions
5. Concrete facts
6. Ideas (abstract)
7. Now
8. Past
9. Future

Use: why a child talks
1. To initiate talk with people
2. To respond to others' talk
3. To get needs met or help
4. To get attention
5. To self to accompany activity
6. To give information
7. To get information
8. To enjoy being with others

Speech clarity

1. Makes approximations to words
2. Individual words are clear
3. Strings of words are clear
4. Repeats when misunderstood
5. Imitates your speech with clearer speech
6. Makes up own words—jargon

Appropriateness of talking

1. Relevant to situation
2. Responsive to what others say
3. Knows when to talk and when not to talk
4. Waits his turn when others talk
5. Talk fits emotionally to the situation

Possible problems

1. Bizarre or inappropriate talk
2. Talk is off the topic
3. Interrupts others' talking
4. Rote or memorized talking
5. Talks *at* more than *with* people
6. Repeats words unnecessarily
7. Unclear or mumbled talking
8. Self-centered talking
9. Short, unelaborated talking

Five strategies to help your child talk socially

The following are ways to help your child become a habitual social talker.

- The goal is not more language but more communicating with language.
- Start with the strategy below that comes most easily for you
- Try one or two as you play with your child, then watch how he responds
- Keep doing the ones that work with your child
- If certain ones seem uncomfortable, do not push yourself. There are many different ways to be effective
- Try new strategies when little is happening with your child
- Determine success by what results in more communicating
- The goal is for your child to talk more frequently and in new ways
- Be patient and feel energized by every new word. However small it seems, it is important for your child

Be balanced and reciprocal

1. Say one thing then wait for your child to respond
2. Talk in a give-and-take turn-taking style
3. Wait with anticipation for your child to respond
4. Allow your child to initiate talking; silent waiting helps
5. Avoid dominating turns with your child
6. Prevent your child from talking in monologues
7. Make sure you and your child talk about the same topic
8. Communicate more like a game of ping-pong than darts

Be matched

1. Communicate in ways your child can try to do
2. Talk about what your child is immediately doing
3. Act like a "living dictionary," i.e. put a word on what your child sees and does
4. Talk about your child's interests
5. Avoid using more words than your child can say

6. Talk not only to be understood but also to show your child what to say

7. "Match up" by giving your child one or two more words to say

8. Show your child new words to say about current things he talks about

9. Show your child how to extend a topic

10. Show your child how his words can become sentences

Be responsive

1. Understand that each of your child's actions can become a word

2. Give your child a word for his actions and experiences

3. Treat your child's experiences as his most important first words

4. Focus on teaching words for what your child already communicates nonverbally

5. Translate your child's actions into words

6. Translate your child's sounds into a word

7. Respond more to positive than negative talking

8. Avoid criticizing your child's language; show him what to say instead

9. Respond to a word with a short sentence

10. Return your child to the topic when he strays

11. Do not respond to inappropriate or undesired talk

Share control

1. Follow your child's topic lead about half the time

2. Encourage your child to stay on your topic about half the time

3. Keep your questions to less than 20 percent of your talking

4. Keep directions and commands to less than 20 percent of your talking

5. Make more comments than questions and commands

6. Silently prevent your child from interrupting

7. Discourage your child from dominating the talking

Be emotionally playful

1. Play with words in enjoyable ways
2. Make talking a part of your child's play
3. Accept any words your child says without criticism
4. Show your child a new way to talk playfully
5. Practice turn-taking games with words
6. Pretend play with words
7. Make talking more like fun than a job
8. Avoid pressuring your child for a certain word
9. Avoid making talking a test for your child
10. Be animated in your talk
11. Act out the words you use

Stage 4: your child's conversational life

Based on years of developing conversations with children, we have found a series of skills that help children become effective and enjoyable conversation partners. Many children with delays have language but do not effectively use it in conversations. Conversation, not language alone, is the key to successful relationships, learning, and success in society. The skills below allow a child to build a conversational life.

Four general attitudes seem essential to become a conversationalist:

1. Interest in sharing knowledge.

2. Interest in what others have to say.

3. Understanding that conversations have many purposes.

4. Confidence and enjoyment in interactions.

With these four attitudes, your child will become a successful conversationalist to the degree they develop the following skills.

Enjoys conversing with others

1. Seeks out others for conversation

2. Makes conversations playful times

3. Converses during literacy activities

4. Converses easily as part of physical play

5. Has pretend conversations

6. Makes games of conversations

7. Wants others to know what he knows

8. Enjoys the attention he gets in conversations

Stays on a mutual topic

1. Takes turns with others

2. Responds to others' meanings and intentions

3. Stays on one topic for several exchanges

4. Allows partner to lead the topic

5. Shows interest in what partner has to say

6. Understands when partner wants to change the topic

Converses for many reasons

1. Converses to get information
2. Converses to enjoy being with others
3. Converses to tell stories
4. Converses to get to know others
5. Converses to argue or compete
6. Converses to manipulate others
7. Converses to solve problems
8. Converses to share ideas
9. Converses during playtime

Possible problems

1. Insists on only his own topic
2. Interrupts others
3. Talks at rather than with others
4. Repeats his ideas excessively
5. Shifts topics rapidly
6. Ignores what others say to him
7. Initiates but does not respond
8. Responds but does not initiate
9. Dominates turns by constantly talking

Five strategies to help your child have conversations

The following are ways to help your child have conversations.

- Conversations mean exchanging words back and forth on a shared topic
- Start with strategies that come most easily for you
- Try one or two as you play with your child, then watch how he responds
- Keep doing the ones that keep your child talking with you
- If certain ones seem uncomfortable, do not push yourself. There are many different ways to be effective
- Try new strategies when little is happening with your child
- Determine success by what results in longer conversations on different topics
- Be patient and feel energized by every new communication. However small it seems, it is important for your child

Be balanced

1. Take turns with your child in conversations
2. Take one turn then wait for your child to take one
3. Avoid dominating the conversation
4. Wait for a turn silently with a clear expectation on your face
5. Make the conversation part of a turn-taking play activity
6. Keep the child for "one more turn" when he stops participating
7. Keep your child on one topic for several turns
8. Try to initiate and respond about equally between the two of you
9. Allow silence when your child does not immediately respond
10. Think of conversation more like a game of ping-pong than darts

Be matched

1. Respond to the personal meaning of what your child says
2. Encourage your child to respond to what you say
3. Talk in ways your child can talk
4. Talk about your child's interests half the time
5. Show your child how to talk about your interests some of the time
6. Discourage your child from talking only about himself

7.   Talk about what your child is doing
8.   Join into his activity and talk about what you are doing together

Be responsive

1.   Respond verbally to what your child is doing
2.   Respond verbally to what your child is saying
3.   Respond once, then wait for your child to say more
4.   Respond by showing your child a little more to say
5.   Respond by staying on the topic
6.   Respond more to positive than negative talking
7.   Respond without judgment or criticism
8.   Respond with a correction without judgment
9.   Respond without demanding the impossible from your child
10.   Respond in the ways that gets the most response from your child

Share control

1.   Talk to behaviors you want more of
2.   Do not talk to behaviors you want less of
3.   Regularly ask yourself: Do I want this behavior to continue?
4.   Look away when your child is doing something you want to decrease
5.   Do not talk to your child when taking him to time-out
6.   Remind yourself that your attention is like a fertilizer to your child
7.   Teach your child's partners to attend to the positive and ignore the negative

Be emotionally playful

1.   Make conversations more playful than task-oriented
2.   Have conversations more for companionship than information
3.   Respond to your child's emotions
4.   Show affection and warmth
5.   Be animated
6.   Be more interesting than your child's distractions
7.   Laugh authentically
8.   Accept your child's ideas without criticism
9.   Talk about your and the child's feelings
10.   Make conversations out of your child's play and pretend

Stage 5: your child's civil behavior

What your child needs to do to become a self-respecting and acceptable social partner

Cooperation

1. Follows directions that are developmentally appropriate
2. Cooperates willingly with out being coerced
3. Cooperates in activities that fit his development
4. Complies willingly but not in a rote or passive manner
5. Responds to others' wishes and behaviors as well as his own
6. Shows more voluntary cooperation than mindless compliance
7. Maintains his own interests and motivations as he cooperates
8. Maintains his own integrity while cooperating

Trust and confidence

1. Approaches people without fear
2. Responds to people without fear or resistance
3. Interacts without needing to have full control
4. Shows comfort and relaxation

Civil behavior

1. Treats others with respect
2. Treats self with respect
3. Treats others with kindness
4. Learns from consequences to his behavior
5. Regulates his emotions reasonably

Self regulation

1. Controls his impulses and emotions reasonably
2. Expresses emotions effectively and without excess
3. Checks himself when beginning to act out or lose control
4. Tolerates frustration without losing control
5. Calms himself when anxious or disrupted

6.   Tolerates transitions without great difficulty

7.   Recovers easily when upset

Emotionally appropriate behavior

1.   Asserts self without aggression

2.   Shows humor

3.   Shows emotion appropriately

4.   Shows positive emotion appropriately

5.   Accepts affection

6.   Shows affection in socially acceptable ways

7.   Recovers easily when upset

8.   Tolerates transitions easily

Emotional attachment

1.   Develops attachments with responsive people

2.   Avoids attachments with people who are not responsive or accepting

3.   Attachments are flexible and not obsessive

4.   Seeks comfort in times of distress or anxiety

5.   Shows similar emotional patterns as his life partners

Empathy

1.   Shows concern for others

2.   Is affected by others' emotions

3.   Listens to others

4.   Actively tries to please others

5.   Actively helps or supports others

6.   Take others' perspective/point of view

Possible problems

1.   Disregards others' feelings or ideas

2.   Talks in rude or insensitive ways

3.   Interrupts others

4. Talks loudly or otherwise inappropriately
5. Dominates conversations
6. Abuses others verbally
7. Abuses others physically
8. Shows little emotion
9. Shows excesive emotion
10. Fails to learn from consequences
11. Ignores others or acts as if they do not exist
12. Fears contact with people
13. Makes attachments to people who are abusive or not accepting
14. Shows little sustained attachment to people

Five strategies to improve your child's civil and appropriate behavior

The following are ways to help your child improve his civil and appropriate behaviour.

- The goal is for your child to communicate in civil and socially acceptable ways
- Start with the strategies below that come most easily for you
- Try one or two as you play with your child, then watch how he responds
- Keep doing the ones that work with your child
- If certain ones seem uncomfortable, do not push yourself. There are many different ways to be effective
- Try new strategies when little is happening with your child
- Determine success by what results in less negative and more positive behaviors
- The goal is for your child to treat others with respect and appreciation
- Be patient and feel energized by each new positive behavior. However small it seems, it is important for your child

Be balanced

1. Avoid doing much more than your child in an interaction
2. Wait for your child to take a turn
3. Wait silently and with clear expectation for him to respond
4. Gently insist on taking your turn
5. Be sure neither of you dominates the interaction
6. Explain the "50/50" rule: when interacting, try hard to do no more than half of the talking
7. Think of communicating as more a "give and take" than just giving information or directions
8. Be sure your "turn" responds to what the child just said or did
9. When the child dominates the interaction, silently terminate it briefly; do not support excessive behavior that will limit your child in society

Be matched

1. The more you act like your child the more he will cooperate
2. The more you talk in ways your child can try, the more he will respond
3. Evaluate your child's environments for over-stimulation
4. Understand and reduce environments that disrupt your child
5. Understand and increase environments where your child behaves well
6. Define "good behavior" as positive interactions, not only as "not doing anything wrong"
7. Change your child's environments so he interacts more positively
8. Be sure to give your child tasks he can succeed with
9. Try doing only one thing at a time when playing with your child

Be responsive

1. Talk to behaviors you want more of
2. Do not talk to behaviors you want less of
3. Regularly ask yourself: Do I want this behavior to continue?
4. Look away when your child is doing something you want to decrease
5. Do not talk to your child when taking him to time-out
6. Remind yourself that your attention is like a fertilizer to your child
7. Teach your child's partners to attend to the positive and ignore the negative

Share control

1. Allow your child to control your interactions at least half the time
2. Follow his ideas and actions at least half the time
3. Be more responsive than directive; that is, respond supportively more than controlling in a directive way
4. Limit your questions to necessary ones and less than 20 percent of your talk with him
5. Make sure that he allows you to have some control
6. Comment on what your child does or says, then wait for a response

7. Make your interactions more a playful flow than a task

8. Avoid pressing your child for specific answers more than 20 percent of the time

9. Teach the child by example that he can have successes in conversation

Be emotionally playful

1. Genuinely enter into your child's activities of interest

2. Play with your child when he is acting positive

3. Comfort your child when he is genuinely fearful

4. Make sure to discipline quietly and quickly

5. Learn to read your child's emotions

6. Show him that you genuinely enjoy him

7. Learn to "read" when he is available

8. Build on his "available" times by joining him in them

9. Respond to the positive things your child does

10. Ignore the undesired things your child does

11. Avoid judging your child's behavior

12. Invite your child into activities you enjoy

13. Understand your child's fears and limitation

14. Reduce stress in your interactions

15. Be more concerned with the interaction continuing than "right" answers

16. Tolerate your child's play even when you do not understand it

17. Be animated and more interesting than your child's distractions

18. Comfort your child when he is distressed

19. Show your child clear boundaries to abusive behavior

13

The Environment Form

How are your child's environments influencing your child's social and language development? Your child will communicate very differently in different environments. As people, activities, and stimulation changes, so will his interest and ability to communicate change. A common question parents ask is: "He talks so much at home, why doesn't he talk outside or in school?" Many children communicate more maturely, more often, and more easily in some situations and rarely or with difficulty in others.

In fact, some environmental features can actually prevent or discourage a child from communicating and socializing with others. It is important not to define your child's abilities by his performance in difficult situations or with people with whom he does not have a real relationship.

Common environmental barriers to a communicative life

Use this scale to discover what might interfere with your child's natural learning to communicate. Then start making changes with the ones you can change easily. The goal is first to make your child's environments more actively allow and help him interact, then communicate and talk. Many parents find that simply changing a small number of these barriers results in the child socializing and communicating much more. You can use the scale that follows for each major environment your child is in, such as home, school, or day-care. Identify two or three changes you can make to help your child socialize and communicate more.

Envoronmental barriers to a child's communication

1. Partners act in ways the child cannot act
2. Partners talk in ways the child cannot talk
3. Child spends little one-to-one time with people
4. His living or learning environment is noisy for him
5. His visual environment is distracting to him
6. He has few boundaries to limit his behavior
7. His peers are overwhelming to him
8. His environment allows him few successes
9. He has little access to quiet time
10. People rarely enter into his choice and style of play
11. Interactions with people are very brief
12. His environment discourages communicating
13. His environment encourages more solo than social behavior
14. Teaching focuses more on performance than conversation
15. His environment encourages or requires passive behavior
16. His environment offers too many choices for him
17. He is not allowed enough time at an activity
18. He is expected to do things on his own without modeling
19. He is regularly corrected and criticized
20. He is regularly pressured to do difficult things

How responsive is your child's environment to his development?

Just as you can respond in ways that help your child develop, so too can his environments be responsive in ways that help him socialize and communicate. Use this scale to determine how responsive and supportive your child's major environments are. Use the scale separately for home, school, and other common situations.

How responsive is your child's environment?

How balanced is the environment?

1. One-to-one interactions are possible
2. Child is allowed to take turns
3. Child is given enough time to respond
4. A general give and take is allowed

How matched is the environment?

1. People act in ways the child can act
2. Expectations are possible for him
3. People communicate in ways he can do
4. Stimulation level fits child's sensitivities

How responsive is the environment?

1. Supports and allows child's interest
2. People respond to what the child communicates about
3. People respond by showing him what to do next
4. More responses to positive than negative behaviors
5. People genuinely accept the child for who he is

How much does the environment allow the child control?

1. Child chooses activity some of the time
2. Child controls interactions some of the time
3. Child is directed by others some of the time
4. Helps child be more active than passive

How playful and emotionally attached is the environment?

1. Enjoyment is valued in the setting
2. Child has flexibility in what he does
3. Affection is shared frequently
4. Adults are animated and more interesting than child's distractions

How effective is the discipline in the setting?

1. Child gets more attention for positive than negative behaviors
2. Consequences to negative behavior are immediate, not delayed
3. Others are not rewarded for behaviors prohibited to child
4. Clear boundaries for unacceptable behavior are apparent

Appendix

Research Support for Communicating Partners

The Communicating Partners approach described in this book evolved through a series of clinical investigations of late-talking children and their families. Chapter 1 provides a chronological history of the issues and approaches as they developed into the model presented in this book. This Appendix summarizes a series of research studies of the model in clinical use with a wide variety of families and children with autistic spectrum disorders.

All of the studies have in common that the clinicians were trained in the Communicating Partners approach with the same video and manual based curriculum. The three part curriculum addressed the following:

1. An introduction to the parent–child relationship model (MacDonald and Carroll 1992).

2. Systematic training in using the CP responsive strategies (balance, match, respond, share control, and emotional play) (MacDonald and Davidson 1992).

3. Demonstration of the parent training process (MacDonald and Wilkening 1993).

Each program began with the interaction goals of social play, imitation, and turn-taking. The central goal of the programs was to help the children interact and communicate more frequently with people who entered the child's experiences, using the responsive strategies. Consequently the programs were evaluated both in terms of the child's development as well as changes in the interaction skills of the parents.

The Ohio State study

A one-year study of 25 pre-school children and their parents was conducted at the Nisonger Center at the Ohio State University. All children exhibited severe social and communicative delays with marked autistic features, including social isolation, self-stimulation, preservation, and unconventional functional play. The study involved training parents to develop responsive play relationships that were tailored to enhance the child's social interaction and communication skills. The training involved three phases: education, professional training, and practice in the home.

The education phase introduced parents to developmental information on how children learned to communicate and how parents can be partners in their child's development. Parents used a developmental map similar to the ARM described in this book to follow their child's development and learn to focus on appropriate next steps. They were also given readings and practical tutorials that were developmentally targeted to their child. Practical examples of conversation routines were used as models for how parents were to interact. From the beginning, parents understood that their child's progress would be their responsibility and not the professional's job.

During the professional training phase, the professional served as teacher and coach for parents, who then integrated the program into their daily lives with their children. The professional demonstrated the responsive strategies with the child and coached the parent to become the child's communicating partner, with the help of video training tapes.

The home practice phase involved parents practicing the strategies within regular daily routines and spontaneous events in the home. Parents focused on no more than two goals for the child, such as sound imitation and turn-taking, and no more than two strategies, such as matching and balancing. Parents provided simple written diary reports of concerns and progress. The tutorials and practice guides were similar to the ones which will be provided in Volume 2 of this book.

The Ohio State study provided findings in two major arenas: the parent and child profiles before treatment and parallel profiles after treatment. The pre-treatment findings addressed the following questions:

- How do preschool ASD children interact and communicate in play with their parents?
- How do parents interact and communicate in play with their ASD children?

The post-treatment findings describe how parents and children changed after one year of training, based on videotaped samples one and two months before and after the program. While no control group was available, the findings were validated in independent evaluations by six uninvolved adults who viewed random samples of the pre- and post-performances. In over 80 percent of the cases, the evaluators judged the children's post-performances to be significantly superior to the pre-performances.

Pre-treatment findings

The pre-treatment findings generally indicated the following patterns. The children interacted much less than their parents. The interactions were usually brief and did not last more than one or two turns. There was little evidence of a give-and-take or reciprocal relationship in the play. The children generally played alone or followed their parents' directions. The parents usually did not join in the children's play but played more of a teacher or regulator role and one of play partner. Parents often talked in adult ways far beyond the child's language level. Since most of the children's behavior was nonverbal, it was striking that the parents usually did not enter the child's nonverbal play but appeared to expect the child to enter their verbal world. There appeared to be few joint activity routines in which the child had practice learning to communicate in developmentally possible ways.

Post-treatment findings

CHILDREN

After treatment the children played more actively with their parents, rather than in the isolated patterns seen before. Most of the children moved from a generally passive role to a more assertively interactive role. More than half the children demonstrated a habit of turn-taking without prompting. They were staying voluntarily in social contacts and initiating much more than before. While the major gains were increases in interaction, more than half the children began speaking during the year of treatment and were evaluated as having made more than one and a half years' progress on communication measures. The children's rate of nonfunctional or "autistic"-like behavior decreased as they became more interactive with their parents. About half of the children maintained "autistic" features as they still improved their interactive life.

PARENTS

The parents changed more in their social play skills than did the children. They generally became more childlike and playful, thus more accessible to the children. Most of the parents learned to match their child in the sense that they acted and communicated more in ways the child could do. They improved considerably in their waiting time since before treatment few parents waited for their children to participate much. The parents also become more responsive in that they usually changed their role from a directive teacher to a play partner who followed the child's lead and made the child the center of the agenda rather than their own teaching goals. The video analyses showed strikingly that the parents did much less after the program, which appeared to be related to the finding that the child did much more. The parents also became more animated and playful and less rigid and structured in the way they had been before treatment.

Summary

The study gave us a major video and database from which we developed the program further and refined the treatment strategies on the basis of those strategies that related to increased child interaction. Parents were by and large able to implement the program in their homes and reported in surveys that they had learned about their child's development and how to continue supporting it at home.

The Discovery Center study: a parent–school collaboration

The Communicating Partners program has been adopted by the Logan County pre-school programs in central Ohio as a model for over 200 children with developmental disabilities since 1997. After receiving a series of in-service training workshops on CP, the school supported a one-year study of the effects of the model on a group of children and both their parents and teachers. The program educated parents and professionals together toward one major goal: to increase the rate, duration, and social quality of the interactive life of a group of young children with ASD. The program combined clinical and educational approaches to train parents and school personnel to have playful and communicative relationships with 19 preschool children, each with one to three year delays in social, communicative, adaptive, cognitive, and emotional skills. The purpose was to extend the Ohio State study described above to a school setting in which the child's teacher would be included in the training as well as the parents. The reasoning was that, for pre-conversational children with ASD, a developmentally appropriate curriculum would have a focus on social and communicative skills before the focus became academic skills. The notion was that in order for children to use academic skills effectively they first needed to have the social and communicative abilities to use those skills in daily living.

A series of video-mediated training workshops introduced Communicating Partners to 19 families as well as to the teachers and assistants in the ten classrooms. The notion was to train one or two children in each classroom along with their responsible teachers. The intention was for the teachers then to extend the program to other children in their classrooms. One speech therapist and one parent with several years' experience with CP met regularly with the family and classroom to reinforce the program by showing and discussing a series of video training tapes on the five responsive strategies. The author then met monthly with the family and school staff for further coaching and program design. An interesting feature of the design was that the child's social and communicative goals were the same for the family as for the classroom, so that the child's major learning environments would be relatively consistent in their expectations of the child. Both teacher and parents also attempted to follow similar strategies in helping the children to be more interactive.

Evaluations of pre- and post-video taped samples, autism profiles, developmental assessments, and parent and teacher surveys indicated that 14 of the 18 children progressed socially, communicatively, or linguistically, with several children progressing in two or three areas. The parents of the progressing children learned to be more developmentally matched and responsive, exhibiting the role of play partner more than one of didactic teacher. The changes in the children were more marked with their parents than with their teacher in the complicated context of the classrooms. The findings suggest that children may need to learn one-to-one communicative relations before they will generalize them to the competitive and stimulating nature of a classroom.

Interviews before the program revealed that most of the parents believed that only professional therapists and teachers could help their children communicate and that they did not value highly the developmental value of their own home play with their child. Fourteen parents reported at the end that they had changed their relationship with their children from one of care-taking and teaching to one of a frequent play partner, finely tuned to the child's current interests and abilities.

The findings

Before the program, the children generally:

- played alone
- interacted rarely with people
- avoided social contact
- showed little eye contact and social imitation
- communicated rarely and mainly to themselves
- showed little interactive turn-taking and responding
- demonstrated little enjoyment with people
- communicated mainly for needs and rarely for affection.

Before the program, the parents generally:

- mismatched the child by communicating far above the child's abilities
- dominated the interactions without waiting for the child to take turns
- interacted little for play and more for directing the child to an adult agenda
- responded more to negative or inappropriate behaviors than to productive ones
- shared little in the children's nonverbal play and communication
- showed more of a serious than playful demeanor
- allowed the child extensive time alone.

After the one school year (August to June), while the children changed to varying degrees, each of the 14 was judged (independently by two professionals and two parents based on video samples and reports) to have made the following changes:

- They were more socially aware.
- They were more responsive to others' speech.
- They were more interactive in terms of frequency and length of turn-taking.

- They were more communicative in terms of both nonverbal and verbal communication.
- They spent less time avoiding or resisting others' contacts.
- They spent more time initiating and responding with both family and three school staff.
- They showed more functional play that demonstrated concepts ready to evolve into words.
- They showed less self-stimulating behaviors.
- They paid more attention to play tasks both with and without people.
- They showed greater affection and perceived enjoyment of others.

Eleven of the children reduced their nonsocial and aggressive behavior. Three did not. In fact, these three appeared more aggressive as they moved from social isolation to more interaction with people. At least seven began to show humor and eight became spontaneously imitative in daily life. Of the eight who began using words, four were using short sentences. While three of the verbal children used words mainly to label things and meet their needs, five children showed marked pragmatic improvement in that they began to talk for social reasons, like commenting, replying, greeting, and conversing.

After the program the parents also changed in varying degrees, with most of the parents making at least the following changes:

- They showed more balanced interaction with more waiting and turn-taking.
- They showed more matching by acting and communicating in ways the child can do.
- They were more playful within the child's physical and nonverbal world.
- They were less directive and controlling of the child.
- They were more attentive and less allowing the child to be alone.
- They were more playful and animated, expressing more enjoyment with the child.
- They were more allowing of the child to initiate and complete tasks.
- They made fewer complaints of behavior problems (except in three cases).
- They reported more happier interactions at home.
- They had greater expectations of the child's development.

When parents were asked how they applied the program at home, there were as great a variety of answers as there were families. It was clear that the lives of the families were spontaneous and unpredictable with few routines. Consequently the programs focused on teaching parents to integrate the strategies into natural daily activities. Ten parents reported that they used the social strategies within daily activities and that the major change was that they now played much more in the child's world than they had before. Most parents reported that they could now teach their child to communicate best by playing with him. They believed that they needed to be the ones who prepared their children for school. While some parents began playing like their children early in the program, others took a few months to be comfortable acting like their child and to overcome their habits of directing and controlling their children.

While both the children and parents showed progress, the test of the program lay in the observation of the quality, emotion, and reciprocity of the relationships between parents and children. In most families, the parent and child moved: from the role of lone observer to one of interactive participant; from a one-sided picture to a reciprocal give-and-take style of relationship; from a mutually unresponsive relationship to one in which parents and children were sensitively aware and responsive to each other's interests and abilities; from a relationship in which parents and children behaved very differently to a relationship reflecting more joint activity and a wide range of social interactions; and from a relationship that was mainly task-oriented with little affection to one with animation, enjoyment, and emotional attachment. The relationships not only involved more interactions, but they lasted longer, required less prompting, and appeared more conversational.

The Family Child Learning Center study

The third major investigation of the model was conducted in collaboration with Gerald Mahoney and Frida Perales at the Family Child Learning Center associated with the Akron Children's Hospital and Kent State University in northern Ohio. The three of us had for many years conducted parallel studies of parent–child relationships with children with disabilities. In 1998, we received a joint research grant to study the responsive relationship approach with 50 children: 20 with ASD and 30 with a variety of language delays. The project provided extensive data analyses that allowed richer investigation of the effects of the model on cognitive and emotional development as well as the social and communicative goals (Mahoney and MacDonald 2003). The four-year project allowed assessments of several developmental domains before and after the training as well as elaborate analyses of the video samples. A full report of the study and multiple analyses is available in the Responsive Teaching Early Intervention curriculum (Mahoney and MacDonald 2003).

For the purpose of this study, the term "Responsive Teaching" was used as the title for the early intervention curriculum. The responsive strategies and developmental goals were virtually similar to those in Communicating Partners and the staff was trained with the series of Communicating Partners video training tapes that were used in the studies described earlier in this Appendix. Each of the 50 parent–child programs began by establishing joint activity routines in which the major interaction goals of social play, imitation, and turn-taking were central to the program. Parents were trained in using the responsive strategies similar to the ones in the ARM in this book.

Ms. Perales trained several graduate students to be the parents' coaches. She had trained with the Communicating Partners program and related video training tapes for several years and was directly responsible for supervising the programs in this study. This was the first formal replication of the model by an independent group of professionals.

Parents and children received training during hourly sessions on a weekly basis for a year. The average number of sessions per year was 32.6. Each session involved instruction of the parent on one developmental goal and demonstration of the strategies to be used in daily routines in the home. Parents reported that they devoted, on average, a little more than two hours a day using the responsive strategies in prescribed activities as well as natural routines.

The findings

The data are based on independent observers who were trained to high reliability on the major variables. Videotaped observations were randomized so observers did not know which sample was before or after treatment and no two families were rated consecutively. In addition to the video analyses, several measures of cognitive, language, and social–emotional functioning were taken before and after the program.

The elaborate analyses provided one of the most detailed evaluations of a parent–child treatment program ever undertaken and resulted in several findings:

1. The parents' interaction styles became more responsive, matched, playful, and balanced with the children.

2. The children had significantly higher ratings at post-treatment in social and communicative skills as well as in related effects such as attention, persistence, cooperation, initiation, joint attention, and affect.

3. Children's use of the trained social and communicative behaviors was highly associated with changes in their mother's responsiveness and use of the five strategies.

4. Children made significant gains in both cognitive and language development beyond that expected within the timespan.

5. Improvements were made in a range of reported and observed behavior problems.

6. Parents' ability to cope with the stress of raising a child with ASD showed some improvement in that parents' stress reduced with regard to their role with the child.

7. Evidence of conventional features of "autistic" behavior was greatly reduced in some children but somewhat reduced in most.

Summary

The one-year program with 50 children and parents yielded several encouraging findings regarding the effectiveness of training parents to be their child's primary responsive partners. We found that, even though the program involved only modest levels of professional contact (one hour per week at most), parents followed through with it an average of two hours per day. The program was effective at encouraging two-thirds of the parents to engage in significantly more responsive interactions with their children. Furthermore, there was a strong relationship between how much parents used the responsive strategies and how much the children became more social and communicative. Nearly three-fourths of the children significantly increased their social and communicative behaviors over the course of intervention. While no claims of cure can or need be made, the findings indicate that the majority of the children increased their developmental rate in the areas of cognition, communication, emotional behavior, and social interaction. Their changes were related to the degrees to which parents became more responsive, balanced, matched, control-sharing, and playful.

The results of this extensive study are impressive not only because of the magnitude of changes children attained, but more importantly because of the consistent relationship between the impact of responsive teaching on parents' interactive behavior and the children's developmental progress. The detailed analyses make us more convinced than ever that parental responsiveness plays a crucial role in intervention because it has an enormous impact on the children's use of pivotal developmental behaviors. Parents cannot teach children everything they need to learn, but parents can profoundly influence the child's fundamental learning habits that are critical to helping children learn from their routine interaction in daily life. Our findings suggest that it is far more critical for children to "learn to learn" in their social relationships than it is for them to learn discrete behaviors or skills in directive teaching. The study also revealed that parents became more enthusiastic and optimistic about their child's future once they experienced personal success in effecting positive changes in their children rather than relying on strangers to help their child develop.

The communicative literacy study

Paula Rabidoux investigated the interactive style of mothers and 20 language-delayed preschoolers. Half of the children were preverbal; the other half were minimally verbal but not conversational. She studied the relationship between the parents' responsive and directive style to the interactive participation of the children. The major finding was that the more parents used the responsive strategies of matching, balancing, sharing control, and being emotionally playful, the more the children stayed interacting, related with the picture book events, and communicated their intentions. A parallel study analyzed the same children's behavior when the investigator deliberately used the Communicating Partners responsive strategies with the same storybook materials. The findings showed that all but one child interacted and communicated more frequently, more maturely, and with fewer off-topic distractions with the "responsive" investigator than with the mothers, who were primarily directive with their children.

The study suggests that storybook times are ideal communication learning times due to three factors:

1. The child is captive rather than on the move.

2. Concrete cues are available to develop semantic relatedness.

3. Communicative interactions facilitate a child's motivation to become literate.

The Ann Arbor group parent therapy program

Ira Glovinski, a psychotherapist, conducted a group parent therapy program with children with autistic and bipolar patterns. The training focused on teaching parents the five CP responsive strategies in play-based therapy. The parents were at first generally directive rather than responsive, dominating rather than balanced, mismatched in action and language, more task-oriented than play-oriented, and more rigid than relaxed in expectations. The children were more passive than interactive, more nonverbal than verbal, played more alone than with others, and showed more resistance than cooperation. In summary, the parent–child pairs were rarely reciprocal, playful, or actively into each other's world. After a 12-week program with video demonstrations, live practice with children, and coaching of parents, the parents and children were more interactive and communicative and spent more time playing than teaching. The children showed more initiative and stayed in longer interactions, engaged the parents more in joint activities, and cooperated more readily. The majority of the parents learned to wait for their child, and the parents' expectations of their child were more realistic and more positive. Parents' anxiety about their parenting and the child's future decreased as they experienced success, effecting small but marked changes in their children.

The Pittsburgh program

Carolyn Glass conducted a two-year group parent education program teaching the principles of Communicating Partners at the Center for Creative Play associated with the University of Pittsburgh. The training involved video training tapes as well as live demonstrations with the children and monthly meetings discussing progress and questions. While no formal evaluations were feasible, surveys of over 40 parents revealed that they felt they had learned both about their child's development and their personal role in it. Over half of the parents reported increased interaction in their children within three months.

References

For more references and practical findings, see the Communicating Partners website (www.jamesdmacdonald.org). You are also invited to join our discussion group on the Internet at *http://groups.yahoo.com/group/communicating.*

Attwood, T. (1998) *Asperger's Syndrome.* London: Jessica Kingsley Publishers.

Bandura, A. (1986) *Modeling and Social Learning Theory.* Englewood Cliffs, NJ: Prentice Hall.

Bandura, A. (1986) *Social Foundations of Thought and Action: A Social Theory.* Englewood Cliffs, NJ: Prentice Hall.

Baron-Cohen, S. (1995) *Mindblindness: An Essay on Autism and Theories of Mind.* Cambridge, MA: MIT Press.

Bates, E. (1976) *Language and Context: The Acquisition of Pragmatics.* New York: Academic Press.

Bloom, L. (1991) *Language Development from Two to Three.* New York: Cambridge University Press.

Bloom, L. (1993) *The Transition from Infancy to Language: Acquiring the Power of Expression.* New York: Cambridge University Press.

Bloom, L. and Lahey, M. (1978) *Language Developmental and Language Disorders.* New York: John Wiley.

Bornstein, M.H. (ed) (1989) 'Maternal responsiveness: Characteristics and consequences.' *New Directions for Child Development 43*, 75–87.

Bornstein, M. (ed) (1995) *Handbook of Parenting.* Mahwah, NJ: Erlbaum Publishers.

Bronfenbrenner, U. (1979) *The Ecology of Human Development.* Cambridge, MA: Harvard University Press

Brown, R. (1973) *A First Language: The Early Stages.* Cambridge, MA: Harvard University Press.

Bruner, J. (1977) 'Early social interaction and language acquisition.' In H.R. Schaffer (ed) *Studies in Mother–Infant Interaction.* New York: Academic Press.

Bruner, J. (1983) *Child Talk.* New York: Norton.

Bruner, J. (1986) *Actual Minds; Possible Worlds.* Cambridge, MA: Harvard University Press.

Bruner, J. (1990) *Acts of Meaning.* Cambridge, MA: Harvard University Press.

Csikszentmihalyi, M. (1990) *Flow: Psychology of Optimal Experience.* New York: Harper-Row.

Dalai Lama, and Goleman, D. (2003) *Destructive Emotions.* New York: Bantam Dell.

Deci, E. (1975) *Intrinsic Motivation.* New York: Plenum Press.

Donnellan, A., Mirenda, P., Mesareos, P., and Fassbender, L. (1984) 'Analyzing the communicative functions of aberrant behavior.' *Journal of the Association for Persons with Severe Handicaps 9*, 210–219.

Duchan, J. (1989) 'Evaluating adults' talk to children: Assessing adult attunement.' *Seminars in Speech and Language 10*, 17–27.

Duchan, J. (1995) *Supporting Language Learning in Everyday Life.* San Diego, CA: Singular.

Elkind, D. (1981) *The Hurried Child: Growing Up Too Fast Too Soon.* Reading, MA: Addison-Wesley Publishing.

Elkind, D. (1987) *Miseducation: Preschoolers at Risk.* New York: Knopf.

Field, T. (1980) *High-risk Infants and Children: Adult and Peer Interactions.* New York: Academic Press.

Gardner, H. (1983) *Frames of Mind: The Theory of Multiple Intelligences.* New York: Basic Books.

Girolometto, L., Verbey, M., and Tannock, R. (1994) 'Improving joint engagement in parent–child interaction: An intervention study.' *Journal of Early Intervention 18*, 2, 155–167.

Goldberg, S. (1977) 'Social competence in infancy: A model of parent–child interaction.' *Merrill-Palmer Quarterly 23*, 163–177.

Goleman, D. (1995) *Emotional Intelligence.* New York: Bantam Press.

Goodman, J. (1992) *When Slow is Fast Enough: Educating the Delayed Preschool Child.* New York: The Guildford Press.

Grandin, T. (1995) *Thinking in Pictures.* New York: Doubleday.

Greenspan, S. (1985) *First Feelings.* New York: Academic Press.

Hart, B. and Risley, T. (1999) *The Social World of Children: Learning to Talk.* Baltimore, MD: Paul Brookes Publishing.

Hobson, R.P. (1993) *Autism and the Development of Mind.* Mahwah, NJ: Erlbaum.

Horstmeier, D. (In press) *Survival Math: Environmental Approaches for Down Syndrome and Other Concrete Learners.* Bethesda, MD: Woodbine Press.

Horstmeier, D. and MacDonald, J. (1978) *Ready Set Go: Talk to Me.* Columbus, OH: Charles Merrill.

Hunt, J.McV. (1971) 'Intrinsic motivation and psychological development.' In H.M. Schroeder (ed) *Personality Theory and Information Processing.* New York: Ronald.

Kaiser, A. and Hester, P. (1994) 'Generalized effects of milieu teaching.' *Journal of Speech and Hearing Research 37*, 63–92.

Kanner, L. (1943) 'Autistic disturbances of affective content.' *Nervous Child 2*, 217–250.

Kaufman, B.N. (1976) *Son Rise.* New York: HarperCollins.

Koegel, R.L., Koegel, L.K., and McNerney, E.K. (2001) 'Pivotal areas in intervention for autism.' *Journal of Clinical Child Psychology 30*, 1, 19–32.

Kohn, A. (1993) *Punished by Rewards: The Trouble with Gold Stars, Incentive Plans, and Other Bribes.* Boston, MA: Houghton Mifflin.

Koschanska, G. (1997) 'Mutually responsive orientation between mothers and their young child: Implications for early socialization.' *Child Development 68*, 94–112.

Koschanska, G. (2001) 'Emotional development in children with different attachment histories: The first three years.' *Child Development 72*, 474–490.

Koschanska, G. and Murray, K. (2000) 'Mother–child mutually responsive orientation and conscience development: From toddler to early school age.' *Child Development 71*, 1424–1440.

Leslie, A.M. (1987) 'Pretense and representation: The origins of "theory of mind".' *Psychological Review 94*, 412–426.

Lewis, M. and Rosenblum, L. (1977) *Interaction, Conversation, and the Development of Language.* New York: John Wiley

Lombardino, L. (1979) 'Maternal speech acts with nondelayed and Down Syndrome children.' Unpublished doctoral dissertation, Ohio State University.

Maccoby, E. (1999) 'The uniqueness of the parent–child relationship.' In W.A. Collins and B. Laursen (eds) *Minnesota Symposia on Child Psychology: Vol. 30. Relationships as Developmental Contexts.* Hillsdale, NJ: Erlbaum.

MacDonald, J. (1972) 'Reliability of naïve raters of normal disfluencies and stuttering behaviors.' Unpublished Ph.D. dissertation, University of Minnesota.

MacDonald, J. (2002) *The Adult–Child Relationship Map (ARM): A Guide for Social and Communication Development.* Columbus, OH: Communicating Partners.

MacDonald, J. and Blott, J. (1974) 'Environmental Language Intervention (ELI).' *Journal of Speech and Hearing Disorders 39*, 244–256.

MacDonald, J. and Caroll, J. (1992) 'A partnership model for communicating with infants at risk for delays.' *Journal of Infant and Young Children 4*, 3, 20–30.

MacDonald, J. and Davidson, S. (1992) *ECO II Video Training Series: Five Responsive Teaching Strategies with Language Delayed Children.* Columbus, OH: Communicating Partners.

MacDonald, J. and Gillette, Y. (1985) 'Turntaking: The key to communication.' *Exceptional Parent 15*, 49–54.

MacDonald, J. and Gillette, Y. (1986) 'Communicating with persons with severe handicaps: Roles of parents and professionals.' *Journal of the Association of Severe Handicaps 11*, 4, 255–265.

MacDonald, J. and Gillette, Y. (1989) *The ECO Language Programs.* Austin, TX: Riverside Press.

MacDonald, J. and Mitchell, B. (2002) 'Communicate with your child: 15 ways to help children communicate.' Columbus, OH: Communicating Partners.

MacDonald, J. and Wilkening, P. (1993) *ECO II Video Training Series: A Parent Based Language Training Model with Later Talking Children.* Columbus, OH: Communicating Partners.

Mahoney, G., Boyce, G., Fewell, R., Spiker, D., and Wheeden, C.A. (1998) 'The relationship of parent–child interactions to the effectiveness of early intervention services for at-risk children and children with disabilities.' *Topics in Early Childhood Special Education 18*, 1, 5–17.

Mahoney, G., Finger, I., and Powell, A. (1985) 'The relationship between maternal behavioral style to the development of developmentally impaired infants.' *American Journal of Mental Deficiency 90*, 296–302.

Mahoney, G. and MacDonald, J. (2003) *Responsive Teaching: Parent-Mediated Developmental Intervention*. Baltimore, MD: Brookes.

Mahoney, G. and Powell, A. (1988) 'Modifying parent–child interaction: Enhancing the development of handicapped children.' *Journal of Special Education 22*, 82–90.

Meisels, S. and Shonkoff, J. (1989) *Handbook of Early Childhood Intervention*. Cambridge: Cambridge University Press.

Nichols, M. (1977) 'Measuring early semantic rules in the speech of children with developmental delays.' Unpublished doctoral dissertation, Ohio State University.

Owens, R. (1979) 'Pragmatic functions in the speech of preschool-aged children with Down Syndrome.' Unpublished doctoral dissertation, Ohio State University.

Owens, R. and MacDonald, J. (1982) 'Pragmatic functions in the speech of preschool-aged Down's and nondelayed children.' *American Journal of Mental Deficiency 86*, 503–511.

Perls, F., Hefferline, R., and Goodman, P. (1977) *Gestalt Therapy*. New York: Bantam Press.

Piaget, J. (1954) *The Construction of Reality in the Child*. New York: Basic Books.

Piaget, J. (1963) *The Language and Thought of the Child*. New York: Basic Books.

Prizant, B. and Wetherby, A. (1989) 'Enhancing language and communication in autism.' In G. Dawson (ed) *Autism: Nature, Diagnosis, and Treatment*. New York: The Guildford Press.

Prizant, B. and Wetherby, A. (1998) 'Toward an integrated view of early language, communication development and socioemotional development.' *Topics in Language Disorders 10*, 1–16.

Rabidoux, P. and MacDonald, J. (2000) 'An interactive taxonomy of mothers and children during storybook interactions.' *American Journal of Speech-Language Pathology 9*, 331–344.

Rabidoux, P. and MacDonald, J. (2001) *Communicative Literacy: Learning to Become Communicative and Literate at the Same Time. A Manual*. Columbus, OH: Communicating Partners.

Resler, C. (1975) 'Semantic rules in the language of 2, 3, and 4 year old children.' Unpublished doctoral dissertation, Ohio State University.

Rogers, S. and Bennetto, L. (2000) 'Intersubjectivity in autism: The roles of imitation and executive function.' In A. Wetherby and B. Prizant (eds) *Autism Spectrum Disorders*. Baltimore, MD: Brookes.

Rogers, S. and Lewis, H. (1992) 'An effective day treatment model for young children with pervasive developmental disorders.' *Journal of the American Academy of Child Psychiatry 28*, 207–214.

Schopler, E., Reichler, R., and Renner, B. (1986) *The Childhood Autism Rating Scale (CARS)*. New York: Irvington Press.

Seligman, M. (1990) *Learned Optimism*. New York: Pocket Books.

Seligman, M. (1996) *The Optimistic Child*. New York: Houghton Mifflin.

Seligman, M. (2002) *Authentic Happiness: Using the New Positive Psychology*. New York: Free Press.

Sigman, M. and Capps, L. (1997) *Children with Autism: A Developmental Perspective*. Cambridge, MA: Harvard University Press.

Sigman, M. and Ungerer, J. (1984) 'Cognitive and language skills in autistic, mentally retarded and normal children.' *Developmental Psychology 20*, 293–3 02.

Siller, M. and Sigman, M. (2002) 'The behaviors of parents with autism predict subsequent development of children's communication.' *Journal of Autism and Developmental Disorders 32*, 2, 77–89.

Sowell, T. (1997) *Late-talking Children*. New York: Basic Books.

Stern, D. (1977) *The First Relationship: Infant and Mother*. Cambridge, MA: Harvard University Press.

Trevarthen, C. (1979) 'Communication and cooperation in early infancy: Primary intersubjectivity.' In M. Bullowa (ed) *Before Speech*. New York: Cambridge University Press

Trevarthen, C., Aitken, K., Papoudi, D., and Robarts, J. (1998) *Children with Autism: Diagnosis and Intervention*. London: Jessica Kingsley Publishers.

Vygotsky, L.S. (1978) *Mind in Society: The Development of Higher Psychological Processes* (trans and eds M. Cole, V. John-Steiner, S. Scribner, and E. Souberman). Cambridge, MA: Harvard University Press

Watzlawick, P., Beavin, J., and Jackson, D. (1967) *Pragmatics of Human Communication*. New York: Norton and Co.

Wells, G. (1986) *The Meaning Makers: Children Learning Language and Using Language to Learn*. Portsmouth, NH: Heinemann Books.

Wertsch, J. (1985) *Culture, Communication and Cognition: Vygotskian Perspectives*. Cambridge: Cambridge University Press.

Willems, S., MacDonald, J., and Lombardino, L. (1983) 'Teaching parents sign language with children with developmental disabilities.' *Exceptional Children 12*, 34–45.

Williams, D. (1994) *Somebody, Somewhere: Breaking Free from the World of Autism*. London: Jessica Kingsley Publishers.

Williams, D. (1996) *Autism: An Inside-Out Approach*. London: Jessica Kingsley Publishers.

Williams, D. (1998) *Autism and Sensing*. London: Jessica Kingsley Publishers.

Winnicott, D.W. (1965) *The Maturational Process and the Facilitating Environment*. London: Hogarth.

Subject Index

Author Index